Issues in Progress
   Impact Validity as a Framework for Advocacy-Based Research
   Sean G. Massey & Ricardo E. Barreras
   Ethnic-racial Stigma and Physical Health Disparities in the United States of America: From Psychological Theory and Evidence to Public Policy Solutions
   Luis M. Rivera & Danielle Beatty

Editorial Advisory Board
   Dominic Abrams, University of Kent at Canterbury, United Kingdom
   Manuela Barreto, University of Exeter, United Kingdom
   Allan B.I. Bernardo, De La Salle University, Philippines
   Chi-yue Chiu, Nanyang Technological University, Singapore
   Jacquelynne Eccles, University of Michigan, United States
   Carolin Hagelskamp, New York University, United States
   Nick Haslam, University of Melbourne, Australia
   Ying-yi Hong, Nanyang Technological University, Singapore
   Melanie Killen, University of Maryland, College Park, United States
   Jason Plaks, University of Toronto, Canada
   Luisa Ramirez, Universidad del Rosario, Colombia
   Jennifer Richeson, Northwestern University, United States
   Lisa Rosenthal, Yale University, United States
   Adam Rutland, University of Kent at Canterbury, United Kingdom
   Isis Settles, Michigan State University, United States
   Beth Shinn, Vanderbilt University, United States
   Maykel Verkuyten, Utrecht University, The Netherlands
   Johanna Vollhardt, Clark University, United States

Past JSI Editors
   Rick H. Hoyle (2006–2009)
   Irene Hanson Frieze (2001–2005)
   Phyllis Katz (1997–2000)
   Daniel Perlman (1993–1996)
   Stuart Oskamp (1988–1992)
   George Levinger (1984–1987)
   Joseph E. McGrath (1979–1983)
   Jacqueline D. Goodchilds (1974–1978)
   Bertram H. Raven (1970–1973)
   Joshua A. Fishman (1966–1969)
   Leonard Solomon (1963)
   Robert Chin (1960–1965)

John Harding (1956–1959)
M. Brewster Smith (1951–1955)
Harold H. Kelley (1949)
Ronald Lippitt (1944–1950)

2013 Vol. 69, No. 3

Uncertainty and Extremism

Issue Editors: Michael A. Hogg, Arie Kruglanski and Kees van den Bos

INTRODUCTION
Uncertainty and the Roots of Extremism 407
Michael A. Hogg, Arie Kruglanski, and Kees van den Bos

SECTION I: CONCEPTUAL ANALYSES
Commitment and Extremism: A Goal Systemic Analysis 419
Kristen M. Klein and Arie W. Kruglanski
Uncertainty–Identity Theory: Extreme Groups, Radical Behavior, and Authoritarian Leadership 436
Michael A. Hogg and Janice Adelman
A Raw Deal: Heightened Liberalism Following Exposure to Anomalous Playing Cards 455
Travis Proulx and Brenda Major
Uncertainty and Status-Based Asymmetries in the Distinction Between the "Good" Us and the "Bad" Them: Evidence That Group Status Strengthens the Relationship Between the Need for Cognitive Closure and Extremity in Intergroup Differentiation 473
Christopher M. Federico, Corrie V. Hunt, and Emily L. Fisher

SECTION II: CULTURE AND MIGRATION
Culture and Extremism 495
Michele J. Gelfand, Gary LaFree, Susan Fahey, and Emily Feinberg
Uncertainty, Threat, and the Role of the Media in Promoting the Dehumanization of Immigrants and Refugees 518
Victoria M. Esses, Stelian Medianu, and Andrea S. Lawson

SECTION III: IDEOLOGY, POLITICS AND RELIGION
Anxious Uncertainty and Reactive Approach Motivation (RAM) for Religious, Idealistic, and Lifestyle Extremes 537
Ian McGregor, Mike Prentice, and Kyle Nash
Compensatory Control and Its Implications for Ideological Extremism 564
Aaron C. Kay and Richard P. Eibach

Determinants of Radicalization of Islamic Youth in the Netherlands:
  Personal Uncertainty, Perceived Injustice, and Perceived
    Group Threat 586
  Bertjan Doosje, Annemarie Loseman, and Kees van den Bos

COMMENTARY
A Millennial Challenge: Extremism in Uncertain Times 605
  Susan T. Fiske

Uncertainty and the Roots of Extremism

Michael A. Hogg*
Claremont Graduate University

Arie Kruglanski
University of Maryland

Kees van den Bos
Utrecht University

Extremism in society is the source of enormous human suffering and represents a significant social problem. In this article, we make a case for the urgency of understanding the psychology of societal extremism, discuss the diverse forms that extremism can take, and identify uncertainty as a correlate of and quite possibly precondition for extremism. We discuss the concept of uncertainty and the burgeoning social psychological research on uncertainty and its links with various forms of extremism. Thus, this article frames and contextualizes the subsequent articles in this issue of the Journal of Social Issues, on the psychology of the relationship, and possible causal link, between uncertainty and societal extremism.

Life is pervaded with uncertainty—ranging from how our interactions with strangers may unfold to the nature of the universe and the meaning of existence. Close relationships can be a source of great uncertainty as they develop, change, and conclude. And at a more macro level immigration, relocation, unemployment, economic crisis, regime collapse, and climate change can all arouse profound and enduring feelings of uncertainty in individuals. Although in some circumstances we seek out uncertainty and find it exhilarating, often we experience feelings of uncertainty as upsetting; something to be confronted and reduced.

In this issue of the *Journal of Social Issues* we focus on a special, and highly socially relevant, class of responses to uncertainty—extremism. People may

---

*Correspondence concerning this article should be addressed to Michael A. Hogg, School of Behavioral and Organizational Sciences, Claremont Graduate University, 123 East 8th Street, Claremont, CA 91711 [e-mail: michael.hogg@cgu.edu].

zealously cling to all-embracing ideologies and world views, engage in aggressive or disruptive behaviors aimed at protecting or promoting their world view, and identify as true believers with rigidly and hierarchically structured social groups or categories that are ethnocentric and intolerant of dissent and diversity. The psychological relationship between uncertainty and extremism is complex and its nature rests on what is meant by uncertainty, how uncertainty relates to neighboring constructs, what the focus of uncertainty is, what we mean by "extremism," what aspects of extremism we focus on, and what the psychological processes are that may translate uncertainty into extremism.

It is important to note that "extremism" is a contested term in so far as it is generally used in day-to-day and societal discourse as a term of disparagement. What may be considered and labeled as extremist by some people may be viewed quite differently by others (the classic notion that one person's terrorist may be another's freedom fighter). However, extremism that manifests as violence, cruelty, and intentional infliction of human suffering is generally decried even if there is "debate" over the cause and justification of the behavior. It is important to note that societal extremism is a human universal—occurring across history, societies, nations, cultures, and ideologies.

The nine articles in this issue of *Journal of Social Issues* adopt a variety of perspectives and foci to address the nature of and psychological relationship between uncertainty and extremism. They are grouped into three thematic sections: conceptual analyses; culture and migration; ideology, politics, and religion. In addition there is a closing commentary and discussion by Susan Fiske (Fiske, 2013), which pulls the thematic strands together, offers an overview of the intriguing aspects of the uncertainty–extremism interface, and takes the broad view in locating and evaluating the validity, scope, applicability, and policy implications of the science in the context of relevant social issues.

The present contributions were selected from a wider group of papers presented at a small conference on uncertainty and extremism that we (Hogg, Kruglanski, & Van den Bos) organized at Claremont Graduate University in November 2009. The meeting was jointly sponsored by the Society for the Psychological Study of Social Issues and the European Association of Social Psychology, and received generous support from the School of Behavioral and Organizational Sciences at Claremont Graduate University.

Uncertainty and Extremism

Intuitively it often seems that periods of large-scale societal instability and uncertainty coincide with sociopolitical and ideological extremism. Narrative accounts to varying degree substantiate this observation (e.g., Brand, 1995; Goodwin, 2011; Lane, 2011; Midlarsky, 2011; Staub, 1989). The British historian Edward Gibbon, in his momentous work on *The History of the Decline and Fall of the*

Roman Empire (published in six volumes between 1776 and 1789), commented on how collapse of the order that Roman rule provided, and the attendant uncertainties that this engendered, lent momentum to a wave of religious fanaticism, and the spawning of a plethora of religious movements that demanded extreme ideological commitment from their adherents.

In the 20th century, the Great Depression of the 1930s witnessed a global rise of national-political extremism, sliding into fascism, communism, and nationalism, and culminating in genocide and a world war that killed between 62 and 78 million people. The postwar nuclear arms race between the Soviet Union and the West created existential uncertainty due to the possibility of nuclear annihilation (captured by the bleak acronym MAD—mutually assured destruction) and spawned profound anti-Western and anticommunist hysteria, on both sides of the East–West divide. The 1960s and early 1970s, particularly in the United States, saw a period of rapid technological, sociocultural, and normative change that raised uncertainty about America's future. Coinciding with, and arguably prompted by, these developments the United States was swept by unprecedented race riots and antiwar demonstrations, and many young people were drawn to extreme countercultural movements, religious cults, and radical political organizations that may well be characterized as "extreme."

Since at least the 1950s substantial demographic changes in the United States and Western Europe have induced uncertainty about what it means to be "White." This has energized a variety of racist groups such as the Ku Klux Klan in the United States, the British National Party in the United Kingdom, the Front Nationale in France, and other similar groups and individuals in Germany, the Netherlands, Norway, and other countries. In a similar vein the decline of global Muslim power and influence over the last 200 years, the inability of secular regimes in the Middle East to provide just governance for people in the region, and the confrontation in Muslim nations between traditionalism and Western style modernism has raised in the minds of many value confusion and gnawing uncertainties about the future.

Over the past 20 years this has energized in various parts of the world a fundamentalist reaction and associated antifeelings, exemplified by the Taliban, as well as Al Qaeda and its affiliates. This reaction has most recently led to terrorist atrocities in Britain, Spain, the United States, Bali, India, Iraq, Afghanistan, Russia, and other countries, which in turn has created existential uncertainties for many people around the globe. This not only paved the way for zealous opposition to Islam in Europe and for wars in Afghanistan and Iraq, but also provided fertile ground for people to endorse wide ranging restrictions to civil rights, and a shift to the right in European politics, fueled by anxieties about the influx of Muslim immigrants into the continent.

Most recently, the global financial collapse of 2008 and its attendant economic uncertainties prompted the introduction of draconian economic measures, spawned violent protests in France and Greece, and a reactionary shift of conservative political ideology in the United States toward radical conservatism. Finally, the wave of uprisings and regime changes across North Africa and the Middle East that erupted in 2011 created sociopolitical uncertainty that has led some current affairs commentators to warn about the specter of extremist organizations filling the void.

Although some forms of extremism (such as behaviors relating to animal rights) may be less strongly associated with feelings of uncertainty and more strongly related to moral principles and sometimes moral rigidity, uncertainty, and extremism often co-occur. But does uncertainty *cause* extremism, and if so how and under what circumstances? In other words, what is the psychology of the relationship between uncertainty and extremism?

Social Psychology of Uncertainty

The idea that uncertainty plays a key motivational role in human behavior is not new (cf. Fromm, 1947). The American pragmatist philosopher John Dewey captured the motivational prominence of uncertainty rather nicely. As he put it: "... in the absence of actual certainty in the midst of a precarious and hazardous world, men cultivate all sorts of things that would give them the *feeling* of certainty" (Dewey, 1929/2005, p. 33).

However, probably the best known social psychological treatment of uncertainty is provided by social comparison theory (Festinger, 1954; see also Suls & Wheeler, 2000). When people feel uncertain about the accuracy of their perceptions, beliefs, and attitudes they seek out people who are similar to themselves in order to make comparisons that largely confirm the veracity and appropriateness of their own attitudes. In this way, attitudinal uncertainty is associated with pressures toward uniformity and the development of mutual bonds of attraction among like-minded people that underpin the cohesiveness of social groups (e.g., Festinger, Schachter, & Back, 1950).

The wider notion here is that when people are uncertain they are more motivated to verify and confirm aspects of themselves, often positive aspects of self, than to obtain accurate information about themselves and their attitudes and perceptions (e.g., Sedikides, 1993; Sedikides & Strube, 1997; Swann, Rentfrow, & Guinn, 2003). Indeed a core tenet of social cognition is that although people's attention is attracted by vivid and distinctive stimuli that stand out as different, people are often motivated to confirm their cognitive representations (schemas, stereotypes) about themselves, other people, and their world (see Fiske & Taylor, 2008). In short, uncertainty can motivate a confirmation bias.

Such bias occurs where people possess opinions on a topic (in the form of relevant schemas, stereotypes, and self-perceptions) that are rendered uncertain. In the absence of relevant opinions, however, people whose need for certainty is aroused may be quite susceptible to social influence and be quick to embrace views, attitudes, or conclusions suggested to them by others (Kruglanski, Webster, & Klem, 1993). People's susceptibility to social influence under conditions of uncertainty can have profound societal consequences by promoting the impact of certainty-promising demagogues of various kinds, discouraging open mindedness to a diversity of viewpoints, and enhancing the appeal of rigidly simplistic, black/white ideologies, and fundamentalist belief systems and practices (e.g., Altemeyer, 2003; Baron, Crawley, & Paulina, 2003; Billig, 1982; Curtis & Curtis, 1993; Doty, Peterson, & Winter, 1991; Hoffer, 1951; Jost, Glaser, Kruglanski, & Sulloway, 2003; Lambert, Burroughs, & Nguyen, 1999; Orehek et al., 2010).

Uncertainty can be considered a demand on the system that calls out for dedication of cognitive resources to resolve the uncertainty. Sometimes people may invest substantial effort in carefully deliberating on and resolving uncertainties—much like people sometimes systematically process persuasive messages (Bohner, Moskowitz, & Chaiken, 1995; Petty & Cacioppo, 1986). However, people have limited cognitive processing capacity and they often employ a range of cognitive shortcuts and heuristics (Kahneman & Tversky, 1973; Tversky & Kahneman, 1974; also see Kahneman, Slovic, & Tversky, 1982) to quickly reduce uncertainty until they are "sufficiently" certain about something to desist from dedicating further cognitive effort. This provides closure, in the gestalt sense (Koffka, 1935), and allows people to move on to dedicate cognitive effort to other things (see Kruglanski, Belanger, Chen, & Kopetz, 2012; Kruglanski & Gigerenzer, 2011).

This same principle of parsimoniously reducing uncertainty also extends to the way that groups reduce uncertainty. For example, when groups embrace a variety of different opinions and are uncertain about what the group's overall position should be they often select an appropriate social decision scheme such as unanimity, majority wins, or two-thirds majority to help them quickly resolve uncertainty (Davis, 1973; Stasser, Kerr, & Davis, 1989). Sometimes groups can be so keen to quickly reach consensus in order to overcome potential disagreement-based uncertainty that they entirely fail to adopt proper rational decision-making procedures—falling prey to groupthink (Janis, 1982; also see Aldag & Fuller, 1993). Finally, certitudes grounded in majority consensus can be so precious that consistent minorities that actively challenge the majority view and ignite uncertainty can be fiercely derogated, suppressed, and excluded—however, once uncertainty raises its head it can be very difficult to brush it aside, and minorities can thus have substantial latent influence over the majority (cf. Moscovici, 1980; see also Hogg, 2010).

People can feel uncertain about many things: for example, their perceptions, beliefs, attitudes, values, relationships, and careers; their future and their place in the world; and even more fundamentally about their very self and identity. The origins of uncertainty can reside in self-reflection, interpersonal relationships, group and intergroup dynamics, or widespread events in the larger society or global community. In addition, the uncertainty can be weak or strong, transitory or enduring, and important or trivial. Uncertainty is multifaceted and thus how people respond to uncertainty is also multifaceted.

Extremism as a Resolution of Uncertainty

In the previous section we have briefly built a case for how badly people can need to reduce feelings of uncertainty. The motivation can be so strong that people take cognitive shortcuts to resolve their uncertainties in ways that are not necessary optimal. This argument can be taken even further.

Probably the most powerful way to reduce uncertainty and protect oneself from the specter of uncertainty is to ground one's beliefs, attitudes, values, and understanding of the world in consensus and repeated exposure to similar other people who share and agree with, and reinforce one's view of the world (e.g., Van den Bos, Poortvliet, Maas, Miedema, & Van den Ham, 2005). People can also insulate themselves from divergent views by effectively living in a world of consensus—for example, consuming only those mass media that share their world view, and navigating largely to fellow-traveler websites on the internet. Following this uncertainty-reducing strategy, people may try to avoid stumbling upon alternative views and when they do they can react strongly by devaluing and discrediting as deviants, heretics, and worse those who think differently. Indeed, there is evidence that dissent and criticism can invite marginalization and rejection, even persecution (e.g., Van den Bos, Euwema, Poortvliet, & Maas, 2007).

People like to feel that their perceptions and understandings of the world are more correct than alternative viewpoints—that there is a clear moral superiority to their own perspectives and thus to themselves and those who share their views. This overlays opinion and interpretation with a stark binary right–wrong classification—it builds a powerful motivation to protect and promote, perhaps at all cost, the ideological integrity and superiority of one's own views. Authority and leadership can become very important here (e.g., Hogg, 2007a; Kruglanski, Pierro, Mannetti, & Degrada, 2006).

People take a lead about what is correct and true from authority figures, who can be contemporary individuals who are strong and directive leaders of a consensus or group that people believe they belong to. There is considerable evidence that where uncertainty is particularly aversive and closure is strongly desired groups prefer strong autocratic leadership where the attainment of consensus is facilitated by reliance on the leader and where consensus-delaying debate and discussion are discouraged (Kruglanski et al., 2005; Kruglanski et al., 2006; Orehek et al., 2010).

Authority can also come from definitive texts that are considered true in an absolute sense—almost all religions and most powerful political ideologies have them. Even scholarly schools of thought can repeatedly refer to a particular body of text as definitive. Those who interpret such texts in an orthodox manner can become highly authoritative and be invested with substantial power as they ground the belief system in a solid and unchanging foundation that is highly attractive to those who seek to manage their uncertainty.

Uncertainty is also reduced if people feel that the relations among people are clear, invariant, and predictable. Thus, stable structural relations between groups and among roles and subgroups within a group can be particularly attractive. People can go to great lengths to support and justify the existing social structure, even if such behavior places themselves and their group in a relatively disadvantaged position—an idea explored by system justification theory (e.g., Jost & Hunyadi, 2002; Jost & Van der Toorn, 2011).

Psychological Relationship between Uncertainty and Extremism

Our argument suggests that the human motivation to reduce or to manage uncertainty is strong and is thus associated with extremism, may lay the groundwork for extremism, and may even lead to extremism. This may be so because extremism connotes clarity and a "black and white" perspective, admitting no ambiguous shades of gray. Extremism also embraces the possibility of people sometimes protecting and promoting their uncertainty-reducing black and white world through assertive, radical actions that may be antisocial, disruptive, and aggressive.

In recent years there has been a growing interest in social psychology in researching and theorizing the role of uncertainty and related constructs in a range of behaviors that speak to the general phenomenon of extremism (e.g., Hogg, 2007b; Kruglanski et al., 2006; Van den Bos, 2009; see also Hogg & Blaylock, 2011). The articles in this issue of *Journal of Social Issues* present this wide-ranging research enterprise—they review the current state of knowledge and describe recent conceptual and empirical developments. This is a diverse and vibrant area of research in which, against a background of common purpose, different researchers and research groups offer different perspectives and foci. The articles in this special issue reflect this fruitful heterogeneity.

We have organized the nine main articles into three subsections to reflect the articles' principal foci. The first four articles (Federico, Hunt, & Fisher, 2013; Hogg & Adelman, 2013; Klein & Kruglanski, 2013; Proulx & Major, 2013) are mainly focused on conceptual issues to do with the nature of uncertainty, the nature of extremism, and the psychological relationship between the two. The next section has two articles (Esses, Medianu, & Lawson, 2013; Gelfand, LaFree, Fahey, & Feinberg, 2013) that focus on uncertainty and extremism in the context of culture, immigration, population migration, and the refugee experience. The final set of three articles (Doosje, Loseman, & Van den Bos, 2013; Kay & Eibach, 2013; McGregor, Prentice, & Nash, 2013) focus on uncertainty and extremism in the context of religious and political zealotry and ideological orthodoxy.

However, these subsections are not insulated from one another—there are common themes, examples, and concepts that thread their way through the narrative. There is discussion of stereotyping, prejudice, dehumanization, and violence, and the role of status asymmetry and perception of injustice. There is discussion of personal and self-uncertainty and the relationship between uncertainty reduction, pursuit of meaning, gaining control, reacting to threat, and the individual's need for cognitive closure. In addition to covering diverse aspects of the uncertainty–extremism relation, the articles also draw on a variety of conceptual frameworks and theories, including social identity theory, uncertainty–identity theory, terror management theory, the meaning maintenance model, and concepts of group centrism and compensatory control and conviction.

Extremism, particularly when it is associated with aggression, violence, and destruction, is a grim and ubiquitous social issue; and so all articles offer, in their closing comments, some discussion of and speculation about how to protect society from harmful extremism. The translational and policy implications of the theory and research presented here are given a more complete treatment in Fiske's (2013) closing summary and commentary.

Postscript

Uncertainty is an inseparable counterpart of historical change and as we enter the second decade of the 21st century the pace of change, driven by ceaseless technological innovations, seems faster than ever before. Arguably then, the challenge of coping with uncertainty and avoiding its potentially dangerous social consequences such as extremism and violence is particularly acute at this historical moment. The social–cognitive study of the interface of uncertainty and extremism is, therefore, of unique poignancy—promising, as it does, evidence-based and theory-grounded scientific insights on a societal problem with wide-ranging and global consequences. We hope that the work described in this special issue constitutes a step toward fulfillment of that promise.

References

Aldag, R. J., & Fuller, S. R. (1993). Beyond fiasco: A reappraisal of the groupthink phenomenon and a new model of group decision processes. *Psychological Bulletin, 113*, 533–552.

Altemeyer, B. (2003). Why do religious fundamentalists tend to be prejudiced. *International Journal for the Psychology of Religion, 13*, 17–28. doi: 10.1207/S15327582IJPR1301_03

Baron, R. S., Crawley, K., & Paulina, D. (2003). Aberrations of power: Leadership in totalist groups. In D. van Knippenberg & M. A. Hogg (Eds.), *Leadership and power: Identity processes in groups and organizations* (pp. 169–183). London: Sage. doi: 10.4135/9781446216170.n13

Billig, M. (1982). *Ideology and social psychology: Extremism, moderation and contradiction*. London: Sage.

Bohner, G., Moskowitz, G. B., & Chaiken, S. (1995). The interplay of heuristic and systematic processing of social information. *European Review of Social Psychology, 6*, 33–68. doi: 10.1080/14792779443000003

Brand, H. A. (1995). *The reckless decade: America in the 1890s*. Chicago, IL: University of Chicago Press.

Curtis, J. M., & Curtis, M. J. (1993). Factors related to susceptibility and recruitment by cults. *Psychological Reports, 73*, 451–460. doi: 10.2466/pr0.1993.73.2.451

Davis, J. H. (1973). Group decision and social interaction: A theory of social decision schemes. *Psychological Review, 80*, 97–125. doi: 10.1037/h0033951

Dewey, J. (1929/2005). *The quest for certainty: A study of the relation of knowledge and action.* Whitefish, MT: Kessinger Publishing.

Doosje, B., Loseman, A., & van den Bos, K. (2013). Determinants of radicalization of Islamic youth in the Netherlands: Personal uncertainty, perceived injustice, and perceived group threat. *Journal of Social Issues, 69*, 586–604.

Doty, R. M., Peterson, B. E., & Winter, D. G. (1991). Threat and authoritarianism in the United States, 1978–1987. *Journal of Personality and Social Psychology, 61*, 629–640. doi: 10.1037/0022-3514.61.4.629

Esses, V. M., Medianu, S., & Lawson, A. S. (2013). Uncertainty, threat, and the role of the media in promoting the dehumanization of immigrants and refugees. *Journal of Social Issues, 69*, 518–536.

Federico, C. M., Hunt, C. V., & Fisher, E. L. (2013). Uncertainty and status-based asymmetries in the distinction between the "good" us and the "bad" them: Evidence that group status strengthens the relationship between the need for cognitive closure and extremity in intergroup differentiation. *Journal of Social Issues, 69*, 473–494.

Festinger, L. (1954). A theory of social comparison processes. *Human Relations, 7*, 117–140. doi: 10.1177/001872675400700202

Festinger, L., Schachter, S., & Back, K. (1950). *Social pressures in informal groups: A study of human factors in housing.* New York: Harper.

Fiske, S. T. (2013). A millennial challenge: Extremism in uncertain times. *Journal of Social Issues, 69*, 605–613.

Fiske, S. T., & Taylor, S. E. (2008). *Social cognition: From brains to culture.* New York: McGraw-Hill.

Fromm, E. (1947). *Man for himself: An inquiry into the psychology of ethics.* New York: Rinehart.

Gelfand, M. J., LaFree, G., Fahey, S., & Feinberg, E. (2013). Culture and extremism. *Journal of Social Issues, 69*, 495–517.

Gibbon, E. (1776–1789). *The history of the decline and fall of the Roman Empire.* London: Strahan & Cadell.

Goodwin, M. (2011). *New British fascism: rise of the British nationalist party.* London: Routledge.

Hoffer, E. (1951). *The true believer.* New York: Time.

Hogg, M. A. (2007a). Organizational orthodoxy and corporate autocrats: Some nasty consequences of organizational identification in uncertain times. In C. A. Bartel, S. Blader, & A. Wrzesniewski (Eds.), *Identity and the modern organization* (pp. 35–59). Mahwah, NJ: Erlbaum.

Hogg, M. A. (2007b). Uncertainty-identity theory. In M. P. Zanna (Ed.), *Advances in experimental social psychology* (Vol. 39, pp. 69–126). San Diego, CA: Academic Press. doi: http://dx.doi.org/10.1016/S0065-2601(06)39002-8

Hogg, M. A. (2010). Influence and leadership. In S. T. Fiske, D. T. Gilbert, & G. Lindzey (Eds.), *Handbook of social psychology* (5th ed., Vol. 2, pp. 1166–1207). New York: Wiley.

Hogg, M. A., & Adelman, J. (2013). Uncertainty-identity theory: Extreme groups, radical behavior, and authoritarian leadership. *Journal of Social Issues, 69*, 436–454.

Hogg, M. A., & Blaylock, D. L. (Eds.) (2011). *Extremism and the psychology of uncertainty.* Boston: Wiley-Blackwell. doi: 10.1002/9781444344073

Janis, I. L. (1982). *Groupthink: Psychological studies of policy decisions and fiascoes* (2nd ed.). Boston, MA: Houghton Mifflin.

Jost, J. T., Glaser, J., Kruglanski, A. W., & Sulloway, F. J. (2003). Political conservatism as motivated social cognition. *Psychological Bulletin, 129*, 339–375. doi: 10.1037/0033-2909.129.3.339

Jost, J. T., & Hunyadi, O. (2002). The psychology of system justification and the palliative function of ideology. *European Review of Social Psychology, 13*, 111–153. doi: 10.1080/10463280240000046

Jost, J. T., & van der Toorn, J. (2011). System justification theory. In P. A. M. van Lange, A. W. Kruglanski, & E. T. Higgins (Eds.), *Handbook of theories of social psychology.* London: Sage. doi: 10.4135/9781446249222.n42

Kahneman, D., & Tversky, A. (1973). On the psychology of prediction. *Psychological Review, 80,* 237–251. doi: 10.1037/h0034747
Kahneman, D., Slovic, P., & Tversky, A. (Eds.) (1982). *Judgment under uncertainty: Heuristics and biases.* New York: Cambridge University Press.
Kay, A., & Eibach, R. P. (2013). Compensatory control and its implications for ideological extremism. *Journal of Social Issues, 69,* 564–585.
Klein, K. M., & Kruglanski, A. W. (2013). Commitment and extremism: A goal systemic analysis. *Journal of Social Issues, 69,* 419–435.
Koffka, K. (1935). *Principles of gestalt psychology.* New York: Harcourt, Brace & Co.
Kruglanski, A. W., Belanger, J., Chen, X., & Kopetz, C. (2012). The energetics of motivated cognition: A force field analysis. *Psychological Review, 119* (1), 1–20. doi: 10.1037/a0025488
Kruglanski, A. W., & Gigerenzer, G. (2011). Intuitive and deliberate judgments are based on common principles. *Psychological Review, 118,* 97–109. doi: 10.1037/a0020762
Kruglanski, A. W., Pierro, A., Mannetti, L., & De Grada, E. (2006). Groups as epistemic providers: Need for closure and the unfolding of group-centrism. *Psychological Review, 113,* 84–100. doi: 10.1037/0033-295X.113.1.84
Kruglanski, A. W., Raviv, A., Bar-Tal, D., Raviv, A., Sharvit, K., Ellis, S., Bar, R., Pierro, A., & Mannetti, L. (2005). Says who?: Epistemic authority effects in social judgment. *Advances in Experimental Social Psychology, 37,* 346–392. doi: 10.1016/S0065-2601(05)37006-7
Kruglanski, A. W., Webster, D. M., & Klem, A. (1993). Motivated resistance and openness to persuasion in the presence or absence of prior information. *Journal of Personality and Social Psychology, 65,* 861–876. doi: 10.1037/0022-3514.65.5.861
Lambert, A. J., Burroughs, T., & Nguyen, T. (1999). Perceptions of risk and the buffering hypothesis: The role of just world beliefs and right-wing authoritarianism. *Personality and Social Psychology Bulletin, 25,* 643–656. doi: 10.1177/0146167299025006001
Lane, C. (2011). *The age of doubt: Tracing the roots of our religious uncertainty.* Newhaven, CT: Yale University Press.
McGregor, I., Prentice, M., & Nash, K. (2013). Anxious uncertainty and reactive approach motivation (RAM) for religious, idealistic, and lifestyle extremes. *Journal of Social Issues, 69,* 537–563.
Midlarsky, M. I. (2011). *Origins of political extremism: Mass violence in the twentieth century and beyond.* New York: Cambridge University Press. doi: 10.1017/CBO9780511975868
Moscovici, S. (1980). Toward a theory of conversion behavior. In L. Berkowitz (Ed.), *Advances in experimental social psychology* (Vol. *13,* pp. 202–239). New York: Academic Press. doi: 10.1016/S0065-2601(08)60133-1
Orehek, E., Fishman, S., Dechesne, M. Doosje, B., Kruglanski, A. W., Cole, A. P., Saddler, B., & Jackson, T. (2010). Need for closure and the social response to terrorism. *Basic and Applied Social Psychology, 32,* 279–290. doi: 10.1080/01973533.2010.519196
Petty, R. E., & Cacioppo, J. T. (1986). The elaboration likelihood model of persuasion. In L. Berkowitz (Ed.), *Advances in experimental social psychology* (Vol. *19,* pp. 123–205). New York: Academic Press. doi: 10.1016/S0065-2601(08)60214-2
Proulx, T., & Major, B. (2013). A raw deal: Heightened liberalism following exposure to anomalous playing cards. *Journal of Social Issues, 69,* 455–472.
Sedikides, C. (1993). Assessment, enhancement, and verification determinants of the self-evaluation process. *Journal of Personality and Social Psychology, 65,* 317–338. doi 10.1037/0022-3514.65.2.317
Sedikides, C., & Strube, M. J. (1997). Self-evaluation: To thine own self be good, to thine own self be sure, to thine own self be true, and to thine own self be better. In M. P. Zanna (Ed.), *Advances in experimental social psychology* (Vol. *29,* pp. 209–296). New York: Academic Press. doi: 10.1016/S0065-2601(08)60018-0
Stasser, G., Kerr, N. L., & Davis, J. H. (1989). Influence processes and consensus models in decision-making groups. In P. B. Paulus (Ed.), *Psychology of group influence* (2nd ed., pp. 279–326). Hillsdale, NJ: Erlbaum.
Staub, E. (1989). *The roots of evil: The psychological and cultural origins of genocide and other forms of group violence.* New York: Cambridge University Press.

Suls, J., & Wheeler, L. (Eds.) (2000). *Handbook of social comparison: Theory and research.* New York: Kluwer/Plenum.
Swann, W. B., Jr., Rentfrow, P. J., & Guinn, J. S. (2003). Self-verification: The search for coherence. In M. R. Leary & J. P. Tangney (Eds.), *Handbook of self and identity* (pp. 367–383). New York: Guilford.
Tversky, A., & Kahneman, D. (1974). Judgment under uncertainty: Heuristics and biases. *Science, 185,* 1124–1131. doi: 10.1126/science.185.4157.1124
Van den Bos, K. (2009). Making sense of life: The existential self trying to deal with personal uncertainty. *Psychological Inquiry, 20,* 197–217. doi: 10.1080/10478400903333411
Van den Bos, K., Euwema, M. C., Poortvliet, P. M., & Maas, M. (2007). Uncertainty management and social issues: Uncertainty as important determinant of reactions to socially deviating people. *Journal of Applied Social Psychology, 37,* 1726–1756. doi: 10.1111/j.1559-1816.2007.00235.x
Van den Bos, K., Poortvliet, P. M., Maas, M., Miedema, J., & Van den Ham, E.-J. (2005). An enquiry concerning the principles of cultural norms and values: The impact of uncertainty and mortality salience on reactions to violations and bolstering of cultural worldviews. *Journal of Experimental Social Psychology, 41,* 91–113. doi: 10.1016/j.jesp.2004.06.001

MICHAEL A. HOGG is Professor of Social Psychology at Claremont Graduate University and president of the Society of Experimental Social Psychology. He is the 2010 recipient of the Diener mid-career award from the Society for Personality and Social Psychology; foundation editor of *Group Processes and Intergroup Relations;* former associate editor of the *Journal of Experimental Social Psychology;* and a fellow of numerous scholarly associations including the Association for Psychological Science and the Society for the Psychological Study of Social Issues. His extensively published research on social identity theory, group processes and intergroup relations, has a recent focus on influence and leadership, and uncertainty and extremism.

ARIE W. KRUGLANSKI is a Distinguished University Professor and co-director of START (National Center for the Study of Terrorism and the Response to Terrorism) at the University of Maryland, College Park. Kruglanski is a recipient of the National Institute of Mental Health Research Scientist Award, the Senior Humboldt Award, the Donald Campbell Award for Outstanding Contributions to Social Psychology, and the Distinguished Scientific Contribution Award from the Society of Experimental Social Psychology. He has served as editor of the *Journal of Personality and Social Psychology,* and *Personality and Social Psychology Bulletin,* and associate editor of the *American Psychologist.* Kruglanski's research focuses on human judgment and decision making, the motivation–cognition interface, and group and intergroup processes. It has been disseminated in over 250 publications, and has been supported by grants from the National Science Foundation and the National Institute of Mental Health, among others.

KEES VAN DEN BOS is Professor of Social Psychology at Utrecht University. His research, which focuses on basic and applied social psychology pertaining to social justice and normative behavior as well as uncertainty and cultural worldviews, has been widely disseminated in more than 130 publications including leading journals and has been supported by numerous competitive and research grants, including a prestigious VICI innovational research grant from the Dutch national science foundation (NWO). In 1996 he received his PhD cum laude, won a dissertation award from the Association of Dutch Social Psychologists, and obtained a fellowship from the Royal Netherlands Academy of Arts and Sciences. He has been associate editor of *Social Justice Research* and the *European Journal of Social Psychology* and currently is senior associate editor of *Personality and Social Psychology Bulletin*. In both 2009 and 2010 he was elected the psychology teacher of the year at Utrecht University.

Commitment and Extremism: A Goal Systemic Analysis

Kristen M. Klein* and Arie W. Kruglanski
University of Maryland, College Park

Growing evidence suggests that uncertainty is related to extremism in its various forms. The aim of the present article is to probe the underlying psychological mechanisms of this relation. We begin by considering two disparate definitions of extremism as: (1) expressed zeal/attitude polarity, and (2) deviation from a norm. Zeal constitutes a direct expression of goal commitment, whereas deviant behavior is likely to occur under high commitment because of the greater perceived instrumentality of such behavior to the goal. We discuss a psychological mechanism that implies this increased instrumentality of deviant behavior to its goal. From this perspective, the relation between uncertainty and extremism represents a special case of the general relation between goal commitment and extremism: An aversively high degree of uncertainty augments commitment to the goal of uncertainty reduction. This in turn increases the appeal of extreme expressions seen as effective ways and means to uncertainty reduction.

In recent years psychological researchers have evinced strong interest in a possible relationship between uncertainty and extremism (Hogg, 2004, 2007, 2012; McGregor, 2003, 2006a, 2006b; McGregor, Zanna, Holmes, & Spencer, 2001; van den Bos, 2009; van den Bos, Ameijde, & van Gorp, 2006; van den Bos, Poortvliet, Maas, Miedema, & van den Ham, 2005). This relationship has been of considerable interest to investigators for both theoretical and pragmatic reasons. For one, research on the relationship between uncertainty and extremism addresses the theoretical link between two fundamental phenomena of potential relevance to

---

*Correspondence concerning this article should be addressed to Kristen M. Klein, Psychology Department, University of Maryland, College Park, MD 20742 [e-mail: kleinkm@umd.edu].

This research was performed under an appointment to the U.S. Department of Homeland Security (DHS) Scholarship and Fellowship Program, administered by the Oak Ridge Institute for Science and Education (ORISE) through an interagency agreement between the U.S. Department of Energy (DOE) and DHS. ORISE is managed by Oak Ridge Associated Universities (ORAU) under DOE contract number DE-AC05-06OR23100. All opinions expressed in this article are the author's and do not necessarily reflect the policies and views of DHS, DOE, or ORAU/ORISE.

numerous situations. Moreover, it is quite possible that in today's rapidly changing world, the relationship between uncertainty and extremism is underlying the recent global trends toward fundamentalism, violence, and terrorism (Hogg, Kruglanski, & van den Bos, 2013).

The research in this domain has indeed found support for the contention that uncertainty is related to extremism, but several issues remain to be addressed. The first is a lack of clarity as to the psychological meaning of extremism and the existence of several definitions of extremism, which are of unclear relation to one another (Hogg et al., 2013). Second, there is a relative lack of clarity as to the underlying psychological reasons for the linkage between uncertainty and extremism. It has been suggested that extremism brings about certainty, or a reduction in uncertainty, but the proposed mechanism for this effect has thus far remained somewhat obscure. Is extremism a necessary condition for certainty (can one be certain without being extreme)? Is extremism a sufficient condition for certainty (if one is extreme, does it mean that one is certain)?

In this article, we address these issues by proposing that the relation between uncertainty and extremism represents a special case of a more general phenomenon, which we describe in goal systemic (Kruglanski et al., 2002) terms. (Although we reserve a fuller explanation of our goal systemic approach for a later section, the goal systemic approach is rooted in goal systems theory [Kruglanski et al., 2002], which outlines patterns of relations between the goals people hold and the means they use to pursue them.) The general phenomenon, known as the dilution effect (Zhang, Fishbach, & Kruglanski, 2007), is that any means that is perceived as *uniquely* instrumental to a goal it serves, even if it is detrimental to other goals, is perceived as *particularly* instrumental to that goal. Any such means that is instrumental to just one goal is what goal systems theory (Kruglanski et al., 2002) calls a *unifinal* means; by contrast, means that are instrumental to multiple goals are called *multifinal* means. Because unifinal means are perceived as particularly instrumental to the goal they serve, individuals may be especially likely to pursue unifinal means when that goal is activated. In terms of the present goal of interest, uncertainty reduction, we propose that the adoption of extreme attitudes or behaviors is perceived as a particularly effective (instrumental) means to uncertainty reduction, because such attitudes and behaviors do not appear to serve other goals. As we will try to show, our goal systemic analysis of the relation between uncertainty and extremism accounts for prior data, and affords new implications that warrant further investigation.

Scholars have previously described uncertainty reduction as a fundamental human motivation, whether directly in terms of personal uncertainty (Hogg, 2004, 2007, 2012; McGregor, 2003, 2006a, 2006b; McGregor et al., 2001; van den Bos et al., 2006) or uncertainty related to the randomness or unpredictability of external events (Kay & Eibach, 2013), or indirectly in terms of need for closure (Dechesne & Kruglanski, 2004; Kruglanski & Webster, 1994; McGregor et al., 2001), mortality salience (Solomon, Greenberg, & Pyszczynski, 2004; van den Bos et al., 2005), or self-threat (McGregor, 2006a, 2006b; McGregor & Jordan, 2007). Common to all these descriptions is the notion that the experience of uncertainty in any domain is generally unpleasant (McGregor, 2003; van den Bos, 2009) and leads to the desire to reduce uncertainty in some domain of one's life (Hogg, 2004, 2007, 2012). People may experience uncertainty reduction as a focal goal that acts to suppress alternative goals when uncertainty reduction becomes highly salient or important, perhaps due to situational pressures (e.g., economic instability; Staub, 1989), cultural factors (see Gelfand, LaFree, Fahey, & Feinberg, 2013), or personality characteristics (e.g., high need for closure; Kruglanski & Webster, 1994). Although this uncertainty reduction goal may typically be unconscious, automatically adopted and pursued (see Proulx & Major, 2013), it can nonetheless powerfully drive individuals toward means they perceive as effective for its pursuit.

This argument provides a goal systemic framework that may help to unify the growing body of literature on uncertainty and extremism. Researchers who study the relationship between these constructs have discussed uncertainty reduction as an important *goal* that drives people to diverse forms of extremism (Hogg, 2004, 2007, 2012; McGregor, 2003; van den Bos, 2009). In this article, we are extending this analysis to describe the various manifestations of extremism as highly instrumental unifinal (and costly) *means* to uncertainty reduction. Using this motivational framework, we can relate uncertainty reduction as a goal to extremism as an instrumental means to that goal. The work of others (e.g., Doosje, Loseman, & van den Bos, 2013; Hogg, 2004, 2007, 2012; Hogg & Adelman, 2013; McGregor, Prentice, & Nash, 2013; McGregor et al., 2001) suggests that people perceive an array of manifestations of extremism as instrumental means to uncertainty reduction, and that they are more likely to endorse or use extreme means under higher levels of uncertainty. In our own work, we have also shown that the quest for certainty, represented by a high need for closure, leads to greater support for and utilization of extreme (costly) means. Therefore, the goal systemic framework we will present is supported by both theoretical analysis and previous research and may afford new insights into the relation between uncertainty and extremism.

As a preview of what is to come, we first consider two popular definitions of extremism, namely its definitions as: (1) deviation from a behavioral norm, (2) zeal, intensity, or attitude polarity. We then present a goal systemic analysis and show how it reveals the inherent relatedness of these two definitions of extremism. Finally, we will consider the implications of our analysis for issues regarding both antisocial and prosocial forms of extremism.

Two Expressions of Extremism

Extremism as Deviation from the Norm

Wintrobe (2006) concisely stated that "the simplest way to think about an extremist is someone whose views are outside the mainstream on some issue or dimension" (p. 6). This is one of the classic definitions of extremism, as deviation from the norm or the majority. For example, an individual might be considered an extremist if he or she holds political opinions that deviate from those held by the majority, or those that are considered normative. Of course, extremism defined in this manner is entirely dependent on the comparison group or majority used to derive a standard of what is normal and, consequently, what is extreme. Sidanius (1985) noted that "the specific social or political ideas, which may be very 'extreme' in one geographical or cultural context, may be very 'moderate' in another context" (p. 639). Jaccard and others (1995) referred to such relativity of extremism as the "nomothetic perspective," meaning that "extremity for one individual depends on how extreme the attitudes are for other individuals included in the analysis" (p. 354).

Extremism as Zeal or Conviction

Many theorists and researchers have also depicted zeal or profound conviction as yet another important manifestation of extremism, characterized variously in terms of "the salience or importance of a belief or set of beliefs" (Breton, Galeotti, Salmon, & Wintrobe, 2002, p. xiii); "intensity of feeling on [an] issue" (Abelson, 1995, p. 38); and "zealot[ry], fanatic[ism], and true believer[hood]" (Hogg, 2007, p. 92). Researchers have operationalized such conviction or zeal using items that reflect firmness of belief, willingness to defend a position, firmness of opinion, and certainty about a position (McGregor et al., 2001). In addition, researchers sometimes designate attitude ambivalence as the inverse of conviction, a sensation of being "'torn' between two sides of the issue," disagreement between the head and heart, "strong mixed emotions," and "gut feeling" in contrast with "rational intellect" (p. 474). From this perspective, extremism as zeal or conviction reflects commitment to a particular position or attitude on a given issue.

Closely akin to the notion of extremism as zeal is its definition as attitude extremity, which originated in traditional attitudes theory and research in social psychology. Attitude extremity "refers to the attitude itself (where, along a bipolar continuum, the attitude falls)" (Visser et al., 2006, p. 55). Abelson (1995) noted that "extremity has been conventionally measured by self-placement of subjects along a numerical scale of attitude position, usually labeled at the end with the respective designations, *extremely unfavorable* and *extremely favorable*" (p. 25). Therefore, attitude extremity is a function of an actor's or observer's subjective perception of the actor's position on an attitude object relative to the positions of others. Note that attitude extremity, much like zealous conviction, can signal commitment to a particular attitude or position on an issue. Indeed, researchers (e.g., Krosnick et al., 1993) have discussed attitude extremity, as well as certainty, intensity, and similar factors, as components of the multifactor, complex construct known as attitude strength, which is conceptually quite similar in meaning and complexity to commitment.

Although several authors have discussed these two popular definitions (Abelson, 1995; Breton et al., 2002; Wintrobe, 2006), the relation between the various expressions of extremism is as yet unclear. Is an individual who possesses great attitude conviction (zealous extremism) also likely to exhibit behavior that deviates from the norm (deviant extremism)? Most people probably feel strongly and positively about survival, protection of loved ones, and self-respect, and likewise feel strongly and negatively about death, disease, and humiliation. Therefore, individuals may hold zealous, intense, and polarized (extremely negative or positive) attitudes with regard to those concerns, but their zeal would not imply deviance; those concerns are shared by a majority of individuals, and thus are normative.

Similarly, individuals who possess great attitude conviction may not behave in ways that deviate from the norm because of the many intervening variables that can weaken the attitude–behavior relation. According to the theories of planned behavior and reasoned action (Ajzen, 1985; Fishbein & Ajzen, 1975), behavioral intentions, the mediating variable between attitudes and behavior, consist of (1) individuals' attitudes toward a behavior, (2) the subjective norms regarding that behavior, and (3) their perceived behavioral control over the performance of that behavior. These factors can all work to strengthen or diminish the likelihood that a given attitude will lead to a specific behavior. For instance, one may possess a positive attitude toward protest as a means of resolving grievances one harbors against a government. However, if the subjective norms are heavily stacked against protests (e.g., in an oppressive regime where protest is widely considered folly) or if the individual doubts his or her perceived behavioral control over the ability to stand one's ground in protest (e.g., if police forces are likely to take offensive measures against protesters), then the individual would be much less likely to engage in protest. Given this apparent absence of a perfect relation between zealous attitudes and non-normative behaviors, manifest in these two common operational definitions of extremism, a critical question remains: What is the conceptual gist of extremism? Psychologically speaking, we propose that extremism is an expression of *goal commitment*. In these terms, zeal constitutes a *direct expression* of commitment. It demonstrates how strongly one feels about the goal and the importance one attaches to the goal. In other words, zeal is both a necessary and sufficient condition for the inference of goal commitment. Observed zeal allows one to infer commitment, and a high degree of commitment means that one feels strongly or is zealous with regard to the goal. By contrast, deviancy is an *indirect expression* of goal commitment. Deviancy from a social norm signifies the relinquishment of goals or benefits desired by most people, which in turn represents the incurrence of costs. This suggests that individuals would not deviate from social norms and incur costs unless they were particularly committed to the goal that the deviant action serves. Therefore, deviancy may be a sufficient condition for the inference of goal commitment, but as noted above, it is hardly necessary.

In the following analysis, we further explore these notions within a goal systemic (Kruglanski et al., 2002) framework, which presents the conceptual gist of extremism and proposes an explanation for the mechanism that relates it to uncertainty. Specifically, attitude extremity and zealous conviction signal commitment to a valued goal (e.g., uncertainty reduction), and such extreme commitment can make the individual willing to sacrifice other goal pursuits (e.g., by deviating from the norm or the majority) in order to achieve the valued goal. Indeed, under high commitment to a focal goal, one tends to be less concerned with alternative goals and even suppresses them (Kopetz, Faber, Fishbach, & Kruglanski, 2011; Shah, Friedman, & Kruglanski, 2002). Therefore, under high goal commitment, an individual may be particularly likely to choose a deviant means, or one that incurs costs with regard to alternative goals about which the individual is not concerned for the moment, simply because the deviant means will be perceived as a particularly effective route to the focal goal.

Goal Commitment and Extremism: A Goal Systemic Approach

According to goal systems theory (Kruglanski et al., 2002), people must choose among available means to pursue their goals. Of course, people regularly possess multiple goals at once, some of which might conflict with one another and thus complicate the choice among means. As an example, inspired by Esses and colleagues' (Esses, Medianu, & Lawson, 2013) analysis of immigration-related extremism, consider an individual who has an uncertainty reduction goal that stems from a perceived threat from immigrants to economic opportunities for Whites in the United States. Such an individual might choose between two means he perceives as available for reducing economic uncertainty that he attributes to an influx of immigrants: (1) joining a lobbyist group that pushes for stricter immigration policies and tougher enforcement of existing laws, or (2) joining a White supremacist group that uses threatening and sometimes violent tactics to intimidate immigrants.

If the actor is also concerned with acting within the confines of the law or using normative channels for action, the choice between the lobbyist group and the supremacist group may be obviated by the presence of the additional legal or normative goal (i.e., clearly the lobbyist group is the best means if both goals matter). If, however, the actor was recently laid off and replaced with an immigrant who was willing to work for less money, thus leaving the actor's family without a source of income, threatening their financial security, and forcing them to move elsewhere to find work or start over in a new career at a relatively late point in life, the uncertainty reduction goal may become more important than the legal or normative goal, perhaps to the point of becoming all-consuming. (Note that this example is intended to provide a simple illustration of a conceptual point in the context of uncertainty and extremism. By no means do we think that lobbying and White supremacy are the *only* options people have or consider when confronting economic uncertainty related to immigration, nor do we think that anti-immigration proponents are necessarily extremists by virtue of their attitudes or behaviors. Likewise, obviously a great many individuals who experience economic uncertainty do not attribute it to immigration, and few if any of those who do actually join lobbyist or White supremacy groups.)

In goal systemic terms, the uncertainty reduction goal described in the above example can be considered the *focal goal*, or a goal that is highly salient or important to an individual at a given time, or to which the individual is highly committed. The legal or normative goal described above is an *alternative goal*, or a goal that the individual might consider in addition to the focal goal when choosing among various means options. Furthermore, the lobbyist group is a *multifinal* means, or one that is instrumental to both the focal and alternative goals (i.e., uncertainty reduction and legal or normative conformity). The violent supremacist group is a *unifinal* means, or one that is instrumental only to the focal goal (i.e., uncertainty reduction) but not to the alternative goal (i.e., legal or normative conformity). One might presume that the multifinal means yields the greatest value due to its instrumentality to multiple goals and hence ought to be chosen by the individual; however, this need not always be the case.

Perceived Instrumentality of Means: The Dilution Effect

Interestingly, research has shown that multifinal means are vulnerable to a perceived reduction in their efficacy: the dilution effect (Zhang et al., 2007). Simply stated, the dilution effect is the inference that if a means is *uniquely* instrumental to a focal goal (but not to alternative goals), then it must be *especially* instrumental to the focal goal. In other words, the greater the number of goals to which a means is instrumental, the less instrumental the means is perceived as being to any one of those goals. The perceived instrumentality of a *multifinal* means to the focal goal is diluted by its instrumentality to alternative goals; therefore, a multifinal means is not perceived as particularly instrumental to the focal goal. From the previous example, the lobbyist group is a multifinal means, as it is instrumental to both the uncertainty reduction and legal or normative goals. A lobbyist group would thus not be perceived as particularly instrumental to the goal of uncertainty reduction, because its association with the additional legal or normative goal dilutes its perceived instrumentality to the uncertainty reduction goal.

By contrast, a *unifinal* means is one that is uniquely instrumental to the focal goal; therefore, the unifinal means' perceived instrumentality to the focal goal is not diluted by (nonexistent) instrumental relations to alternative goals. As a result, people perceive a unifinal means as more instrumental than a multifinal means in pursuing a focal goal, a phenomenon documented in several studies (Zhang et al., 2007). As an example, consider the supremacist group as a potential means to uncertainty reduction. A violent supremacist group in this case is a unifinal means, as it is uniquely instrumental to the uncertainty reduction goal but not to the legal or normative goal. Therefore, the supremacist group would be perceived as *especially* instrumental to the focal goal of uncertainty reduction, and as *more* instrumental to the uncertainty reduction goal than the normative lobbyist group. Simply, the added benefits a multifinal means accords make it *less* appealing for pursuit of any one among those benefits (i.e., goals).

Importantly, in many cases unifinal means that serve a particular focal goal are not only noninstrumental to alternative goal pursuits, but are costly or *detrimental* to them. In such cases, the unifinal means should, due to the dilution effect, be perceived as particularly instrumental to the focal goal that the means *does* serve, regardless of the costs to alternative goals one may incur by its use. Still, however, one may be reluctant to actually employ such a costly, unifinal means, due to its apparent detrimentality to alternative goal pursuits. Indeed, these alternative goal constraints have been shown to limit the range of means one will consider for focal goal pursuit to include only multifinal means, or those that will serve both the focal goal *and* alternative goals (Kopetz et al., 2011). So the critical question becomes: when will those alternative goal constraints be relaxed, such that people also consider using the unifinal and costly means for focal goal pursuit?

The answer resides in the notion of intense focal goal commitment: Specifically, under high commitment to a focal goal, people tend to suppress or inhibit alternative goals, which would otherwise drain valuable resources away from pursuit of the valued focal goal (Shah, Friedman, & Kruglanski, 2002). Moreover, once those alternative goals have been suppressed, the individual's means set for pursuing the focal goal expands to include not only multifinal means, but also unifinal means to the focal goal, including those which may be costly to the prior alternative goal considerations (Kopetz et al., 2011). This allows for the dilution effect to operate on the individual's choice among means for focal goal pursuit: Because costly, unifinal means seems particularly *instrumental* to the valued focal goal (due to the dilution effect), such means may be perceived not only as one among several potential means for focal goal pursuit, but as the *optimal* means, or the one that will afford the highest probability of attaining the focal goal.

A goal systemic framework thus elucidates the linkage between uncertainty as a *goal* to which one may be highly committed and extremism as a variety of costly, unifinal *means* to that goal. Under conditions in which one is highly committed to uncertainty reduction, alternative goals to which extreme means would be detrimental may be suppressed, freeing the way for the individual to employ extreme (costly) means in pursuit of uncertainty reduction. If an individual is highly committed to the focal goal, then he or she may prefer to use such a unifinal means, whatever its costs for alternative goals, because the dilution effect leads the individual to perceive such a means as highly instrumental to the valued focal goal, and because the alternative goals are now suppressed. For instance, due to the dilution effect, a person may perceive a unifinal (and costly) supremacist group as more instrumental to the uncertainty reduction goal than a lobbyist group. If she feels particularly threatened by immigrants (or *committed* to reducing economic uncertainty that she feels is caused by immigrants), she may temporarily suppress her alternative legal or normative conformity goals and choose the unifinal and costly, and thus (seemingly) potently instrumental supremacist group over the multifinal lobbyist group.

On the Relativity of Extremism

As we have argued, the dilution effect suggests that under high commitment to a focal goal, one might prefer to use a means that is uniquely instrumental to the focal goal, even if it is detrimental to alternative goals. Moreover, those who are less committed to the focal goal might perceive such a unifinal and costly means as a relatively poor or extreme choice, because the means would not help them to achieve other important goals and, in fact, would harm their pursuit of alternative goals. In this manner, those who are highly committed to a focal goal would perceive a unifinal and costly means as nonextreme, whereas those who are less committed would perceive the very same means as extreme. Put differently, the *perception* of extremism is relative to a particular point of view, or "in the eye of the beholder" (Kruglanski & Orehek, 2009).

Thus, our characterization of extremism is expanded to include not only the *process* leading to "extreme" behavior, but also the *perception* of "extremism" by both the actor and observers. An individual may possess an extreme attitude ("extreme" in terms of zealous conviction) that leads to extreme behavior ("extreme" in terms of its deviance from the norm). However, the extremity of the attitude and of the behavior may be perceived differently by the actor and others who share his or her perspective, versus observers who do not. For instance, individuals who share an extremely negative attitude toward immigrants may not view their attitude as "extreme," although others who do not share this attitude may. Likewise, individuals who join White supremacy groups may not view their behavior as deviant or "extreme" (particularly if they are joined by a multitude of likeminded White supremacists), whereas onlookers may perceive them as the prototypical instantiation of extremism.

Essentially, the perception of extremism is a judgment about a behavior, an opinion, or an emotional reaction. As with all judgments, those concerning the extremity of a given attitude or action depend on the psychology of the individual who is making the judgment. If the individual is the so-called actor, who is choosing among means to pursue a highly valued goal, he or she may not perceive a unifinal and costly means as extreme, because the dilution effect suggests that it is highly instrumental to the highly valued goal. However, if the individual is an observer who is less committed to the actor's focal goal, he or she may perceive the very same means as extreme. Because high commitment to a focal goal results in the inhibition of alternative goals (Shah, Friedman, & Kruglanski, 2002), the costs incurred by use of a deviant means will be more apparent to an observer who is *less* committed the actor's focal goal, and thus more aware of the alternative goals that the means may fail to deliver, or even undermine.

Uncertainty and Extremism: Goal and Instrumental Means

Our discussion thus far has concerned commitment and extremism, and the goal systemic framework presented here could pertain to any goal at all, irrespective of content. For example, a person committed to the goal of health might carry out extreme health-related activities (e.g., run marathons, exercise for hours, join Rocky in his run up the courthouse steps), devote considerable time to learning about the nutritional value of various foods, and so on. Similarly, a person committed to work-related goals will not only exhibit zeal in her pursuits, but also deviate from what most people would do by staying at the office late, working on weekends, and so on. Another person who is committed to the goal of a slim figure, avoiding a large figure, or (unconsciously) being in control of some aspect of her life might engage in anorexic or bulimic behaviors, which are detrimental to health and deviate from most people's eating habits.

The question remains, though: What has any of this to do with uncertainty? We propose that the relationship between uncertainty and extremism is nonunique. Rather, it is an instantiation, or a special case, of the relation between goal commitment and extremism. In other words, if uncertainty is upsetting or uncomfortable enough, then it will induce high commitment to the goal of uncertainty reduction. Under these conditions, individuals will pursue uncertainty reduction with abandon ("forgetting all else") and will do whatever it takes to attain uncertainty reduction. For example, they may join fundamentalist movements that proclaim a Truth and eschew debate and discussion, they might become members of bigoted organizations intolerant of cultural diversity, and so on. Because the extreme groups adopt beliefs that are detrimental to mainstream norms and concerns, they are "unifinal" and hence perceived as particularly effective means to the uncertainty reduction goal.

Previous research on the need for cognitive closure provides support for this notion. People under high need for closure are more likely to exhibit group-centric characteristics (e.g., intergroup biases, autocracy, opinion uniformity),

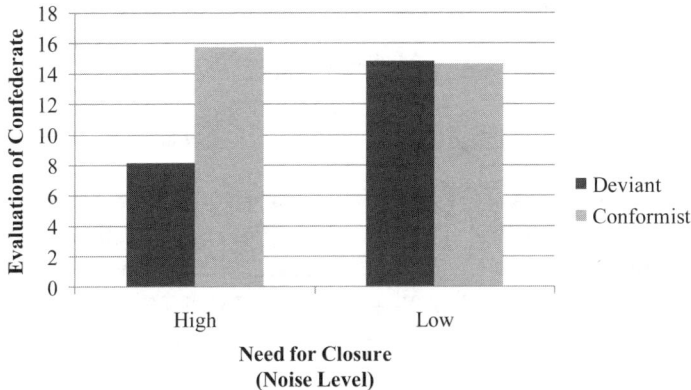

Fig. 1. Evaluations of deviant versus conformist confederates under high versus low need for closure, induced via the presence or absence of a noisy printer.

which are defining features of many extreme or deviant groups (Hogg, 2004, 2012; Kruglanski, Pierro, Mannetti, & DeGrada, 2006). This need for closure–group centrism relation may be particularly strong when people perceive legitimate reasons for group centrism such as a large ingroup–outgroup status differential (see Federico, Hunt, & Fisher, 2013) or beliefs in ingroup superiority even when real status differences suggest otherwise, which can in turn lead to support for and intentions to engage in violence against outgroups (Doosje et al., 2013). While group centrism uniquely serves to bolster a deviant minority group's worldview (i.e., reduce uncertainty), it is also costly to alternative goals, such as personal freedom and voice. A high need for closure also leads to zealous *seizing and freezing* on early information, hence relinquishing a concern for accuracy and the consideration of all relevant information (Kruglanski & Webster, 1996). High need for closure is further related to the rejection of opinion deviates in the group, again at the cost of tolerance, acceptance, and a thorough consideration of information, as shown by Kruglanski and Webster (1991). For example, in their Study 2, small groups of participants were instructed to discuss information and arrive at unanimous consensus on drug testing policies for campus athletes. Both the participants and information were biased in favor of mandatory drug testing, as was one of two experimental confederates in each group; however, the other confederate in the group held a deviant opinion from that of the majority (i.e., against compulsory drug testing). Each group discussed the issue with either a noisy printer working in the background (to induce high need for closure) or no background noise (thus affording relatively low need for closure) and then evaluated each of the other group members, including the confederates. As shown in Figure 1, participants rated the deviant confederate much less positively than the conformist confederate, but *only* when need for closure was elevated. This and the other aforementioned need for closure effects can be seen as the adoption of extreme (and otherwise costly) means for the pursuit of uncertainty reduction.

Implications for Future Research

Portraying the relation between uncertainty and extremism as a special case of the general psychological relation between goal commitment and extremism has several implications following from a goal systemic analysis. We outline these implications below, along with pertinent illustrative examples and novel research questions that warrant further investigation:

Implication 1. It is not uncertainty per se that induces extremism but rather a given, sufficient level of uncertainty that does so. The uncertainty should be aversive enough for the individual to inhibit the alternative goals that the extreme means would undermine. This suggests that the functional relationship between uncertainty and extremism may not be linear, but rather take a step-wise form. That is, up to a given point, increasing uncertainty may not lead to systematic increases in extremism. However, beyond that point, there might be a sharp jump in extremism. A search for this "uncertainty threshold" may yield promising results.

Implication 2. The step-wise jump in extremism at the "uncertainty threshold" should be correlated with suppression of the alternative goal concerns to which an extreme means to the goal of uncertainty reduction would seem inimical. In other words, at levels of uncertainty greater than or equal to the uncertainty threshold, the endorsement or use of extreme means should increase with the suppression of alternative goals to which the means is detrimental.

Implication 3. Even at relatively high levels of uncertainty, activating alternative goal concerns (e.g., via priming) should reduce individuals' tendency to embrace extreme uncertainty-reducing measures. Such alternative goal activation would essentially reactivate alternative goals, thus reminding the individual of the costs incurred by use of the extreme means and potentially reducing the likelihood that he or she would endorse or use the extreme means. Policymakers may be able to use this implication to their advantage by identifying alternative goals that would-be extremists value and reminding them of the importance of those goals to them and the costs they may incur to those goals by use of extreme means. For instance, as Fiske (2013) suggests, fostering dual ingroup identities among immigrants may increase their commitment to normative concerns within the new country, thus rendering deviant, extreme means for uncertainty reduction unappealing. In some cases, such alternative goal activation may be sufficient to deter extreme behavior.

Implication 4. Actor–observer differences in perceived extremity of given uncertainty-reducing activities should be apparent. Actors whose need to reduce uncertainty is elevated should regard their instrumental actions and opinions as less extreme than observers whose desire for uncertainty reduction is lower. For instance, a highly uncertain individual might consider joining a cult to be a perfectly rational means to uncertainty reduction; by contrast, the average person might view cult membership as extreme, because reducing uncertainty is not as important to him, and he or she may also entertain alternative goals that a highly uncertain individual may have eschewed. In other words, for the observer who is less committed to the actor's focal goal, any perceived benefits of extremism would simply not be worth the costs. In terms of policy, one obvious implication lies in the realm of political rhetoric that paints various groups as extreme—but only if those groups feel or act differently than "we" do. The relativity of perceptions of extremism should serve as a constant reminder to politicians and other key players that finding common ground in terms of shared goals, as well as being sensitive to others' concern for unshared goals, is critical to avoiding the sort of Black-and-White, us versus them thinking that so often alienates the other and gives rise to extreme action.

Implication 5. The actor–observer difference could be replicated within subjects. Individuals whose alternative concerns are primed (versus not primed) should regard given uncertainty-reducing actions and opinions as more extreme. This implies that an actor who is highly committed to uncertainty reduction and employs an extreme means may later look back on his or her actions and regret the use of that means. This might occur if, for instance, an individual initially joined an extremist group in order to reduce uncertainty, but over time became less concerned with uncertainty reduction and more concerned with the social acceptance goal to which she incurred costs by joining the extreme group. Such an individual may decide to leave the extremist group despite its potent uncertainty reduction, because the alternative social acceptance goal has now become an important consideration, as well.

This implication could be useful to policymakers as a strategy for deradicalization or deprogramming efforts. Increasing the salience of costs to alternative goals, even after the extreme behavior has occurred, may induce a sense of regret among extremists. Although a few particularly hardened extremists may continue to doggedly take pride in the sacrifices they have made for the cause (rather than regretting them), the majority may come to realize that they grossly underestimated those costs and now wish to move forward peaceably, trying to restore what was lost during whatever time is left for them.

Implication 6. Although unifinal means that are costly to alternative goals (i.e., extreme) may be perceived as more effective than multifinal means, a means' status as unifinal or multifinal is not the only factor that may impact its perceived instrumentality to a focal goal. Other variables that lead individuals to perceive multifinal, or at least noncostly means as particularly instrumental to a focal goal could sometimes operate more strongly than the dilution effect. For instance, individuals may be deradicalized through repeated exposure to trusted epistemic authorities who denounce extremism and endorse less violent means to uncertainty reduction. Indeed, several deradicalization programs for suspected terrorist detainees employ the services of moderate Muslim clerics (where the conflicts involve Islamic extremism), who eschew violence and espouse peaceful, nonviolent action and lifestyles (Rabasa et al., 2010). Even if extreme means are still perceived as most instrumental to uncertainty reduction, less extreme alternative means may be newly perceived as sufficiently instrumental, or "instrumental enough" to the goal of uncertainty reduction. Providing an alternative means may give individuals another way out and thus prevent them from embracing extremism.

Conclusion

One final implication of our goal systemic analysis is that extremism is not necessarily bad or good. Zealotry and deviance can be employed in the service of goals that may be valued either positively or negatively by a given individual or group. Viewing the uncertainty–extremism relation highlights for us the negative aspects of extremism, because the goal of uncertainty reduction may induce close-mindedness, bigotry, autocracy, and all things that (predominantly liberal) academia tends to evaluate negatively. However, we might applaud similarly high commitment to a goal that academics tend to value positively, such as the zealous publication pursuits of a graduate student. Note that those outside academia might view the lengths to which such a student would go in pursuit of an extensive CV as quite excessive or simply "not worth it." Indeed, recent high-profile cases of scientific misconduct in our own field of psychology serve as sobering reminders of academics' equal vulnerability to this very process of high focal goal commitment, inhibition of alternative considerations, and use of costly (extreme) means for pursuing tenure, grants, fame, and so on.

The crux of our argument is that those with different values and goals may differentially perceive a given attitude or action as extreme. These values and goals may vary across individuals, groups, or cultures, and such differences can lead to no small amount of misunderstanding and interpersonal or intergroup conflict. Just as Saddam Hussein, Adolf Hitler, and Muammar Gaddafi could be considered extremists, so could Nelson Mandela, Mahatma Gandhi, Jesus Christ, and countless others throughout history who have been venerated for their zealous pursuits of what those who venerate them consider noble causes. Extremists of all stripes share a common deviance from the norm in order to pursue a highly valued goal, often sacrificing much in the process. The difference between whom we consider to be good and bad extremists lies in what and whom they were willing to sacrifice, and whether or not we care about those costs.

References

Abelson, R. P. (1995). Attitude extremity. In R. E. Petty & J. A. Krosnick (Eds.), *Attitude strength: Antecedents and consequences* (pp. 25–41). Hillsdale, NJ: Erlbaum Press.
Ajzen, I. (1985). From intentions to actions: A theory of planned behavior. In J. Kuhl & J. Beckman (Eds.), *Action-control: From cognition to behavior* (pp. 11–39). Heidelberg: Springer.
Breton, A., Galeotti, G., Salmon, P., & Wintrobe, R. (Eds.) (2002). *Political extremism and rationality*. New York: Cambridge University Press. doi: 10.2277/0521804418
Dechesne, M., & Kruglanski, A. W. (2004). Terror's epistemic consequences: Existential threats and the quest for certainty and closure. In J. Greenberg, S. L. Koole, & T. A. Pyszczynski (Eds.), *Handbook of experimental existential psychology* (pp. 247–262). New York: Guilford Press.
Doosje, B., Loseman, A., & van den Bos, K. (2013). Determinants of radicalization of Islamic youth in the Netherlands: Personal uncertainty, perceived injustice, and perceived group threat. *Journal of Social Issues, 69*, 586–604.
Esses, V. M., Medianu, S., & Lawson, A. S. (2013). Uncertainty, threat, and the role of the media in promoting the dehumanization of immigrants and refugees. *Journal of Social Issues, 69*, 518–536.
Federico, C. M., Hunt, C. V., & Fisher, E. L. (2013). Uncertainty and status-based asymmetries in the distinction between the "good" us and the "bad" them: Evidence that group status strengthens the relationship between the need for cognitive closure and extremity in intergroup differentiation. *Journal of Social Issues, 69*, 473–494.
Fishbein, M., & Ajzen, I. (1975). *Belief, attitude, intention, and behavior: An introduction to theory and research*. Reading, MA: Addison-Wesley.
Fiske, S. T. (2013). A millennial challenge: Extremism in uncertain times. *Journal of Social Issues, 69*, 605–613.
Gelfand, M. J., LaFree, G., Fahey, S., & Feinberg, E. (2013). Culture and extremism. *Journal of Social Issues, 69*, 495–517.
Hogg, M. A. (2004). Uncertainty and extremism: Identification with high entitativity groups under conditions of uncertainty. In V. Yzerbyt, C. M. Judd, & O. Corneille (Eds.), *The psychology of group perception: Perceived variability, entitativity, and essentialism* (pp. 401–418). New York: Psychology Press.
Hogg, M. A. (2007). Uncertainty-identity theory. In M. P. Zanna (Ed.), *Advances in experimental social psychology* (Vol. 39, pp. 69–126). San Diego, CA: Academic Press. doi: 10.1016/S0065-2601(06)39002-8
Hogg, M. A. (2012). Uncertainty-identity theory. In P. A. M. Van Lange, A. W. Kruglanski, & E. T. Higgins (Eds.), *Handbook of theories of social psychology* (pp. 62–80). Thousand Oaks, CA: Sage. doi: 10.4135/9781446249222
Hogg, M. A., & Adelman, J. (2013). Uncertainty-identity theory: Extreme groups, radical behavior, and authoritarian leadership. *Journal of Social Issues, 69*, 436–454.
Hogg, M. A., Kruglanski, A., & van den Bos, K. (2013). Uncertainty and the roots of extremism. *Journal of Social Issues, 69*, 407–418.
Jaccard, J., Radecki, C., Wilson, T., & Dittus, P. (1995). Methods for identifying consequential beliefs: Implications for understanding attitude strength. In R. Petty & J. Krosnick (Eds.), *Attitude strength: Antecedents and consequences* (pp. 337–360). Hillsdale, NJ: Erlbaum Press.
Kay, A. C., & Eibach, R. P. (2013). Compensatory control and its implications for ideological extremism. *Journal of Social Issues, 69*, 564–585.
Kopetz, C., Faber, T., Fishbach, A., & Kruglanski, A. (2011). Multifinality constraints effect: How goal multiplicity narrows the means set to a focal end. *Journal of Personality and Social Psychology, 100*(5), 810–826. doi: 10.1037/a0022980

Krosnick, J. A., Boninger, D. S., Chuang, Y. C., Berent, M. K., & Carnot, C. G. (1993). Attitude strength: One construct or many related constructs? *Journal of Personality and Social Psychology*, *65*(6), 1132–1151.

Kruglanski, A.W., & Orehek, E. (2009). Toward a relativity theory of rationality. *Social Cognition*, *27*(5), 639–660. doi: 10.1521/soco.2009.27.5.639

Kruglanski, A. W., Pierro, A., Mannetti, L., & DeGrada, E. (2006). Groups as epistemic providers: Need for closure and the unfolding of group-centrism. *Psychological Review*, *113*(1), 84–100. doi: 10.1037/0033-295X.113.1.84

Kruglanski, A. W., Shah, J. Y., Fishbach, A., Friedman, R., Chun, W. Y., Sleeth-Keppler, D. (2002). A theory of goal systems. In M. P. Zanna (Ed.), *Advances in experimental social psychology* (Vol. *34*, pp. 331–376). New York: Academic Press.

Kruglanski, A. W., & Webster, D. M. (1991). Group members' reactions to opinion deviates and conformists at varying degrees of proximity to decision deadline and of environmental noise. *Journal of Personality and Social Psychology*, *61*(2), 212–225. doi: 10.1037/0022-3514.61.2.212

Kruglanski, A. W., & Webster, D. M. (1994). Individual differences in need for cognitive closure. *Journal of Personality and Social Psychology*, *67*(6), 1049–1062. doi: 10.1037/0022-3514.67.6.1049

Kruglanski, A. W., & Webster, D. M. (1996). Motivated closing of the mind: "Seizing" and "freezing." *Psychological Review*, *103*(2), 263–283. doi: 10.1037/0033-295X.103.2.263

McGregor, I. (2003). Defensive zeal: Compensatory conviction about attitudes, values, goals, groups, and self-definitions in the face of personal uncertainty. In S. J. Spencer, S. Fein, M. P. Zanna, & J. M. Olson (Eds.), *Motivated social perception* (pp. 73–92). Mahwah, NJ: Lawrence Erlbaum Associates.

McGregor, I. (2006a). Offensive defensiveness: Toward an integrative neuroscience of compensatory zeal after mortality salience, personal uncertainty, and other poignant self-threats. *Psychological Inquiry*, *17*(4), 299–308. doi: 10.1080/10478400701366977

McGregor, I. (2006b). Zeal appeal: The allure of moral extremes. *Basic and Applied Social Psychology*, *28*(4), 343–348. doi: 10.1207/s15324834basp2804_7

McGregor, I., & Jordan, C. H. (2007). The mask of zeal: Low implicit self-esteem, threat, and defensive extremism. *Self and Identity*, *6*, 223–237. doi: 10.1080/15298860601115351

McGregor, I., Prentice, M., & Nash, K. (2013). Anxious uncertainty and reactive approach motivation (RAM) for religious, idealistic, and lifestyle extremes. *Journal of Social Issues*, *69*, 537–563.

McGregor, I., Zanna, M. P., Holmes, J. G., & Spencer, S. J. (2001). Compensatory conviction in the face of personal uncertainty: Going to extremes and being oneself. *Journal of Personality and Social Psychology*, *80*(3), 472–488. doi: 10.1037/0022-3514.80.3.472

Proulx, T., & Major, B. (2013). A raw deal: Heightened liberalism and conservatism following exposure to anomalous playing cards. *Journal of Social Issues*, *69*, 455–472.

Rabasa, A., Pettyjohn, S. L., Ghez, J. J., & Boucek, C. (2010). Deradicalizing Islamic extremists. Santa Monica, CA: RAND Corporation. Retrieved from http://www.rand.org/pubs/monographs/MG1053

Shah, J. Y., Friedman, R., & Kruglanski, A. W. (2002). Forgetting all else: On the antecedents and consequences of goal shielding. *Journal of Personality and Social Psychology*, *83*(6), 1261–1280.

Sidanius, J. (1985). Cognitive functioning and sociopolitical ideology revisited. *Political Psychology*, *6*(4), 637–661. doi: 10.2307/3791021

Solomon, S., Greenberg, J., & Pyszczinski, T. (2004). The cultural animal: Twenty years of terror management theory and research. In J. Greenberg, S. Koole, & T. Pyszczinski (Eds.), *Handbook of experimental existential psychology* (pp. 13–34). New York: Guilford Press.

Staub, E. (1989). *The roots of evil: The origins of genocide and other group violence*. New York: Cambridge University Press.

Van den Bos, K. (2009). The social psychology of uncertainty management and system justification. In J. T. Jost, A. C. Kay, & H. Thorisdottir (Eds.), *Social and psychological bases of ideology and system justification* (pp. 185–209). New York: Oxford University Press, Inc. doi: 10.1093/acprof:oso/9780195320916.001.0001

Van den Bos, K., Ameijde, J., & van Gorp, H. (2006). On the psychology of religion: The role of personal uncertainty in religious worldview defense. *Basic and Applied Social Psychology, 28*(4), 333–341. doi: 10.1207/s15324834basp2804_6

Van den Bos, K., Poortvliet, P. M., Maas, M., Miedema, J., & van den Ham, E. (2005). An enquiry concerning the principles of cultural norms and values: The impact of uncertainty and mortality salience on reactions to violations and bolstering of cultural worldviews. *Journal of Experimental Social Psychology, 41*, 91–113. doi: 10.1016/j.jesp.2004.06.001

Visser, P. S., Bizer, G. Y., & Krosnick, J. A. (2006). Exploring the latent structure of strength-related attitude attributes. In M. P. Zanna (Ed.), *Advances in experimental social psychology* (Vol. *38*, pp. 1–68). San Diego, CA: Academic Press. doi: 10.1016/S0065-2601(06)38001-X

Wintrobe, R. (2006). *Rational extremism: The political economy of radicalism*. New York: Cambridge University Press. doi: http://dx.doi.org/10.1017/CBO9780511511028

Zhang, Y., Fishbach, A., & Kruglanski, A. W. (2007). The dilution model: How additional goals undermine the perceived instrumentality of a shared path. *Journal of Personality and Social Psychology, 92*(3), 389–401. doi: 10.1037/0022-3514.92.3.389

KRISTEN M. KLEIN is a doctoral candidate in the Social, Decision, and Organizational Sciences program in the University of Maryland's Department of Psychology. She was a Graduate Fellow funded by the Department of Homeland Security's Scholarship and Fellowship Program and participated in the Max Planck Summer Institute for Bounded Rationality in Berlin. In addition to her research on the psychology of extremism, she serves as Project Manager on a database of individual- and organizational-level motives for suicide attacks. She has also worked with researchers at SUNY Albany on social networks in the IRA and suicide attacks as an organizational tactic, as well as basic research on judgment and decision processes that may underlie extremism.

ARIE W. KRUGLANSKI (PhD, UCLA) is Professor of Psychology at the University of Maryland. He has published widely on human judgment and decision making, motivation, group processes, and the psychology of terrorism. His awards include the Donald Campbell Award from Society of Personality and Social Psychology, and the Distinguished Scientific Contribution Award from the Society for Experimental Social Psychology. He has served as editor of the *Journal of Personality and Social Psychology*: Attitudes and Social Cognition section, editor of the *Personality and Social Psychology Bulletin*, and Associate Editor of the *American Psychologist*. Dr. Kruglanski is presently a senior investigator at University of Maryland's National Center for the Study of Terrorism and the Response to Terrorism (START).

Uncertainty–Identity Theory: Extreme Groups, Radical Behavior, and Authoritarian Leadership

Michael A. Hogg[*] and Janice Adelman
Claremont Graduate University

This article describes uncertainty–identity theory's analysis of how self-uncertainty may lead, through social identity and self-categorization processes, to group and societal extremism. We provide details of empirical evidence from direct tests of the theory that focus on four aspects of extremism: (1) studies of self-uncertainty and student support for extreme campus protest groups that promote a radical agenda; (2) studies of uncertainty, identity centrality, and support for violent group action in the context of the Israel–Palestine conflict; (3) studies of the role played by self-uncertainty in support for leadership per se and for authoritarian leadership in particular; and (4) studies of the conjunction of group-membership factors that lead specific individuals within a group to go to greater extremes than others on behalf of the group. The article ends with a discussion of policy implications and principles that might help prevent uncertainty leading, through group identity processes, to societal extremism.

Although society contains individuals, both human endeavor and the operation of human cognition tend to organize society into discrete social categories and human groups. The nature of such groups and their relationships to one another govern much of who we are, specifically our social identity, and our associated perceptions, attitudes, feelings and behaviors, as well as the way others perceive and treat us. Because groups and identity are so fundamental to social life and so consequential for individuals, people are highly motivated to belong to and be accepted by those groups that best satisfy these motivations.

In this article we discuss one such motive: reduction of feelings of uncertainty about or reflecting on one's self and identity. The process of self-categorization that underpins group identification and generates group behaviors is uniquely

---

[*]Correspondence concerning this article should be addressed to Michael Hogg, School of Behavioral and Organizational Sciences, Claremont Graduate University, 123 East 8th Street, Claremont, CA 91711 [e-mail: michael.hogg@cgu.edu].

well equipped to satisfy this motive. However, some types of groups and identities are better suited than others to self-uncertainty reduction through self-categorization—specifically, distinctive and well-structured groups that have clear boundaries and membership criteria, and consensual and prescriptive attitudinal and behavioral attributes grounded in a relatively homogeneous world view. To reduce self-uncertainty people seek these groups out, or try to transform preexisting membership groups to have these attributes.

It is but a short step from here to the popular notion of "extremism." These types of groups can, under uncertainty, become extremist groups that have orthodox ideologies and hierarchical authority structures, promote homogeneity through intolerance of dissent, and sponsor extremist behavioral agenda (Hogg, Kruglanski, & Van den Bos, 2013). However, it is important to note that the analysis proposed in this article focuses on social cognitive and social interactive processes associated with extremism, not the larger scale and more collective sociopolitical forces that play a role and often provide the distal context for these more individual level processes (cf. Moghaddam & Love, 2011).

We describe uncertainty–identity theory (e.g., Hogg, 2007a, 2012), specifically its analysis of the relationship between uncertainty and extremism, and then go into more detail to describe relevant empirical evidence from direct tests of the theory. We discuss studies of self-uncertainty and student support for extreme campus protest groups that promote a radical action agenda; studies conducted in Israel of uncertainty, identity centrality, and support for different forms of violent group action in the context of the Israel–Palestine conflict; studies of the role played by self-uncertainty in support for leadership per se and for authoritarian leadership in particular; and studies of the conjunction of group membership–related factors that lead specific individuals within a group to go to greater extremes than others on behalf of the group. The article ends with a discussion of specific policy implications of this theory and research—general policy principles that might help prevent uncertainty leading to societal extremism.

Social Identity and Intergroup Conflict

Over the past 40 years, social identity theory (Tajfel & Turner, 1979; Turner, Hogg, Oakes, Reicher, & Wetherell, 1987) has become a major and very widely cited social psychological explanation of processes within and between human groups and social categories (also see Abrams & Hogg, 2010; Hogg & Abrams, 1988). The theory explicates social cognitive, social interactive, and social structural processes and their interactions that reciprocally link self-conception as a group member with group and intergroup phenomena.

Although social identity theory does not explicitly talk about "extremism" it does map out conditions under which intergroup behavior can become overtly competitive and assertive; for example, a lower status group will quite possibly "rise up" against the dominant group if it feels its status position is illegitimate, that the status quo is unstable and susceptible to change, and if it has a realistic and practical road map to overturn the status quo (e.g., Ellemers, 1993). Underpinning this analysis of competitive intergroup behavior is the motivational assumption that because groups define and evaluate who we are, our social identity, groups, and their members continually struggle to protect or achieve a favorable social identity based on evaluatively positive distinctiveness from relevant outgroups. Overt intergroup conflict is only one of an array of different ways to achieve this, depending on people's understanding of the nature of relations between groups.

The group level dynamic of positive social identity is in turn underpinned by an individual level motivation associated with protection and pursuit of self-esteem (Tajfel & Turner, 1979). Research on this "self-esteem hypothesis" finds that people do indeed feel positive about themselves if they identify with a positive group, but that lowered self-esteem does not reliably motivate people to actually join or identify more strongly with groups (Abrams & Hogg, 1988; Rubin & Hewstone, 1998). At the very least, therefore, some other motivation must be involved in causing people to identify with and belong to groups—and perhaps features of this motivation can also account for group level extremism. It was to answer this question that uncertainty–identity theory was originally developed.

Uncertainty–Identity Theory

Uncertainty–identity theory (Hogg, 2000, 2007a, 2012) is a conceptualization of the motivational underpinnings of social identity processes and associated group and intergroup behaviors. The key premise is that feelings of uncertainty are aversive, because uncertainty makes it difficult to anticipate events and plan action—uncertainty motivates behavior aimed at reducing uncertainty.

The experience of uncertainty can vary from an exciting challenge that people feel they have the resources to deal with to a fearsome threat that they feel they do not have the resources to deal with (cf. Blascovich & Tomaka, 1996). In both cases there is a motivation to reduce uncertainty, but the path taken differs: where uncertainty is experienced as a challenge people may adopt promotive or approach behaviors, where it is experienced as a threat people may adopt more protective or avoidant behaviors (cf. Higgins's, 1998, regulatory focus theory).

A key resource for uncertainty reduction is the cognitive capacity to resolve the uncertainty. Because uncertainty reduction can be cognitively demanding, people will only invest cognitive energy in resolving uncertainties that are important to them (cf. cognitive miser or motivated tactician models of social cognition, e.g., Fiske & Taylor, 1991). Even then they typically work to reduce uncertainty until they are only "sufficiently" certain (Pollock, 2003) to provide some sense of closure, which allows them to move on and dedicate cognitive energy to other things.

Perhaps the most significant determinant of the subjective importance of an uncertainty is the extent to which self is involved. We are particularly motivated to reduce uncertainty if we feel uncertain about things that reflect on or are relevant to self, or if we are uncertain about our self and identity directly. It is self-uncertainty that is particularly motivating. People need to know who they are, how to behave and what to think, and who others are and how they might behave, think, and treat us. Being properly located in this way renders the social world and one's place within it relatively predictable and allows one to plan effective action, avoid harm, know who to trust, and so forth.

There are potentially many ways to reduce or protect against self-uncertainty, but group identification is particularly effective. This is because identification is associated with social categorization of self and others—a process that depersonalizes behavior and perception of self and others to conform to group prototypes that describe and prescribe how people (including oneself) will and ought to behave and interact with one another. Social categorization of self and others generates a sense of ingroup identification and belonging, and regulates perception, inference, feelings, behavior, and interaction to conform to prototype-based knowledge one has about one's own group and relevant outgroups. Furthermore, because group prototypes are shared ("we" agree "we" are like this, "they"' are like that) one's world view and self-concept are consensually validated by the overt and verbal behavior of fellow group members. Social categorization makes one's own and others' behavior predictable, and allows one to avoid harm, plan effective action, and know how one should feel and behave.

Entitativity and Self-Uncertainty Reduction

Uncertainty–identity theory has several basic key predictions: that uncertainty triggers the process of identification with a self-inclusive category; that people identify more strongly with groups when they feel uncertain; that uncertainty-based identification reduces uncertainty, and that people who feel uncertain will identify even with a group that mediates low status. All of these predictions have been robustly supported across numerous studies—studies that have used different paradigms, different group contexts, and different manipulations and measures of uncertainty (e.g., Grieve & Hogg, 1999; Mullin & Hogg, 1998; Reid & Hogg, 2005; see Hogg, 2007a, for overview). Studies have also explored a variety of boundary conditions or moderators of the uncertainty–identification relationship. Of most relevance here is the important moderating role of group entitativity.

Although uncertainty motivates identification, some types of groups and some properties of groups are more effective at reducing uncertainty through identification. According to uncertainty–identity theory entitativity, that property of a group, resting on clear boundaries, internal homogeneity, social interaction, clear internal structure, common goals, and common fate, which makes a group "groupy"

(Campbell, 1958; Hamilton & Sherman, 1996), moderates the relationship between self-uncertainty and identification (Hogg, 2004).

Under elevated self-uncertainty people prefer to identify with or identify more strongly with high than low entitativity groups. The reason for this is that self-categorization reduces uncertainty most effectively if the group prototype that prescribes cognition, affect, and behavior, is simple, clear, unambiguous, prescriptive, focused, and consensual rather than vague, ambiguous, unfocused, and dissensual. Clear prototypes grounded in consensus and a shared world view, such as the former, are more likely to be found in high than low entitativity groups. Under high uncertainty, people may loosen their ties to, weaken their identification with, and even disidentify altogether from low entitativity groups as they do little to resolve self-uncertainty.

A pair of studies by Hogg, Sherman, Dierselhuis, Maitner, and Moffitt (2007) provides direct support for this idea. Self-uncertainty was experimentally primed to be high or low, and the perceived entitativity of participants' political party was measured (Study 1) or the perceived entitativity of participants' ad hoc lab group was manipulated (Study 2). Group identification was measured by a multi-item scale. In both cases, participants identified significantly more strongly when they were uncertain and their group was highly entitative. There is also indirect support for this general idea from research by Yzerbyt and his colleagues (see Yzerbyt, Castano, Leyens, & Paladrino, 2000). In addition, a pair of field studies of political party supporters and workers on strike, by Sherman, Hogg, and Maitner (2009), found support for the related idea that self-uncertainty can lead people to accentuate the perceived entitativity of a group they are already members of.

Beyond Entitativity: Extreme Group Structure and Radical Group Action

The uncertainty–entitativity logic may be extrapolated to help explain radicalism and zealotry (Hogg 2004, 2005a, 2007b; Hogg, Adelman, & Blagg, 2010; cf. Kruglanski, Pierro, Mannetti, & De Grada, 2006). Taken to an extreme, entitativity could embody rigid, closed boundaries, internal homogeneity and consensus, orthodox and ideological belief systems and associated world view, ritualized practices, profound ethnocentrism, hierarchical structure, and emphatic leadership. A group structured in this way would certainly be considered extremist, and able to provide a very certain sense of self in an uncertain world. Under more extreme uncertainty people may prefer to identify with these extreme manifestations of group structure—such groups are especially well equipped to resolve or protect people from more extreme self-uncertainty.

However, the construct of entitativity is primarily a perceptual construct that describes group structure—it does not speak to what a group does; the extent to which a group adopts a moderate or more radical course of action to protect or promote its identity and the welfare of its members. The most societally problematic feature of extremist or radical groups is precisely that their members identify strongly with a group that advocates and systematically pursues radical actions.

This action component of a group's identity is likely to become more important when what the group stands for is self-relevant and viewed as under threat. When, for example, people feel their security, prosperity, and lifestyle are threatened, or their group is "deprived" relative to another group (cf. Runciman, 1966; Walker & Pettigrew, 1984; Walker & Smith, 2002) they yearn to identify strongly with a group that can actually get things done to remove or buffer the threat—a radical group that has a forceful behavioral agenda. Against this background self-uncertainty will strengthen identification with assertive radical groups, perhaps transforming members into fanatics, zealots, true believers, and ideologues, and may also weaken identification with less assertive moderate groups.

Such groups can often be beleaguered numerical or power minorities that feel their identity is under threat from a more powerful majority. In which case, in the absence of material power, the pursuit of a diachronically and synchronically consistent and assertive behavioral style will effectively render them highly entitative. Research on minority influence has shown that although such a strategy may appear to have little initial impact on the majority, it often leads to latent change through a process akin to conversion—change that quite effectively promotes the minority's position (Moscovici, 1980; Mugny & Pérez, 1991; also see Crano & Seyranian, 2009; Martin & Hewstone, 2008), and thus, from an uncertainty–identity theory perspective, serves a self-uncertainty reduction function. Groups that behave in a consistent and radical manner are thus attractive to people who are self-conceptually uncertain.

Identification with a radical group is particularly problematic for society if members themselves express intentions to engage in the group's extreme behavior—and even more so if people actually engage in those behaviors. Radical behavior is often risky; even if people fully support such behavior they may be disinclined to actually engage in the behavior until they feel confident that it will be effective and that others will also as a group engage in it. Social identity research on attitude–behavior correspondence shows that the strongest attitude–behavior correspondence occurs if attitudes are normative of a self-inclusive ingroup that people identify with (e.g., Hogg & Smith, 2007; Terry & Hogg, 1996), and research on collective protest underscores, among other things, the role of perceived collective efficacy in transforming supporters into actors (e.g., Klandermans, 1997; Stürmer & Simon, 2004; Van Zomeren, Postmes, & Spears, 2008).

Empirical Tests

For obvious reasons it can be difficult to conduct experiments on uncertainty and extremism that deal with real extreme groups and behaviors (e.g., terrorist cells, gangs, drug cartels, cults). So, experiments have tended to focus on "safer" alternatives, but nevertheless ones that have attributes that are clearly relevant to the concepts under examination.

Radicalism on Campus

One direct test of the uncertainty–identity theory hypothesis that self-uncertainty should strengthen identification with and motivation to behave in terms of extreme groups, and perhaps weaken identification with and support for more moderate groups focused on student radicalism (Hogg, Meehan, & Farquharson, 2010). The context of this experiment was Australian higher education at a time when students were faced with significant uncertainty and threats concerning higher education in general and student funding and resources on campus more specifically. In particular, they were unanimously opposed to planned tuition and fee increases and payment schemes—numerous campus groups had formed to protest these changes.

Students on a large Australian university campus ($N = 82$) watched a carefully constructed video of an interview with an ostensive campus protest group's leadership pair (a male and a female) who described their group. In one condition (the radical group condition) the group was described in extreme terms, as being hierarchically structured and organized with strong disciplinary leadership imposing focus and direction and tightly monitoring membership criteria. "Members were expected to be fully committed and adhere tightly to a single vision and agree completely on strategy and tactics—there was no tolerance for disagreement, dissent, or anything less than full commitment. The group pursued its goals single-mindedly and uncompromisingly, adopting relatively extreme and radical tactics—'we're about action, not talk ... Protest—and vigorously. Rallies—large, loud ones—lecture march outs. We'll blockade the campus if we have to. The students can't be pushed around.'" (Hogg et al., 2010, p. 1063).

In the other condition (moderate group) the group was described as having a more open and informal organizational structure, with a less autocratic and directive leadership—leadership by guidance rather than edict—and relatively open membership criteria. "Members were expected to have varying degrees of commitment, and relatively diverse views that they were encouraged to explore within the group. Individual initiative was encouraged within a relatively open atmosphere. The group adopted relatively less radical tactics—letters to newspapers, leafleting, and meetings." (Hogg et al., 2010, p. 1063).

After having watched the video interviews participants were primed to feel uncertain or less uncertain about themselves. They watched another short video, of fellow students expressing high or low uncertainty about their educational future, and then they were asked to spend time thinking about things that made them feel uncertain/certain about themselves and to write down those things that made them feel most uncertain/certain. This priming methodology was based on previous uncertainty–identity theory research (e.g., Hogg et al., 2007; Sherman et al., 2009). Finally there were two dependent variables—a 9-item measure of identification with the protest group and a 6-item measure of intention to engage in behaviors on behalf of the group.

Because pilot research on a sample ($N = 168$) of the same student population had shown, as expected, a significant preference for the moderate over the radical group, Hogg and associates expected that uncertainty would at very least significantly weaken this preference, and only at best abolish it or reverse it. The key results showed a strong main effect for the type of group—participants identified significantly more strongly with and had stronger behavioral intentions for the moderate than radical group. However, the critical finding was the significant interaction showing that uncertainty moderated this effect as predicted—causing the preference for a moderate group to entirely disappear. Uncertainty significantly strengthened identification with and behavioral intensions for the radical group and weakened identification with and behavioral intentions for the moderate group (this effect was a nonsignificant trend for identification, but reliable for intensions.

This tendency for uncertainty to weaken identification with moderate groups and thus undermine the general preference, in Western societies, for moderate over extreme groups has been further confirmed in a pair of studies by Hogg, Farquharson, Parsons, and Svensson (2012). These studies ($N = 168$ and 84) were conducted on the same population and used almost identical methods to the Hogg et al. (2010) study—the differences were that different ostensive student protest groups were used and the groups were presented in a different form (text manifesto in one study and audio interview in the other), and in both studies self-uncertainty was measured rather than primed. Once again uncertainty abolished preferential identification with the moderate group; and in these studies this was entirely due to significant weakening of identification with the moderate group under uncertainty.

Support for Extremism in the Middle East

Although these studies reported above provide good support for the uncertainty–identity theory analysis of the role played by uncertainty in identification with extreme groups and in intentions to engage in behaviors on behalf of these groups (and the inverse for moderate groups), it is understandable that some commentators might wonder if the popular notion of "extremism" is fully captured by contemporary student protest groups on a Western university campus. To address this potential concern, we collected data via a series of separate field studies and field experiments over a 2-year period in Israel and the Palestinian Territories—a region of the world long characterized by sociopolitical uncertainty, intergroup conflict, and group-based violence. The entire data set exceeded 1,600 self-identified Israeli and Palestinian participants of all major religious affiliations.

Here we focus on only two of these studies (Adelman, Hogg, & Levin, 2012) embedded in this larger enterprise. The studies, which were conducted in Israel, had the aim of examining how strength and centrality of national identity (Palestinian or Israeli) interacted with aspects of self-uncertainty (measured in Study 1 and primed in Study 2) to influence support for extreme actions to protect and promote national identity. The clear prediction from uncertainty–identity theory was that the strongest support for more extreme behaviors would be where both uncertainty was high and national identity was reported to be central and strong.

Regarding the key criterion/dependent measures we noted that the intergroup context in Israel/Palestine is one that casts Israeli Jews as the dominant high status numerical majority, and Palestinian Muslims as the lower status subordinate numerical minority. The two groups have starkly different positions of material power, and associated with this they have ready access to quite different resources to promote and protect their identities. Each group will have different beliefs about what actions are realistically likely to be effective for them as a group. Israeli Jews have substantially greater resources, including a large, well-equipped modern conventional military, than do Palestinian Muslims. Thus the two groups are constrained to resort to different tactics to promote their respective agendas—if they turn to extremism and resort to violence they are likely to employ and support different forms of violence that they believe have the greatest collective efficacy (cf. Van Zomeren et al., 2008; see above). Israelis will resort to conventional military actions rather than suicide bombings, as they do not need to do the latter; whereas Palestinians will resort to suicide bombing rather than military actions, as they cannot do the latter.

In Study 1 ($N = 319$) participants indicated whether they identified as Israeli or Palestinian, then completed standard measures of national identity importance (either Israeli or Palestinian), uncertainty, and justification for a number of conflict behaviors, including the use of military tactics in populated cities, targeted assassinations, and suicide bombs. The key finding here was that among Palestinian Muslims support for the use of suicide bombs was, as predicted, notably stronger among those who identified strongly as Palestinian and reported higher levels of uncertainty, particularly self-uncertainty related to the Middle East conflict, $F(1, 82) = 3.69$, $p = .058$ (both relevant simple main effects were significant at $p < .01$). Among Israeli Jews national identification predicted support for military tactics, but this was not moderated by uncertainty.

Study 2 ($N = 375$) was very similar except that uncertainty was experimentally primed as in previous studies described above. The critical finding here was among Israeli Jews—as predicted, they supported the use of military tactics most strongly when they identified strongly as Israelis and were primed to feel uncertain, $F(1, 233) = 2.99$, $p = .085$ (the simple main effect for national identification was highly significant among Israelis primed to feel uncertain). In this study there were no significant effects among Palestinian Muslims.

Taken together, these two studies provide some initial support for uncertainty–identity theory in a real-world conflict setting—strong national identification coupled with high context-relevant uncertainty is a potent cocktail that strengthens support for group-based intergroup violence that employs whatever resources and methods are readily available to the group. However, the results of the studies are not as robust across the two national groups and the two different methods of operationalizing uncertainty. Further "real-world" studies are needed.

Leadership under Uncertainty

Extremist groups typically tend to be very clearly structured in terms of roles, functions, and membership status. This produces or is associated with a hierarchical authority and leadership structure in which leaders are strong and directive and to varying degrees authoritarian. One of the most obvious and vivid features of extreme groups is their "extreme" leaders. Extremist groups typically need strong leadership in order to secure and protect the group's clear and consensual identity and action agenda, and such leadership is exercised over ingroup members and projected against outgroups. No discussion of group and societal extremism is complete without consideration of influence through leadership.

The social identity theory of leadership (Hogg, 2001; Hogg & van Knippenberg, 2003; Hogg, van Knippenberg, & Rast, 2012) argues that when group membership and social identity are important people are highly attentive to information about their group's prototype and tend to be influenced much more strongly by fellow members who are perceived to be prototypical. Such individuals are trusted to be the most reliable source of prototype information and, de facto, occupy a leadership role in the group. Thus, group members support prototypical leaders more strongly than nonprototypical leaders, and prototypical leaders are more influential and effective than nonprototypical leaders.

Building on this, uncertainty–identity theory argues that under uncertainty people not only seek high entitativity groups but have an accentuated thirst for leadership per se, and particularly for leadership that is clear, directive and authoritative. This preference may steer people toward support for genuinely authoritarian leadership (Hogg, 2005b, 2007b). A number of studies have been conducted to directly test the impact of uncertainty on social identity related leadership.

Leadership at any Cost

Rast and associates (Rast, Gaffney, Hogg, & Crisp, 2012) have conducted two studies to test the hypothesis that because uncertainty generates a thirst for leadership it will weaken the usual enhanced support for a prototypical leader over a nonprototypical leader, especially when members of a group only have one viable leadership candidate. Furthermore, the effect will be due to enhanced support for a nonprototypical leader, rather than due to weakened support for a prototypical leader.

In Study 1 ($N = 98$) student participants in Southern California read a short personal manifesto from a prospective student leader who was ostensibly under consideration for a student–faculty liaison leadership position at their college. The manifesto was constructed to present the leadership candidate as being a good fit to the college (high prototypicality) or a poor fit to the college (low prototypicality). Participants also self-reported the extent to which they felt uncertain at that time. The dependent variable was a 7-item measure of support for the candidate.

Results replicated the robust finding that people support a prototypical leader more strongly than a nonprototypical leader. However, this was significantly moderated by uncertainty. The significant association between leader prototypicality and support was present under low uncertainty but disappeared completely under high uncertainty; and this was entirely due to uncertainty strengthening support for the nonprototypical leader. Uncertainty did not affect support for the prototypical leader.

Study 2 ($N = 132$), which was run in the United Kingdom, was almost identical to Study 1 except (i) leader prototypicality was conveyed through ostensive analysis of data on the match between the leader's attitudes and the attitudes of the student body, and most importantly (ii) leader prototypicality was a within-subjects variable—participants had a choice of two leaders to express their support for. Results again confirmed greater support for the prototypical than nonprototypical leader. However, this was significantly moderated by uncertainty. Preferential support for a prototypical over a nonprototypical leader, which was significant under low uncertainty, remained significant under high uncertainty but less markedly so. More critically, and in line with Study 1, uncertainty did not significantly affect support for a prototypical leader, but did significantly increase support for a nonprototypical leader.

Authoritarian Leaders

Rast et al.'s (2012) studies confirm how uncertainty motivates an enhanced desire for leadership per se that can weaken the usual preferential support for prototypical leaders by strengthening support for a nonprototypical leader—even when group members can compare low and high ingroup prototypical leaders or leader options within their group. These studies, however, focus only on prototype-relevant attributes of the leader, not on the leader's behavior or leadership style. The uncertainty–identity theory prediction is that uncertainty should increase support for a leader who has an autocratic leadership style.

Rast, Hogg, and Giessner (in press) recently conducted a study to test this idea. They surveyed organizational employees in the United Kingdom ($N = 215$); measuring self-uncertainty on a 7-item scale, and perceptions of how autocratic they felt their organizational leader was on a 6-item scale. The criterion variables were two 6-item scales measuring (i) support for the leader and (ii) trust in the leader. As predicted, there was a significant association between the interaction of leadership style and uncertainty on the one hand and both support and trust on the other. Under low uncertainty, support and trust were significantly associated with decreasingly autocratic leadership; but under high uncertainty, the relationship was inversed so that support was significantly positively associated with increasingly autocratic leadership and trust was unrelated to leadership style. Perhaps of key interest here is that both support and trust for an autocratic leader increased significantly as a function of increasing uncertainty, whereas for a nonautocratic leader support and trust actually diminished as a function of increasing uncertainty.

Extremist Individuals

The research described so far builds a case showing that feelings of uncertainty about oneself or reflecting on oneself (1) strengthen identification with highly entitative or extreme groups, (2) enhance intentions to behave in more extreme group-serving ways and to support extreme measures to protect and promote one's group, (3) enhance the desire for ingroup leadership per se, such that even relatively less ingroup prototypical leaders become a viable leadership option, and (4) build a preference for strong, hierarchy-based, autocratic leadership. Uncertainty also has the effect of weakening identification with low entitativity, moderate groups and weakening support for moderate leadership.

Against the background of these data, one question that comes to mind is why some individuals in extremist groups, or groups that define themselves to a greater or lesser degree in terms of the exercise of power over and violence against others, engage in violent or antisocial acts whereas others do not. Why, for example, do only some not all members of the military humiliate and brutalize prisoners, some not all police assault suspects, some not all Christians murder employees of clinics that perform abortions, and some not all gang members regularly engage in murder?

Goldman and Hogg (2013) propose that a conjunction of normal social-cognitive and social interactive processes relating to group identification and group belonging can cause people to go to extremes to be accepted as bona fide members of their group. In particular, they argue that people who go to or support extremes of antisocial or aggressive behavior for their group are (1) in a group that is entitative and has norms that are not anathema to extreme, antisocial or aggressive intergroup behavior, (2) are highly identified with that group, (3) feel they are peripheral rather than central members, and (4) believe that through extreme/antisocial ingroup-serving behavior there is a realistic probability of securing greater acceptance as central members. A key point here is that self-uncertainty related to group membership can be assumed to be high when people really want to belong to a group and be acknowledged as full members but feel that they are relatively marginal nonprototypical members.

To examine this idea Goldman and Hogg (2013) conducted a field experiment on members of fraternities and sororities in Southern California ($N = 218$). These groups meet the first two conditions above—they are highly entitative, provide central identities for members, and do not shy away from assertive, aggressive, and antisocial intergroup behaviors in relation to other fraternities and sororities. Participants were primed to think of themselves as relatively central or peripheral members of their fraternity or sorority—they thought carefully about ways in which they possessed typical (nontypical) characteristics of their fraternity/sorority, and then wrote down three examples. They were also primed to think carefully about how easy (difficult) it was to behave in ways that would make them more fully accepted by their fraternity/sorority, and then write down three examples of these behaviors. The primes were counterbalanced across the experiment, and a key dependent variable was an 8-item measure of likelihood of participating in and supporting others to participate in antisocial aggressive behaviors, which included vandalizing others' property and houses, poisoning their food, and fighting with them.

Across the experiment, participants identified strongly with their fraternities and sororities, M of 6.35 on a 9-point scale. Against this background and exactly as predicted, the two independent variables interacted significantly such that marginal members who believed there was a high probability of acceptance were both more likely to participate in and more likely to support others engaging in extreme antisocial and aggressive behaviors on behalf of their fraternity or sorority. Not surprisingly given robust evidence that males are more prepared to engage in physically aggressive behavior (see Bushman & Huesmann, 2010), the interactive effect was, as Goldman and Hogg predicted, stronger among males than females.

From the perspective of self-uncertainty and extremism, this study shows that people whose membership in an important group is uncertain and who believe they can reduce this uncertainty by going to extremes for the group are those who are most likely to embrace, support and engage in extreme behaviors.

Concluding Comments and Policy Implications

In this article, we have presented one particular conceptual analysis of the relationship between uncertainty and extremism—a social cognitive and social interactive analysis firmly focused on group extremism and grounded in uncertainty–identity theory (Hogg, 2007a, 2012). We have characterized "extremism" broadly as referring to a particular type of group structure and manifestation of group life—this includes high group entitativity, rigid and closed group boundaries, internal homogeneity and pressures toward consensus, orthodox and ideological belief systems, ritualized practices, profound ethnocentrism, hierarchical structure, strong or autocratic leadership, and radical action agendas aimed at protecting and promoting the group and its identity (cf. Kruglanski et al., 2006). It also includes powerful or zealous group identification.

Groups can have a moderate or extremist structure with respect to pretty much any constellation of attitudes, values, and behaviors, and people can accordingly adjust the extremity of their attitudes, values, and behaviors to appear to better fit the group they (wish to) identify with. In this article, we argue that self-uncertainty can be one factor that may incline people to identify with more extreme groups. For example, self-uncertainty may steer a Christian toward fundamentalist Christianity or a conservationist toward eco-terrorism.

According to uncertainty–identity theory feelings of uncertainty directly or indirectly about one's self and identity in society are aversive and motivate uncertainty reduction. Self-categorization as a group member reduces this type of uncertainty very effectively because it transforms self-conception so that it is governed by a group prototype that defines self and prescribes perceptions, attitudes, feelings, and behaviors, and describes how others view and treat you. In addition, one's sense of self and one's world view are consensually validated by fellow ingroup members.

Extreme groups, as described above, have precisely the properties that are ideally suited to reduce self-uncertainty because they provide a clear and unambiguous sense of self and place in the world. However, such groups restrict individual freedom to some extent and in many situations can be considered unattractive vehicles for self-definition and identity grounding. People are unlikely to be strongly attracted to them unless uncertainty is relatively chronic, pervasive, or acute, or they have few other viable identity options (see below). In addition, the nature of such groups makes entry and achievement of full membership difficult and peripheral members can be treated badly and readily rejected from group. Using the language of Brewer's optimal distinctiveness theory (Brewer, 1991; Leonardelli, Pickett, & Brewer, 2010), extreme groups usually oversatisfy the need for inclusion and are thus not optimally distinctive—causing people not to identify with them, unless the point of optimal distinctiveness shifts toward greater inclusiveness due to an accentuated need for self-uncertainty reduction.

In this article, we overviewed a program of ongoing research testing the uncertainty–identity theory analysis of extremism. These studies provide evidence that feelings of uncertainty about or reflecting on oneself (1) strengthen identification with highly entitative or extreme groups, (2) enhance intentions to behave in more extreme group-serving ways and to support extreme measures to protect and promote one's group, (3) create a yearning for leadership per se, such that even relatively less ingroup prototypical leaders become a viable leadership option, and (4) build preference for strong, hierarchy-based, autocratic leadership. Uncertainty also weakens identification with low entitativity, moderate groups and weakens support for more moderate leadership. In addition, those individuals who are most likely to embrace, support and engage in extreme behaviors are people (1) whose membership status and thus full inclusion in an important group is uncertain and (2) who believe they can reduce this uncertainty by going to extremes for the group.

Group and societal extremism are serious social issues that cry out for resolution (Fiske, 2013). The analysis presented here has some clear policy implications at the societal, organizational, and community level. The most obvious strategy is to prevent conditions that sponsor chronic, widespread, and acute identity- and self-related uncertainty in the first place. However, this can be very difficult as the most pernicious uncertainties arise from economic crises, ethnic, religious and national conflicts, and natural disasters. These are all very difficult to anticipate or control—and there is no overarching global authority that can effectively step up to the plate.

Another more realistic strategy is to have provisions in place to translate uncertainty that is experienced as a fearful threat into uncertainty that is viewed more positively as a challenge—the key mechanism is making people believe they have the resources to resolve their feelings of self-related uncertainty. Community-based organizations can play a pivotal role here—offering guidance, support, and new identities. There is, of course, a dark side—local religious and political fundamentalist groups can step in, as can gangs, cults, and other extremist groups.

One powerful individual level buffer against extremism, but a buffer that can be encouraged and developed at the societal, organizational, and community level, is for people to have a rich and complex social identity. People who have multiple valued and distinct social identities and group memberships are more resilient if uncertainty impacts one of these identities than are those who have few identities or a single monolithically integrated identity structure. For example, someone whose entire self-concept is tied to his or her religion is likely to cling strongly to an extremist religious ideology in the face of an uncertain world, whereas someone whose self-concept is nourished by a number of strong and separate identities based on religion, profession, workplace, ethnicity, political ideology, (extended) family, and so forth is better able to cope with uncertainty without being seduced by extremism.

This idea, which draws on Roccas and Brewer's (2002; Miller, Brewer, & Arbuckle, 2009) concept of identity complexity, has recently been explored from an uncertainty–identity theory perspective. Hogg, Siegel, and Hohman (2011) applied the analysis to speculate about ways to combat adolescent attraction to and identification with groups that engage in extreme behaviors that put members' health at risk. In another paper, Grant and Hogg (2012) introduced the notion of identity prominence and conducted two experiments showing that uncertainty is less likely to lead to strong identification with a group if rather than having a single prominent social identity people have many prominent social identities (Study 2,

$N = 87$), or their single identity is less prominent relative to other social identities (Study 1, $N = 90$).

Uncertainty and social identity are facts of life, part of the experience of being human. Together the interrelationship of uncertainty and social identity can create extremism and all the associated human and societal costs. However, a conceptual understanding of the causal nexus of these processes and phenomena may help us combat the most damaging consequences of societal extremism, and instead focus on the positive aspects of the uncertainty–identity relationship—such as group commitment and loyalty that underpin motivation to suppress selfish motives and instead exert effort to work for the collective good of the group and its members.

References

Abrams, D., & Hogg, M. A. (1988). Comments on the motivational status of self-esteem in social identity and intergroup discrimination. *European Journal of Social Psychology, 18*, 317–334. doi: 10.1002/ejsp.2420180403

Abrams, D., & Hogg, M. A. (2010). Social identity and self-categorization. In J. F. Dovidio, M. Hewstone, P. Glick & V. M. Esses (Eds.), *The SAGE handbook of prejudice, stereotyping and discrimination* (pp. 179–193). London: Sage. doi: 10.4135/9781446200919

Adelman, J. R., Hogg, M. A., & Levin, S. (2012). *Uncertainty and extremism in the Middle East: The role of Israeli and Palestinian social identity dynamics.* Manuscript submitted for publication, Claremont Graduate University.

Blascovich, J., & Tomaka, J. (1996). The biopsychosocial model of arousal regulation. In M. Zanna (Ed.), *Advances in experimental social psychology* (Vol. *28*, pp. 1–51). New York: Academic Press. doi: 10.1016/S0065-2601(08)60235-X

Brewer, M. B. (1991). The social self: On being the same and different at the same time. *Personality and Social Psychology Bulletin, 17*, 475–482. doi: 10.1177/0146167291175001

Bushman, B. J., & Huesmann, L. R. (2010). Aggression. In S. T. Fiske, D. T. Gilbert, & G. Lindzey (Eds.), *Handbook of social psychology* (5th ed., Vol. 2, pp. 833–863). New York: Wiley.

Campbell, D. T. (1958). Common fate, similarity, and other indices of the status of aggregates of persons as social entities. *Behavioral Science, 3*, 14–25. doi: 10.1002/bs.3830030103

Crano, W. D., & Seyranian, V. (2009). How minorities prevail: The context/comparison-leniency contract model. *Journal of Social Issues, 65*, 335–363. doi: 10.1111/j.1540-4560.2009.01603.x

Ellemers, N. (1993). The influence of socio-structural variables on identity management strategies. *European Review of Social Psychology, 4*, 27–57. doi: 10.1080/14792779343000013

Fiske, S. T. (2013). A millennial challenge. Extremism in uncertain times. *Journal of Social Issues, 69*, 605-613.

Fiske, S. T., & Taylor, S. E. (1991). *Social cognition* (2nd ed.). New York: McGraw-Hill.

Goldman, L., & Hogg, M. A. (2013). *Going to extremes for one's group: The role of prototypicality and group acceptance.* Manuscript submitted for publication. Claremont Graduate University.

Grant, F., & Hogg, M. A. (2012). Self-uncertainty, social identity prominence and group identification. *Journal of Experimental Social Psychology, 48*, 538–542. doi: 10.1016/j.jesp.2011.11.006

Grieve, P., & Hogg, M. A. (1999). Subjective uncertainty and intergroup discrimination in the minimal group situation. *Personality and Social Psychology Bulletin, 25*, 926–940. doi: 10.1177/01461672992511002

Hamilton, D. L., & Sherman, S. J. (1996). Perceiving persons and groups. *Psychological Review, 103*, 336–355. doi: 10.1037/0033-295X.103.2.336

Higgins, E. T. (1998). Promotion and prevention: Regulatory focus as a motivational principle. In M. P. Zanna (Ed.), *Advances in experimental social psychology* (Vol. *30*, pp. 1–46). New York: Academic Press. doi: 10.1016/S0065-2601(08)60381-0

Hogg, M. A. (2000). Subjective uncertainty reduction through self-categorization: A motivational theory of social identity processes. *European Review of Social Psychology, 11*, 223–255. doi: 10.1080/14792772043000040

Hogg, M. A. (2001). A social identity theory of leadership. *Personality and Social Psychology Review, 5*, 184–200. doi: 10.1207/s15327957pspr0503_1

Hogg, M. A. (2004). Uncertainty and extremism: Identification with high entitativity groups under conditions of uncertainty. In V. Yzerbyt, C. M. Judd, & O. Corneille (Eds.), *The psychology of group perception: Perceived variability, entitativity, and essentialism* (pp. 401–418). New York: Psychology Press.

Hogg, M. A. (2005a). Uncertainty, social identity and ideology. In S. R. Thye & E. J. Lawler (Eds.), *Advances in group processes* (Vol. 22, pp. 203–230). New York: Elsevier. doi: 10.1016/S0882-6145(05)22008-8

Hogg, M. A. (2005b). Social identity and misuse of power: The dark side of leadership. *Brooklyn Law Review, 70*, 1239–1257.

Hogg, M. A. (2007a). Uncertainty-identity theory. In M. P. Zanna (Ed.), *Advances in experimental social psychology* (Vol. 39, pp. 69–126). San Diego, CA: Academic Press. doi: 10.1016/S0065-2601(06)39002-8

Hogg, M. A. (2007b). Organizational orthodoxy and corporate autocrats: Some nasty consequences of organizational identification in uncertain times. In C. A. Bartel, S. Blader, & A. Wrzesniewski (Eds.), *Identity and the modern organization* (pp. 35–59). Mahwah, NJ: Erlbaum.

Hogg, M. A. (2012). Uncertainty-identity theory. In P. A. M. Van Lange, A. W. Kruglanski, & E. T. Higgins (Eds.), *Handbook of theories of social psychology* (pp. 62–80). Thousand Oaks, CA: Sage. doi: 10.4135/9781446249222

Hogg, M. A., & Abrams, D. (1988). *Social identifications: A social psychology of intergroup relations and group processes*. London & New York: Routledge.

Hogg, M. A., Adelman, J. R., & Blagg, R. D. (2010). Religion in the face of uncertainty: An uncertainty-identity theory account of religiousness. *Personality and Social Psychology Review, 14*, 72–83. doi: 10.1177/1088868309349692

Hogg, M. A., Farquharson, J., Parsons, A., & Svensson, A. (2012). When being moderate is not the answer: Disidentification with moderate groups under uncertainty. Manuscript submitted for publication, Claremont Graduate University.

Hogg, M. A., Kruglanski, A., & Van den Bos, K. (2013). Uncertainty and the roots of extremism. *Journal of Social Issues, 69*, 407–418.

Hogg, M. A., Meehan, C., & Farquharson, J. (2010). The solace of radicalism: Self-uncertainty and group identification in the face of threat. *Journal of Experimental Social Psychology, 46*, 1061–1066. doi: 10.1016/j.jesp.2010.05.005

Hogg, M. A., Sherman, D. K., Dierselhuis, J., Maitner, A. T., & Moffitt, G. (2007). Uncertainty, entitativity, and group identification. *Journal of Experimental Social Psychology, 43*, 135–142. doi: 10.1016/j.jesp.2005.12.008

Hogg, M. A., Siegel, J. T., & Hohman, Z. P. (2011). Groups can jeopardize your health: Identifying with un-healthy groups to reduce self-uncertainty. *Self and Identity, 10*, 326–335. doi: 10.1080/15298868.2011.558762

Hogg, M. A., & Smith, J. R. (2007). Attitudes in social context: A social identity perspective. *European Review of Social Psychology, 18*, 89–131. doi: 10.1080/10463280701592070

Hogg, M. A., & van Knippenberg, D. (2003). Social identity and leadership processes in groups. In M. P. Zanna (Eds.), *Advances in experimental social psychology* (Vol. 35, pp. 1–52). San Diego, CA: Academic Press. doi: 10.1016/S0065-2601(03)01001-3

Hogg, M. A., van Knippenberg, D., & Rast, D. E. III. (2012). The social identity theory of leadership: Theoretical origins, research findings, and conceptual developments. *European Review of Social Psychology, 23*, 258–304. doi: 10.1080/10463283.2012.741134

Klandermans, B. (1997). *The social psychology of protest*. Oxford, UK: Blackwell.

Kruglanski, A. W., Pierro, A., Mannetti, L., & De Grada, E. (2006). Groups as epistemic providers: Need for closure and the unfolding of group-centrism. *Psychological Review, 113*, 84–100. doi: 10.1037/0033-295X.113.1.84

Leonardelli, G. J., Pickett, C. L., & Brewer, M. B. (2010). Optimal distinctiveness theory: A framework for social identity, social cognition and intergroup relations. In M. P. Zanna (Eds.), *Advances in experimental social psychology* (Vol. *43*, pp. 65–115) San Diego, CA: Elsevier. doi: 10.1016/S0065-2601(10)43002-6

Martin, R., & Hewstone, M. (2008). Majority versus minority influence, message processing and attitude change: The source-context-elaboration model. In M. P. Zanna (Eds.), *Advances in experimental social psychology* (Vol. *40*, pp. 237–326). San Diego, CA: Elsevier. doi: 10.1016/S0065-2601(07)00005-6

Miller, K., Brewer, M. B., & Arbuckle, N. (2009). Social identity complexity: Its correlates and antecedents. *Group Processes and Intergroup relations, 12,* 79–94. doi: 10.1177/1368430208098778

Moghaddam, F. M., & Love, K. (2011). Collective uncertainty and extremism: A further discussion. In M. A. Hogg & D. L. Blaylock (Eds.), *Extremism and the psychology of uncertainty* (pp. 246–262). Oxford, UK: Wiley-Blackwell. doi: 10.1002/9781444344073.ch15

Moscovici, S. (1980). Toward a theory of conversion behavior. In L. Berkowitz (Eds.), *Advances in experimental social psychology* (Vol. *13,* pp. 202–239). New York: Academic Press. doi: 10.1016/S0065-2601(08)60133-1

Mugny, G., & Pérez, J. A. (1991). *The social psychology of minority influence.* Cambridge, UK: Cambridge University Press.

Mullin, B.-A., & Hogg, M. A. (1998). Dimensions of subjective uncertainty in social identification and minimal intergroup discrimination. *British Journal of Social Psychology, 37,* 345–365. doi: 10.1111/j.2044-8309.1998.tb01176.x

Pollock, H. N. (2003). *Uncertain science ... uncertain world.* Cambridge, UK: Cambridge University Press. doi: 10.1017/CBO9780511541377

Rast, D. E. III, Gaffney, A. M., Hogg, M. A., & Crisp, R. J. (2012). Leadership under uncertainty: When Leaders who are non-prototypical group members can gain support. *Journal of Experimental Social Psychology, 48,* 646–653. doi: 10.1016/j.jesp.2011.12.013

Rast, D. E. III, Hogg, M. A., & Giessner, S. R. (in press). Self-uncertainty and support for autocratic leadership. *Self and Identity.* doi: 10.1080/15298868.2012.718864

Reid, S. A., & Hogg, M. A. (2005). Uncertainty reduction, self-enhancement, and ingroup identification. *Personality and Social Psychology Bulletin, 31,* 804–817. doi: 10.1177/0146167204271708

Roccas, S., & Brewer, M. B. (2002). Social identity complexity. *Personality and Social Psychology Review, 6,* 88–106. doi: 10.1207/s15327957pspr0602_01

Rubin, M., & Hewstone, M. (1998). Social identity theory's self-esteem hypothesis: A review and some suggestions for clarification. *Personality and Social Psychology Review, 2,* 40–62.

Runciman, W. G. (1966). *Relative deprivation and social justice.* London: Routledge and Kegan Paul.

Sherman, D. K., Hogg, M. A., & Maitner, A. T. (2009). Perceived polarization: Reconciling ingroup and intergroup perceptions under uncertainty. *Group Processes and Intergroup Relations, 12,* 95–109. doi: 10.1177/1368430208098779

Stürmer, S., & Simon, B. (2004). Collective action: Towards a dual-pathway model. *European Review of Social Psychology, 15,* 59–99. doi: 10.1080/10463280340000117

Tajfel, H., & Turner, J. C. (1979). An integrative theory of intergroup conflict. In W. G. Austin & S. Worchel (Eds.), *The social psychology of intergroup relations* (pp. 33–47). Monterey, CA: Brooks/Cole.

Terry, D. J., & Hogg, M. A. (1996). Group norms and the attitude–behavior relationship: A role for group identification. *Personality and Social Psychology Bulletin, 22,* 776–793. doi: 10.1177/0146167296228002

Turner, J. C., Hogg, M. A., Oakes, P. J., Reicher, S. D., & Wetherell, M. S. (1987). *Rediscovering the social group: A self-categorization theory.* Oxford, UK: Blackwell.

Van Zomeren, M., Postmes, T., & Spears, R. (2008). Toward an integrative social identity model of collective action: A quantitative research synthesis of three socio-psychological perspectives. *Psychological Bulletin, 134,* 504–535. doi: 10.1037/0033-2909.134.4.504

Walker, I., & Pettigrew, T. F. (1984). Relative deprivation theory: An overview and conceptual critique. *British Journal of Social Psychology, 23,* 301–310. doi: 10.1111/j.2044-8309.1984.tb00645.x

Walker, I., & Smith, H. J. (Eds.), (2002). *Relative deprivation: Specification, development, and integration*. Cambridge, UK: Cambridge University Press. doi: 10.1017/CBO9780511527753

Yzerbyt, V., Castano, E., Leyens, J.-P., & Paladino, M.-P. (2000). The primacy of the ingroup: The interplay of entitativity and identification. *European Review of Social Psychology, 11*, 257–295. doi: 10.1080/14792772043000059

MICHAEL A. HOGG is Professor of Social Psychology at Claremont Graduate University and President of the Society of Experimental Social Psychology. He is a Fellow of numerous associations, including the Association for Psychological Science, the Society for Personality and Social Psychology, and the Society for the Psychological Study of Social Issues. A past associate editor of the *Journal of Experimental Social Psychology* and foundation co-editor of the journal *Group Processes and Intergroup Relations*, he was the 2010 recipient of the Carol and Ed Diener Award in Social Psychology from the Society for Personality and Social Psychology. Michael Hogg's research on group processes, intergroup relations, social identity, and self-conception is closely associated with the development of social identity theory. He has more than 300 scientific publications on these topics.

JANICE ADELMAN is currently a freelance applied social psychologist. Her research focuses on processes of identity and support for political violence and terrorism. She is an active member of the Society for the Psychological Study of Social Issues, where she is current Newsletter Editor and past chair of the Graduate Student Committee; and of the International Society of Political Psychology, where she is past chair of the Junior Scholars Committee. She received her PhD in applied social psychology from Claremont Graduate University, and holds an MSc in neurobiology from The Hebrew University of Jerusalem.

A Raw Deal: Heightened Liberalism Following Exposure to Anomalous Playing Cards

Travis Proulx[*]
Tilburg University

Brenda Major
University of California, Santa Barbara

According to the meaning maintenance model, people may respond to meaning violations by affirming unrelated beliefs to which they are committed. While this affirmation generally moves in the direction of social inequality, meaning violations that are not personally threatening—but that nevertheless evoke uncertainty—should evoke a heightened preference for social equality (i.e., a socially liberal judgment). We tested this hypothesis in an experiment that exposed participants to reverse colored playing cards, where participants were subsequently more supportive of Affirmative Action if they were relatively committed to a belief that social inequality is unjust. This study demonstrates that people will make heightened socially liberal judgments following a meaning violation that is not personally threatening, and that is unrelated to the affirmed meaning frameworks.

It is generally understood that Western Liberalism was born during the French Revolution. On July 14, 1789, populist insurgents swept into the Bastille under a banner of "Liberty, Equality, Fraternity." In short order, the monarchy was abolished, feudalism was discarded and a document was drafted that enshrined the crowning ideals of the Age of Enlightenment: The Declaration of the Rights of Man and the Citizen. Over the next 3 years, however, civil society began to unravel. In the face of continuing foreign wars, counter-insurgencies and economic chaos, notions of "Liberty" and "Fraternity" were set aside, and the "Committee of Public Safety" imposed a brutal means of establishing extreme "Equality": massacring the remaining aristocracy. In just over a year, close to 17,000 people were led to

---

[*]Correspondence concerning this article should be addressed to Travis Proulx, Tilburg School of Social and Behavioural Sciences, Tilburg University, Tilburg, 5000 LE, The Netherlands [e-mail: t.proulx@uvt.nl].

the guillotine before the architect of the Reign of Terror, Maximilien Robespierre, was himself placed under the blade. On into the 20th century, radicalized equality ideologies have continually arisen in the face of general social upheaval, from the Bolshevik purging of the bourgeoisie, to the Khmer Rouge executing anyone with an education.

Given the historical reemergence of extremist equality ideologies, it would seem likely that psychologists would have developed numerous theoretical accounts to explain why equality beliefs may become radicalized in the face of social upheaval. However, to the extent that psychologists address the link between upheaval and extremist belief, it is not in terms of extremist equality. Rather, it has been generally understood in terms of extremist *in*equality beliefs—the right-wing advocation of social hierarchy, which is understood to follow from unequal distributions of human capacity and effort (e.g., Kirk, 1953). This focus on upheaval and right-wing extremism is especially salient in the social psychological literature, where experimental manipulations of threatening scenarios appear to lead—unilaterally—toward heightened out-group derogation, and an advocating of social inequality, more generally. So reliable is this finding in the social psychological literature, theoretical perspectives have arisen which understand inequality ideologies largely in terms of external threat, where social Conservatism itself is construed as motivated social cognition aimed at establishing an unequal, hierarchical social order by means of out-group derogation (e.g., Jost, Glaser, Kruglanski, & Sulloway, 2003).

If history provides numerous examples of extremist equality ideologies in the face of apparent external threat, why do common lab experiments fail to manifest this societal phenomenon? Why, instead, are extremist *in*equality beliefs the common outcome of social psychological manipulations involving threatening or unpleasant scenarios? In what follows, we will explore a potential explanation for this puzzling incongruity, and present a laboratory experiment aimed at directly testing a hypothesis that arises from this conjecture: while experiences characterized mainly by *personal threat* will evoke a heightened preference for social inequality, experiences characterized mainly by *uncertainty* will evoke a heightened preference for social inequality or social equality, depending on one's prior ideological commitment.

To date, most laboratory experiments that evoke a heightened preference for social inequality are characterized by personally threatening content. By presenting a manipulation that would arouse uncertainty—without any personally threatening implications—we expected participants to make decisions indicative of a heightened preference for social equality (i.e., liberalism) or inequality (i.e., conservatism; Jost et al., 2007) depending on their committed social justice beliefs. This uncertainty-arousing manipulation involves the presentation of anomalous playing cards; while unusual and disorienting, the implicit awareness of this trivial anomaly presumably has no explicitly negative implications for oneself or one's general wellbeing. Nevertheless, we were able to demonstrate that this experience can evoke a heightened preference for social equality as manifested by increased support for Affirmative Action programs. This study may point to a reason why social upheavals marked by prolonged, generalized uncertainty can evoke extreme preferences for social equality or inequality, relative to prior ideological commitments.

The Psychology of Personal Threat

Imagine a typical undergraduate student looking for a bit of extra cash. They spot an advertisement recruiting participants for a psychology experiment with an innocuous title, like "Personality and Belief." They sign up, and at their appointed day and time, a social psychologist leads them to believe that people do not like them (Williams & Nida, 2011), or asks them to recall a time when they felt uncertain about themselves (Hogg, 2007, 2012; Hogg & Adelman, 2013) or lacked control over their life (Kay & Eibach, 2013; Kay, Whitson, Gaucher, & Galinski, 2009), or leads them to believe that their cherished beliefs are not true (Major, Kaiser, O'Brien, & McCoy, 2007), or asks them to behave in a way that goes against those beliefs (Steele and Liu, 1983)—or maybe they are let off easy, and are merely asked to describe the thoughts and feelings aroused by their own death (and what they think physically happens to their body when they die; Greenberg, Porteus, Simon, Pyszczynski, & Solomon, 1995).

How might they respond to these personally threatening experiences? If they are like most people, they will likely engage in compensatory behaviors, such as system justification (Jost, Banaji, & Nosek, 2004), compensatory conviction (McGregor, Zanna, Holmes, & Spencer, 2001), worldview verification (Major et al., 2007), or worldview defense (Greenberg et al., 1995). They might find themselves more motivated to be around people who are similar (Hart, Shaver, & Goldenberg, 2005) and reject people who are not (Fein & Spencer, 1997). They might be more reliant on negative social stereotypes (Burris & Rempel, 2004). They would likely be more punitive toward those who criticize their country (McGregor et al., 1998) or break the law (Rosenblatt, Greenberg, Solomon, Pyszczynski, & Lyon, 1989). Most commonly, they will find themselves motivated to make judgments that have been construed as socially conservative insofar as the behaviors demonstrate an increased preference for social inequality (Jost et al., 2003). And if they understand themselves as someone who is socially liberal—with a corresponding preference for social equality—they may wonder: why would I only make socially conservative judgments after the social psychologist violated everything I'd like to believe about myself (then gave me 15 dollars)?

Uncertainty versus Personal Threat

The answer, according to the threat-uncertainty model (Jost et al., 2007), may lie in the nature of these negative experiences, namely, the extent to which they involve two distinguishable psychological constructs: *uncertainty* and *personal threat* (also see Janoff-Bulman, 1992). At the outset, these personally negative experiences involve some of the beliefs people are most committed to, or would most like to believe. When these beliefs are violated by contradictory experiences, it is understood to elicit a psychological state of *uncertainty* (also see McGregor et al., 2001; Van den Bos, 2001). Following a belief-violating experience, efforts to manage subsequent uncertainty should direct people toward a heightened commitment to their established beliefs, whether they involve a preference for social equality or inequality. Evidence that belief violations, on their own, are not sufficient to evoke a unilaterally heightened preference for social inequality follows from the correlation between measures of uncertainty avoidance (e.g., Ambiguity Intolerance; Budner, 1962) and a general reluctance to alter *any* established social order, whether it advocates social equality or inequality. As well, other established measures of uncertainty avoidance (Personal Need for Structure; Neuberg & Newsom, 1993; Need for Closure; Kruglanski & Webster, 1996) are not strongly correlated with measures of social conservatism understood in terms of a pointed preference for social inequality (e.g., right-wing authoritarianism F-Scale; Sanford, Adorno, Frenkel-Brunswik, & Levinson, 1950).

There is, however, another element embedded in these self-relevant, belief-violating experiences: *personal threat*. Unlike cognitive processes aimed at avoiding *uncertainty*, responses to personal threat have been construed as implicit efforts to assign blame following an aversive experience of threat or loss (Jost et al., 2003; also see Lerner, 1980). These efforts are unilaterally associated with an overall heightened preference for social inequality, insofar as they manifest as defensive efforts aimed at derogating social outgroups (e.g., heightened punishment of a criminal following a mortality reminder; Rosenblatt et al., 1989). Evidence for this unilateral association follows from the correlation between measures of personal threat avoidance (e.g., Dangerous World scale; Duckitt, Wagner, du Plessis, & Birum, 2002) and a pointed preference for social inequality, along with the attendant derogation of social outgroups. Taken together, Jost et al. (2007) understand these findings to be "consistent with Jost et al.'s (2003) conjecture that uncertainty avoidance would motivate resistance to change, whereas threat would motivate opposition to equality" (p. 1002).

If it is the personally threatening element of these common lab manipulations that primarily motivates opposition to social equality, then it should be of little surprise that outgroup derogation and ingroup preference are so widely reported in the experimental literature. It is overwhelmingly the case that the belief-violating experiences employed by social psychologists are explicitly self-relevant, and negatively so. Nevertheless, the special relationship between personally threatening belief violations and social conservatism leaves open the following possibility: *uncertainty* arousing belief violations that are not *personal threats* may initiate a heightened preference for social inequality *or* social equality, depending on the social justice meaning framework to which one is most committed.

The Psychology of Uncertainty

Evidence following from the meaning maintenance model (Heine, Proulx, & Vohs, 2006; Proulx & Inzlicht, 2012) suggests that this should be the case. According to the meaning maintenance model, people structure their experiences as expected relationships—meaning frameworks—that allow them to understand themselves, their world, and their relationship to the world (also see Baumeister, 1991; Peterson, 1999). Violations of these meaning frameworks are understood to arouse a common syndrome of physiological arousal (e.g., Mendes, Blascovich, Hunter, Lickel, & Jost, 2007) and neurocognitive activation (e.g. Inzlicht & Tullett, 2010), often termed *uncertainty* (e.g., Klein & Kruglanski, 2013; Van den Bos, 2001) or *anxious uncertainty* (e.g., McGregor, Nash, Mann, & Phills, 2010).

In recent years, there has been growing evidence that this syndrome is initiated following the violation of any committed meaning framework, whether or not it is relevant to the self, or whether the experience is positive or negative in valence. For example, people will predictably demonstrate markers of anxious uncertainty (e.g., increased heart rate coupled with constricted blood vessels) when their self-understanding is violated. However, they will show this same response following meaning violations unrelated to the self, such as interacting with an Asian experimenter who has an Alabama accent (Mendes et al., 2007). Conversely, providing people with information that violates their meaning frameworks in a manner that *is* self-relevant—in a *positive* way—will also evoke this response. For example, minorities who believe that discrimination is rampant will demonstrate anxious uncertainty if they are *not* being discriminated against (Major et al., 2007). These recent findings join examples of consciously reported anxiety following positively self-relevant experiences that violate meaning frameworks. For example, people feel anxious after learning that their test scores have improved, if this knowledge violates their understanding of how people learn (Plaks & Stetcher, 2007).

Emerging evidence from the cognitive and affective neurosciences suggests that the origin of this anxious uncertainty may lie in brain structures associated with the detection of simple violations of expected relationships—whether these violations are relevant to the self or not, and regardless of their positive or negative valence (Proulx, Inzlicht, & Harmon-Jones, 2012). For example, heightened activation of the anterior cingulate cortex (ACC) has traditionally been associated with conflicting cognitive processes (e.g., Gehring, Goss, Coles, & Meyer, 1993), where this activation can follow from expectancy violations as trivial as those embedded in the Stroop task, i.e., reading the word "RED" when it is coloured green.

More recently, activation of the ACC following these "low-level" violations have been demonstrated following "higher-level" conflicts, such as the attitude–behavior conflicts associated with cognitive dissonance theory (e.g., Harmon-Jones & Harmon Jones, 2008; van Veen, Krug, Schooler, & Carter, 2009). Furthermore, these violations may follow from positive or negative experiences. According to the "reward prediction error hypothesis," midbrain dopamine levels signal the occurrence of a mismatch between expectancy and outcome in the ACC (Holroyd & Coles, 2002). However, the firing of dopaminergic neurons may follow from unpredicted negative feedback, but also from unpredicted positive feedback, and in turn, this activation of the ACC is also implicated in the anxious affective states associated with felt uncertainty (Shackman et al., 2011). In the wake of this anxious uncertainty, approach-oriented behaviors may be triggered that reduce aversive arousal (McGregor, Prentice, & Nash, 2013), where these behaviors often involve a heightened affirmation of committed beliefs.

Taken together, these findings suggest that meaning violations may produce a state of anxious uncertainty in the absence of any personally threatening content, along with subsequent compensation behaviours. In a series of studies following from the meaning maintenance model, it has been demonstrated that, indeed, meaning violations with no personally threatening implications will evoke the heightened affirmation of committed beliefs, where these affirmation behaviors appear prompted by aversive arousal. For example, if the experimenter that a participant is interacting with is secretly switched with a different person—wearing the same clothes—they generally retain no conscious awareness of this meaning violation. Nevertheless, they will respond to the generalized uncertainty this violation produces with heightened affirmation of an unrelated social commitment—derogating an outgroup member by punishing a prostitute more harshly than those in a control condition (Proulx & Heine, 2008). Following the same manipulation, if participants are given the opportunity to (mis)attribute any implicit uncertainty they may be feeling to an alternative source, the heightened affirmation behavior is extinguished (also see Zanna & Cooper, 1974).

In subsequent manipulations, it has been shown that this same heighted affirmation of committed beliefs follows from other sources of uncertainty, such as absurdist humor (Proulx, Heine, & Vohs, 2010) or subliminally perceived nonsense words (Randles, Proulx, & Heine, 2011). While none of these meaning violations could reasonably be construed as personally threatening, they nevertheless provoke the same heightened affirmation of social beliefs as what follows from a classic personal threat manipulation—a reminder of one's mortality (e.g., Rosenblatt et al., 1989).

It must be noted, however, that moral affirmation following these meaning violations—whether they are personally threatening (i.e., mortality), or unrelated to the self (i.e., perceptual anomalies)—all appear to move in a socially conservative direction: greater derogation of a social outgroup member. What has yet to be demonstrated is that the *uncertainty* following meaning violations that are unrelated to the self may also evoke the affirmation of socially liberal beliefs, insofar as these violations are devoid of *personal threat*. Specifically, it has yet to be demonstrated that these nonpersonally threatening meaning violations can also evoke a pointed preference for social equality. This may be largely due to the dependent measure used in these prior studies, insofar as the opportunity to punish a prostitute is not well suited to detecting a pointed preference for social equality. This measure involves a unidirectional judgment, providing only an opportunity to derogate this (presumed) outgroup member to some degree (e.g., there is no option to drop the charges and give the prostitute a commendation). To detect the presence of socially liberal meaning maintenance following a nonpersonally threatening meaning violation, we instead used a bidirectional dependent measure that allows people to actively affirm a preference for social inequality as well as social equality.

Protestant Work Ethic and Affirmative Action

Following from classic political theory (Kirk, 1953), inequality is understood as inherently justified if it follows from how much effort individuals have invested in advancing their social status. As such, inequality is tolerated among social Conservatives—or even preferred—insofar as it is indicative of genuine variability in work ethic within a society. Conversely, Liberals view social inequality as inherently unjust insofar as it is viewed primarily as the result of forces beyond the individual's control, rather than as an absence of work ethic. Protestant work ethic (PWE) is a construct that is commonly discussed and assessed in the social sciences, and is pervasive in Western culture—especially the United States. A cornerstone of the "American Dream" ideal, PWE is a social equity assumption that construes success in terms of personal effort—and lack of success as a failure to work hard or well enough. This latter construal underlies the role of PWE in *justifying* social inequality as an equitable outcome (Levy, West, Ramirez, & Karafantis, 2006), such that PWE is negatively correlated with support of political programs aimed at reducing social inequality (Rosenthal, Levy, & Moyer, 2011).

One such program is Affirmative Action, which is a redistributive program based on the assumption that opportunities for success are unequal for minorities. Begun as an executive order by President Lyndon Johnson in 1965, Affirmative Action initially manifested as a directive to make hiring "color blind" in an effort to address racial discrimination. Later, into the 1970s and 1980s, the mandate of Affirmative Action changed such that race would be explicitly taken into account in favor of hiring minorities, with the aim of addressing historical discrimination that was understood to underlie current inequalities (Niemann & Maruyama, 2005).

To date, Western societies remain deeply ambivalent about Affirmative Action, likely due to the potential conflict between such programs and a deeply ingrained PWE (Crosby, 2004)—especially among European Americans who can imagine themselves passed over for educational or employment opportunities in favor of minority candidates.

This relationship between PWE and Affirmative Action support has been demonstrated experimentally, insofar as reminding European Americans about the implementation of Affirmative Action policies is sufficient to activate PWE construals that justify social inequality (Levy, West, & Ramirez, 2005). Given this general relationship between PWE and Affirmative Action, we would also expect the following experimental outcome: those reminded of their relative PWE beliefs prior to a nonself relevant meaning violation will judge Affirmative Action policies accordingly, demonstrating a heightened support (socially liberal) or opposition (socially conservative) compared to those in a control condition.

Anomalous Cards and Affirmative Action

In this experiment, we used a bidirectional dependent measure that would allow an equal opportunity to demonstrate a heightened preference for inequality (social conservatism) or equality (social liberalism). This judgment would be made following a meaning violation that is manifestly unrelated to the self: an implicit perception of reverse colored playing cards (Bruner and Postman, 1949). Given that this meaning violation does not constitute a *personal threat*, we predicted that the resulting *uncertainty* would motivate people to make judgments indicative of a preference for social inequality or equality relative to a control condition. Whether people make this relatively conservative or liberal social judgment should depend on whichever social justice meaning framework they happen to be affirming following the meaning violation.

Specifically, we expected that those committed to a belief that social inequality is not justified (low PWE) would affirm those commitments by demonstrating relatively more support for a social program that aims to correct social inequality (Affirmative Action). This would be a socially liberal response. Conversely, we expected that those committed to a belief that social inequality is justified (high PWE) would demonstrate relatively more opposition to this same program. This would be a socially conservative response.

Method

Participants. Fifty-two undergraduate students at a west coast North American university (35 women) participated for course credit. To facilitate homogeneity of students' personal experience with Affirmative Action, African American and Latino participants were excused from the study, leaving

40 students (17 women, 4 Asian, mean age = 20.47 years). Since there were no main effects for gender, nor gender-by-condition interactions analyses are collapsed across gender.

Materials and procedure. Participants entered the lab and completed a short questionnaire assessing a relevant social justice meaning framework. In previous research, an abbreviated version of the PWE scale (Mirels & Garrett, 1971) has been used as a face valid means of assessing whether one believes that social inequality is justified or unjustified (e.g., O'Brien, Kinias, & Major, 2008). In the present experiment, this scale was presented both as a means of determining participants' relevant social justice commitments and as a means of making these commitments more accessible prior to participants' exposure to a meaning violation. The scale consisted of 4 Likert items (1 = *Strongly Agree*; 7 = *Strongly Agree*; $\alpha = .73$) (i.e., "If people work hard they almost always get what they want; If people work hard enough, they can be whatever they want to be in life; Getting ahead in life does n't always depend on hard work; Even if people work hard, they don't always get ahead.")

Participants were then randomly assigned to one of two conditions: Control (No Meaning Violation) and Anomalous Cards (Nonself Relevant Meaning Violation). In the Control condition, participants played a game of "21" against the experimenter with a standard deck of Bicycle brand playing cards. After each round it was recorded who had come closest to 21 without going over, and the game ended when the entire deck had been played through. The Anomalous Cards condition was identical in all respects, save for the nature of the playing cards. In this condition, the game was played with a special deck of Bicycle brand playing cards where the 10s, Jacks, Queens, Kings, and Aces are reverse colored (e.g., Hearts are black; Clubs are red, see Figure 1).

Participants in both conditions then completed the Positive and Negative Affect Schedule (PANAS; Watson, Clark, & Tellegen, 1988; PA $\alpha = .85$, NA $\alpha = .91$) to assess whether mood had been influenced by either condition. Given that previous studies have not demonstrated a change in conscious affect following implicitly perceived perceptual anomalies (e.g., Proulx & Heine, 2008), we did not expect mood differences. Following the PANAS, participants completed a distractor task (sorting objects according to their relative usefulness on a camping trip) because previous work on meaning violations has shown that a distraction period facilitates the emergence of compensatory affirmation efforts (e.g., Greenberg et al., 1992).

Following this, all participants were presented with two questions meant to determine their general support or opposition to Affirmative Action. On a scale of 1–9 (1 = *Not At All*; 9 = *Extremely*), participants were asked "How much do you support Affirmative Action?; How much do you oppose Affirmative Action?" (in random order). These two items were highly negatively correlated ($r = -.91$,

Fig. 1. Reverse color playing card.

$p < .001$). We therefore created a difference score of these two questions to indicate participants' overall support (or lack of support) for Affirmative Action, with higher numbers indicating greater support. Participants then completed a demographics questionnaire, were probed for suspicion and debriefed.

Results and Discussion

Prior to analysis, one participant was excluded for not completing all study materials, and one participant was excluded for consciously detecting the anomalous playing cards.

We computed a difference score from the positive and negative affect subscales of the PANAS. Condition had no effect on this affect measure ($F < 1$), nor on the number of "21" rounds participants won ($F < 1$).

To test our primary hypothesis, we conducted a regression analysis predicting support for Affirmative Action scores from PWE scores, dummy coded variables representing Condition (Control = Reference; Anomalous Cards = Contrast), and the interaction of Condition and (centered) PWE scores. This model was significant ($F(3, 34) = 3.06, p = .04$). There was no main effect by Condition ($\beta = -.19, p = .23$). However, as predicted, we observed a significant interaction between PWE and Condition ($\beta = .57, p = .02$) (see Figure 2).

In the Control condition, there was no relationship between PWE and support for Affirmative Action ($\beta = .07, p = .71$). In contrast, in the Anomalous Cards condition, there was a significant, negative relationship between social justice meaning framework and support for Affirmative Action, ($\beta = -.70, p < .01$).

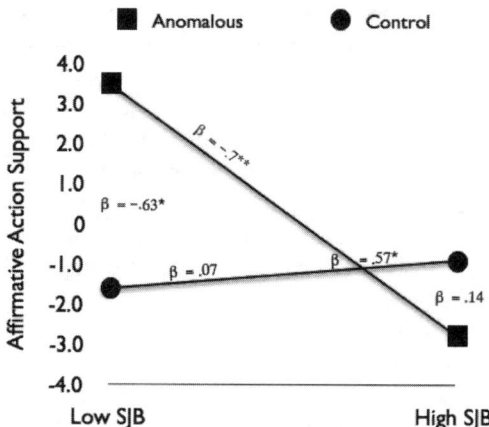

Fig. 2. The relationship between support for affirmative action and condition among those who accept or reject a meritocracy worldview. $*p < .05$; $**p < .01$.

Among those with a strong belief that inequality is not justified (one SD below the mean on PWE), those in the Anomalous Cards condition were more supportive of Affirmative Action than those in the Control condition ($\beta = -.63, p = .01$). In contrast, among those with a strong belief that inequality is justified (at one SD above the mean on PWE), those in the Anomalous Cards condition were not significantly more opposed to Affirmative Action than were those in the Control condition ($\beta = .14, p = .48$).

Nevertheless, among participants in the Anomalous Cards condition, Affirmative Action attitude scores for those with a strong belief that inequality is justified (one SD above the mean on PWE) were marginally lower than the zero point of the attitudes scale ($t_{(38)} = -2.02, p = .052$), while this was not the case for the Control condition ($t_{(38)} = -.64, p = .53$). It was also the case that among those in the Anomalous Cards condition, Affirmative Action attitude scores for those with a strong belief that inequality is not justified (one SD below the mean on PWE) were significantly higher than the "zero" point of the attitudes scale ($t_{(38)} = 2.25, p = .03$), while this was not the case for the Control condition ($t_{(38)} = -1.13, p = .2$).

As we had expected, participants responded to the anomalous cards by heightening their support for a socially liberal position if this judgment was in keeping with their relevant social justice commitments. Specifically, those who were committed to a belief that inequality is not justified (low PWE) became more supportive of Affirmative Action if they played "21" with anomalous playing cards than if they played with a standard deck of cards. In contrast, we expected that those who were committed to a belief that inequality is justified would become less supportive of Affirmative Action if exposed to anomalous playing cards than those exposed to standard cards. However, this effect was not significant.

We speculate that this is due to a floor effect for Affirmative Action opposition among those who generally believe that inequality is justified. That is, they already had an actively negative attitude toward Affirmative Action (below the "zero" point) in the Control condition; this made it less likely that they could oppose it to a significantly greater degree following a meaning violation. However, we do note that among those who had been exposed to anomalous cards and who were committed to a belief that inequality is justified (high PWE), Affirmative Action attitude scores were below the "zero" point of the scale with marginal significance—unlike corresponding scores in the control condition—suggesting that these participants did shift in a socially conservative direction following the meaning violation. Taken together, the novel findings reported here suggest that people will make judgments that heighten support for equality (social liberalism), and to a lesser extent, opposition to equality (social conservatism) following a meaning violation that is not personally threatening.

General Discussion

For decades, unsuspecting undergraduates have been lured into social psychology laboratories. They come with the promise of course credits and cash. What they find is social rejection (Baumeister & Leary, 1995), subjective uncertainty (Hogg, 2007, 2012), and reminders of their own death (Greenberg et al., 1995). Their typical response: heightened outgroup derogation. (Jost et al., 2003, 2007). However, in an experiment following from the meaning maintenance model, we presented a meaning violation that was stripped of personally threatening content insofar as it was manifestly unrelated to the self: reverse colored playing cards. Despite the fact that people lacked an explicit awareness of this trivial anomaly, they responded to the implicit awareness of this meaning violation by affirming an entirely unrelated meaning framework, namely, their relevant social justice meaning framework. Those who were most committed to a belief that social inequality is unjustified demonstrated the first direct evidence for heightened affirmation of social equality following a meaning violation: increased support for Affirmative Action.

General Uncertainty and General Extremes

In a laboratory setting, social psychologists have spent the better part of 30 years exposing people to experiences that evoke a heightened commitment to core beliefs. Like broad historical events involving cultural upheaval, these experiences are characterized by both *uncertainty* and *personal threat*. When participants are asked to recall times when they lacked personal control (Kay et al., 2010), or felt uncertainty about themselves and their goals (Hogg, 2007; 2012), or are made to feel socially rejected (Williams & Nida, 2011), or are reminded of their eventual death (Rosenblatt et al., 1989), it is likely that both of these psychological states are aroused. To the extent that people are reminded of events that represent the unknown, or violate deeply help commitments, they feel a sense of uncertainty. To the extent that these experiences have strongly aversive consequences for oneself—in terms of self-concept, self-esteem, or physical wellbeing—there can be little doubt that they are also experienced as personal threat. And as such, there should be little surprise that these experiences lead, almost unilaterally, to a heighted propensity toward outgroup derogation and a pointed preference for social inequality.

However, to the extent that uncertainty and personal threat can be disentangled, it should be the case that a heightened preference for social equality may also manifest itself, just as its extreme instantiations may manifest at the social and cultural level. This should especially be the case if participants are given a judgment that allows them to directly advocate for these views, in accordance with their prior commitments relative to matters of social equality or inequality. In the present experiment, participants who were relatively committed to a belief that social inequality is not justified (low PWE) strongly affirmed this belief following a trivial source of uncertainty: reverse colored playing cards. While their sudden support for Affirmative Action is not an instance of Maoist fanaticism, it is nevertheless a pointed shift in judgment advocating social equality. The sheer triviality of this meaning violation, coupled with the pronounced effects, speak to the power of uncertainty to dramatically amplify the impact of committed meaning frameworks on relevant social judgments.

At the societal level, it is nothing new to suggest a link between extremist behaviors and a pervasive climate of anxious uncertainty. Much has been made of the increased frequency of lynching during times of economic uncertainty (Tolnay & Beck, 1995), or the rise of fascism amid the chaos of interbellum Germany (Laqueur, 1974). History is rife with examples of social upheaval associated with extreme outgroup derogation and preference for social hierarchy. These behaviors have been understood by theorists as a generalized attempt to lay blame following salient threats of unspecified origins. The ruin and hardship that follows from social upheaval is relatively concrete in its consequences, though the concrete source of these threats may not be as easily determined. More broadly, human impulses in the face of anxious uncertainty have been understood as giving rise to ideological perspectives that entrench social inequality as a political ideal (Jost et al., 2003).

There have been, of course, fanatics of both inequality and equality—both Hitlers and Robespierres—and it has not always been clear why periods of upheaval should also lead to the proliferation of radically *equalizing* ideologies, such as Maoism or Bolshevism, along with their own repressions and killing fields. We are suggesting that part of the answer may lie in two separate and distinguishable dimensions of social upheaval—the general sense of uncertainty that arises during a chaotic and unpredictable era, and the negative, threatening implications for one's safety and well-being.

While personally threatening events may lead to a unilaterally extreme move toward outgroup derogation and increased social inequality, uncertainty—in and of itself—may be associated with a more extreme commitment to any existing elements of ones worldview, whether it advocates equality or inequality. In epochs associated with intense uncertainty and extreme threat, the cumulative effect of these conditions should move people to engage in extreme outgroup derogation, especially among those with strong preexisting commitments to ideologies that understand inequality as an ideal. However, among those with strong commitments to ideologies of equality—or those who do not feel the personal threat as acutely—there may be an equal and opposite shift toward a radicalized leveling of social distinction.

Implications for the Present and Future

Coming at the tail end (or midst?) of the "Great Recession," we find ourselves living during an era that may be characterized as "interesting times." For many, the current economic climate is experienced as both a salient threat to personal well-being, and—as the malaise drags on—a source of generalized uncertainty. While the current crisis may not yet be characterized as "cultural upheaval," we have already witnessed the rise of political and social movements that shift to the left and right of the mainstream. These movements range from the equality advocating "occupy" demonstrations, to the inequality justifying "Tea Party" rallies, and while (almost) no one would claim that they constitute extreme or otherwise dangerous social movements, they have arisen in a time of general uncertainty, and, we would suggest, they are motivated by the same general psychological forces that we have reproduced in laboratory setting, and that have been shown to eventually drive harder shifts to the left and right in similar historical contexts. Moving forward, there are two general policy issues that we'd like to highlight:

First, we simply note the central finding of this empirical work—that both liberal and conservative commitments can be made more extreme following sources of general uncertainty. Over the course of the current crisis, societies and governments will likely heighten their vigilance against destructively extremist commitments. In the political and social psychological literatures, extremism in the face of uncertainty is typically understood as originating from the Right (Jost et al., 2003)—perhaps out of an enhanced sympathy for the equality ideals of the Left (Inbar & Lammers, 2012)—rather than the complete absence of Left-wing extremism as motivated cognition in the face of uncertainty. The current crisis has already shifted equality and inequality commitments further from the mainstream, and these shifts may become more mainstream, and more extreme, as this crisis continues.

Second, societies and governments have often understood uncertainty as a psychological resource to be harnessed rather than quelled—especially when the source of uncertainty is ongoing, without an obvious or immediate resolution. To the extent that generalized uncertainty motivates palliative approach behaviors toward heightened belief commitment (McGregor et al., 2010), democratic (and nondemocratic) governments will continue to harness our current crisis to achieve broader social aims. It is our sincere hope that these aims involve common commitments that unite—rather than divide—segments of societies and nations.

Conclusion

People experience even trivial anomalies as meaning violations, and the resulting uncertainty motivates the heightened affirmation of unrelated meaning frameworks to which they are committed. In the absence of any personally threatening elements of the meaning violation, this uncertainty may lead to heightened socially conservative *or* liberal judgments. While the outcome of this laboratory experiment does not capture the degree of ideological extremism that follows from broad social upheaval, this difference may remain one of degree, rather than kind. We submit that the findings presented here represent a core psychological process that is initiated by the presence of general uncertainty—whatever its source—and which underlies relatively extreme judgments, both on the political right, and the political left, relative to committed social justice beliefs.

References

Baumeister, R. F. (1991). *Meanings of life*. New York: Guilford Press.
Baumeister, R. F., & Leary, M. R. (1995). The need to belong: Desire for interpersonal attachments as a fundamental human motivation. *Psychological Bulletin, 117*, 497–529.
Bruner, J., & Postman, L. (1949). On the perception of incongruity: A paradigm. *Journal of Personality, 18*, 206–223. doi: 10.1111/j.1467-6494.1949.tb01241.x
Budner, S. (1962). Intolerance of ambiguity as a personality variable. *Journal of Personality, 30*, 29–50. doi: 10.1111/j.1467-6494.1962.tb02303.x
Burris, C. T., & Rempel, J. K. (2004). "It's the end of the world as we know it": Threat and the spatial-symbolic self. *Journal of Personality and Social Psychology, 86*, 19–42. doi: 10.1037/0022-3514.86.1.19
Crosby, F. (2004). *Affirmative action is dead: Long live affirmative action*. New Haven, CT: Yale University Press.
Duckitt, J., Wagner, C., du Plessis, I., & Birum, I. (2002). The psychological bases of ideology and prejudice: Testing a dual process model. *Journal of Personality and Social Psychology, 83*, 75–93. doi: 10.1037/0022-3514.83.1.75
Fein, S., & Spencer, S. J. (1997). Prejudice as self-image maintenance: Affirming the self through derogating others. *Journal of Personality and Social Psychology, 73*, 31–44. doi: 10.1037/0022-3514.73.1.31

Gehring, W. J., Goss, B., Coles, M. G., & Meyer, D. E. (1993). A neural system for error detection and compensation. *Psychological Science, 4(6)*, 385–390. doi: 10.1111/j.1467-9280.1993.tb00586.x

Greenberg, J., Simon, L., Solomon, S., Pyszczynski, T., & Chatel, D. (1992). Terror management & tolerance: Does mortality salience always intensify negative reactions to other's who threaten one's worldview? *Journal of Personality and Social psychology, 63*, 212–220. doi: 10.1037/0022-3514.63.2.212

Greenberg, J., Porteus, J., Simon, L., Pyszczynski, T., & Solomon, S. (1995). Evidence of a terror management function of cultural icons: The effects of mortality salience on the inappropriate use of cherished cultural symbols. *Personality and Social Psychology Bulletin, 21*, 1221–1228. doi: 10.1177/01461672952111010

Harmon-Jones, E., & Harmon-Jones, C. (2008). Cognitive dissonance theory: An update with a focus on the action-based model. In J. Y. Shah, W. L. Gardner, J. Y. Shah, & W. L. Gardner (Eds.), *Handbook of motivation science* (pp. 71–83). New York: Guilford Press.

Hart, J., Shaver, P. R., & Goldenberg, J. L. (2005). Attachment, self-esteem, worldviews, and terror management: Evidence for a tripartite security system. *Journal of Personality and Social Psychology, 88*, 999–1013. doi: 10.1037/0022-3514.88.6.999

Heine, S. J., Proulx, T., & Vohs, K. D. (2006). The meaning maintenance model: On the coherence of social motivations. *Personality and Social Psychology Review, 10*, 88–111. doi: 10.1207/s15327957pspr1002_1

Hogg, M. A. (2007). Uncertainty-identity theory. In M. P. Zanna (Ed.), *Advances in experimental social psychology* (Vol. *39*, pp. 69–126). San Diego, CA: Academic Press.

Hogg, M. A. (2012). Uncertainty-identity theory. In P. A. M. Van Lange, A. W. Kruglanski, & E. T. Higgins (Eds.), *Handbook of theories of social psychology* (pp. 62–80). Thousand Oaks, CA: Sage. doi: 10.4135/9781446249222.n29

Hogg, M. A., & Adelman, J. (2013). Uncertainty-identity theory: Extreme groups, radical behavior, and authoritarian leadership. *Journal of Social Issues, 69*, 436–454.

Holroyd, C. B., & Coles, M. H. (2002). The neural basis of human error processing: Reinforcement learning, dopamine, and the error-related negativity. *Psychological Review, 109*(4), 679–709. doi: 10.1037/0033-295X.109.4.679

Inbar, Y., & Lammers, J. (2012). Political diversity in social and personality psychology. *Perspectives on Psychological Science, 7*, 496–503.

Inzlicht, M., & Tullett, A. M. (2010). Reflecting on God: Religious primes can reduce neurophysiological response to errors. *Psychological Science, 21*, 1184–1190. doi: 10.1177/0956797610375451

Janoff-Bulman, R. (1992). *Shattered assumptions*. New York: The Free Press.

Jost, J., Glaser, J., Kruglanski, A., & Sulloway, F. (2003). Political conservatism as motivated social cognition. *Psychological Bulletin, 129*(3), 339–375. doi: 10.1037/0033-2909.129.3.339

Jost, J., Banaji, M., & Nosek, B. (2004). A decade of system justification theory: Accumulated evidence of conscious and unconscious bolstering of the status. *Political Psychology, 25*(6), 881–920. doi: 10.1111/j.1467-9221.2004.00402.x

Jost, J., Napier, J., Thorisdottir, H., Gosling, S., Palfai, T., & Ostafin, B. (2007). Are needs to manage uncertainty and threat associated with political conservatism or ideological extremity? *Personality and Social Psychology Bulletin, 33*(7), 989–1007. doi: 10.1177/0146167207301028

Kay, A., Whitson, J., Gaucher, D., & Galinsky, A. (2009). Compensatory control: Achieving order through the mind, our institutions, and the heavens. *Current Directions in Psychological Science, 18*(5), 264–268. doi: 10.1111/j.1467-8721.2009.01649.x

Kay, A. C., Moscovitch, D. A., & Laurin, K. (2010). Randomness, attributions of arousal, and belief in God. *Psychological Science, 21*(2), 216–218. doi: 10.1177/0956797609357750

Kay, A. C., & Eibach, R. P. (2013). Compensatory control and its implications for ideological extremism. *Journal of Social Issues, 69*, 564–585.

Kirk, R. (1953). *The conservative mind: From Burke to Eliot*. New York: Avon Books.

Klein, M. K., & Kruglanski, A. (2013). Commitment and extremism: A goal systemic analysis. *Journal of Social Issues, 69*, 419–435.

Kruglanski, A. W., & Webster, D. M. (1996). Motivated closing of the mind: "Seizing" and "freezing." *Psychological Review, 103*, 263–283. doi: 10.1037/0033-295X.103.2.263

Laqueur, W. (1974). *Weimar, a cultural history, 1918–1933*. London: Weidenfeld and Nicolson.

Lerner, M. J. (1980). *The belief in a just world: A fundamental delusion.* New York: Plenum Press.
Levy, S. R., West, T. L., & Ramirez, L. (2005). Lay theories and intergroup relations: A social-developmental perspective. *European Review of Social Psychology, 16,* 189–220.
Levy, S. R., West, T. L., Ramirez, L., & Karafantis, D. M. (2006). The protestant work ethic: A lay theory with dual intergroup implications. *Group Processes and Intergroup Relations, 9*(1), 95–115. doi: 10.1177/1368430206059874
Major, B., Kaiser, C., O'Brien, L., & McCoy, S. (2007). Perceived discrimination as worldview threat or worldview confirmation: Implications for self-esteem. *Journal of Personality and Social Psychology, 92,* 1068–1086. doi: 10.1037/0022-3514.92.6.1068
McGregor, H., Lieberman, J., Greenberg, J., Solomon, S., Arndt, J., Simon, L., & Pyszczynski, T. (1998). Terror management and aggression: Evidence that mortality salience motivates aggression against worldview-threatening others. *Journal of Personality and Social Psychology, 74*(3), 590–605. doi: 10.1037/0022-3514.74.3.590
McGregor, I., Zanna, M. P., Holmes, J. G., & Spencer, S. J. (2001). Compensatory conviction in the face of personal uncertainty: Going to extremes and being oneself. *Journal of Personality and Social Psychology, 80,* 472–488. doi: 10.1037/0022-3514.80.3.472
McGregor, I., Nash, K., Mann, N., & Phills, C. E. (2010). Anxious uncertainty and reactive approach motivation (RAM). *Journal of Personality and Social Psychology, 99*(1), 133–147. doi: 10.1037/a0019701
McGregor, I., Prentice, M., & Nash, K. (2013). Anxious uncertainty and reactive approach motivation (RAM) for religious, idealistic, and lifestyle extremes. *Journal of Social Issues, 69,* 537–563.
Mendes, W. B., Blascovich, J., Hunter, S., Lickel, B., & Jost, J. T. (2007). Threatened by the unexpected: Physiological responses during social interactions with expectancy-violating partners. *Journal of Personality and Social Psychology, 92,* 698–716. doi: 10.1037/0022-3514.92.4.698
Mirels, H. L., & Garrett, J. B. (1971). The Protestant Ethic as a personality variable. *Journal of Consulting and Clinical Psychology, 36*(1), 40–44. doi: 10.1037/h0030477
Neuberg, S., & Newsom, J. (1993). Personal need for structure: Individual differences in the desire for simple structure. *Journal of Personality and Social Psychology, 65,* 133–131. doi: 10.1037/0022-3514.65.1.113
Niemann, Y., & Maruyama, G. (2005). Inequities in higher education: Issues and promising practices in a world ambivalent about affirmative action. *Journal of Social Issues, 61*(3), 407–426. doi: 10.1111/j.1540-4560.2005.00414.x
O'Brien, L., Kinias, Z., & Major, B. (2008). How status and stereotypes impact attributions to discrimination: The stereotype-asymmetry hypothesis. *Journal of Experimental Social Psychology, 44*(2), 405–412. doi: 10.1016/j.jesp.2006.12.003
Peterson, J. (1999). *Maps of meaning: The architecture of belief.* New York: Routledge.
Plaks, J., & Stecher, K. (2007). Unexpected improvement, decline, and stasis: A prediction confidence perspective on achievement success and failure. *Journal of Personality and Social Psychology, 93*(4), 667–684.
Proulx, T., & Heine, S. J. (2008). The case of the transmogrifying experimenter: Affirmation of a moral schema following implicit change detection. *Psychological Science, 19,* 1294–1300. doi: 10.1111/j.1467-9280.2008.02238.x
Proulx, T., Heine, S., & Vohs, K. (2010). When is the unfamiliar The Uncanny? Meaning affirmation after exposure to absurdist literature, humor, and art. *Personality and Social Psychology Bulletin, 36,* 817–829. doi: 10.1177/0146167210369896
Proulx, T., Inzlicht, M., & Harmon-Jones, E. (2012). Understanding all inconsistency compensation as a palliative response to violated expectations. *Trends in Cognitive Sciences, 16*(5), 285–291. doi: 10.1016/j.tics.2012.04.002
Proulx, T., & Inzlicht, M. (2012). The five 'A's of meaning maintenance: Making sense of the theories of sense-making. [Target Article] *Psychological Inquiry. 23,* 317–335. doi: 10.1080/1047840X.2012.702372
Randles, D., Proulx, T., & Heine, S. J. (2011). Turn-frogs and careful-sweaters: Subliminal presentations of incongruous word pairings invoke meaninglessness. *Journal of Experimental Social Psychology. 47,* 246–249. doi: 10.1016/j.jesp.2010.07.020

Rosenblatt, A., Greenberg, J., Solomon, S., Pyszczynski, T., & Lyon, D. (1989). Evidence for terror management theory: I. The effects of mortality salience on reactions to those who violate or uphold cultural values. *Journal of Personality and Social Psychology, 57,* 681–690. doi: 10.1037/0022-3514.57.4.681

Rosenthal, L., Levy, S. R., & Moyer, A. (2011). Protestant work ethic's relation to intergroup and policy attitudes: A meta-analytic review. *European Journal of Social Psychology, 41*(7), 874–885. doi: 10.1002/ejsp.832

Sanford, R. N., Adorno, E., Frenkel-Brunswik, E., & Levinson, D. J. (1950). The measurement of implicit antidemocratic trends. In E. Adorno, E. Frenkel-Brunswik, D. J. Levinson, & R. N. Sanford (Eds.), *The authoritarian personality* (pp. 222–279). New York: Harper & Row.

Shackman, A. J., Salomons, T. V., Slagter, H. A., Fox, A. S., Winter, J. J., & Davidson, R. J. (2011). The integration of negative affect, pain and cognitive control in the cingulate cortex. *Nature Reviews Neuroscience, 12*(3), 154–167. doi: 10.1038/nrn2994

Steele, C. M., & Liu, T. J. (1983). Dissonance processes as self-affirmation. *Journal of Personality and Social Psychology, 45,* 5–19. 10. doi: 1037/0022-3514.45.1.5

Tolnay, E., & Beck, E. (1995). *A festival of violence: An analysis of Southern lynchings, 1882–1930.* Chicago, IL: University of Illinois Press.

Van den Bos, K. (2001). Uncertainty management: The influence of uncertainty salience on reactions to perceived procedural fairness. *Journal of Personality and Social Psychology, 80,* 931–941. doi: 10.1037/0022-3514.80.6.931

Van Veen, V., Krug, M. K., Schooler, J. W., & Carter, C. S. (2009). Neural activity predicts attitude change in cognitive dissonance. *Nature Neuroscience, 12*(11), 1469–1474. doi: 10.1038/nn.2413

Watson, D., Clark, L. A., & Tellegen, A. (1988). Development and validation of brief measures of positive and negative affect: The PANAS scales. *Journal of Personality and Social Psychology, 53,* 1063–1070. doi: 10.1037/0022-3514.54.6.1063

Williams, K. D., & Nida, S. A. (2011). Ostracism: Consequences and coping. *Current Directions in Psychological Science, 20*(2), 71–75. doi: 10.1177/0963721411402480

Zanna, M., & Cooper, J. (1974). Dissonance and the pill: An attribution approach to studying the arousal properties of dissonance. *Journal of Personality and Social Psychology, 29,* 703–709. doi: 10.1037/h0036651

TRAVIS PROULX is currently an assistant professor at Tilburg University. His research focuses on on how people make sense of their experiences, and how people respond to violations of relevant expectations.

BRENDA MAJOR is currently a Distinguished Professor in the Department of Psychological and Brain Sciences at the University of California, Santa Barbara. Her research interests include social stigma, resilience, the psychological justification of inequality, and the antecedents and consequences of perceived discrimination and unfair treatment. Her work has been funded by the National Science Foundation, the National Institutes of Health, and the American Philosophical Foundation, among others. Major is Past President of the Society of Experimental Social Psychology and of the Society for Personality and Social Psychology. Her current research projects examine the impact of organizational diversity initiatives on minorities' and majorities' perceptions of fairness and acceptance within organizations, and the impact of perceived ethnic, gender, and weight-based discrimination on physiological stress responses, health behaviors, and interpersonal relationships.

Uncertainty and Status-Based Asymmetries in the Distinction Between the "Good" Us and the "Bad" Them: Evidence That Group Status Strengthens the Relationship Between the Need for Cognitive Closure and Extremity in Intergroup Differentiation

Christopher M. Federico[*]
University of Minnesota, Twin Cities

Corrie V. Hunt
Hart Research Associates

Emily L. Fisher
Hobart and William Smith Colleges

In this article, we look at how a key index of discomfort with uncertainty—the need for cognitive closure—interacts with perceived group status to influence a key antecedent of extremism: intergroup differentiation. Because high status provides people with a clear basis for superiority claims, we predicted that individuals with a high need for closure would accentuate intergroup differences in favor of the ingroup when they believe the latter to have higher status relative to outgroups. Two studies provided support for this hypothesis. In Study 1, Whites who were high in need for closure differentiated in favor of the ingroup when they perceived a larger status difference between the high-status ingroup and lower-status Black and Latino outgroups. In Study 2, individuals high in need for closure who were

---

[*]Correspondence concerning this article should be addressed to Christopher M. Federico, Department of Psychology, University of Minnesota, 75 East River Road, Minneapolis, MN 55455 [e-mail: federico@umn.edu].

randomly assigned to a high-status (vs. low-status) group displayed the same pattern.

What is the psychological basis of extremism in the sociopolitical realm? While the answer to this question is obviously complex, a key ingredient in the genesis of extremism is a polarization in evaluations of the ingroup and outgroup—that is, a tendency to parse the social world in binary, black-and-white terms, as a Manichean confrontation between a "good" us and "bad" them (Hogg, 2012; Hogg & Blaylock, 2012). Of course, this tendency toward "group-centrism" is ubiquitous and does not always rise to the level of pathology implied by the term "extremism" (Hogg, 2003; Mullen, Brown, & Smith, 1992; Tajfel & Turner, 1986; Yzerbyt & Demoulin, 2010). Nevertheless, the crucial role of the evaluatively laden division of the world into ingroup and outgroup in extremist outlooks raises the question of what leads this division to be stronger in some cases than in others.

In this study, we address this question by examining how individual differences related to one's orientation toward uncertainty explain variation in the tendency to differentiate between ingroup and outgroup that is one of the "deep" roots of extreme outlooks (e.g., Golec de Zavala, Federico, Cislak, & Sigger, 2008; Hogg, 2012; Sidanius & Pratto, 1999). In this vein, recent studies have focused on how individual differences in the *need for cognitive closure*—the desire for knowledge that is certain and firm—influence intergroup differentiation (Kruglanski, 2004). This work suggests that ingroups are epistemic providers: they offer their members a consensually validated shared reality, overcoming uncertainty. As a result, individuals with a high need for closure—who possess a stronger need to overcome uncertainty—differentiate between ingroup and outgroup more extremely (Kruglanski, Pierro, Mannetti, & DeGrada, 2006; Shah, Kruglanski, & Thompson, 1998). Nevertheless, recent findings also suggest that the relationship between the need for closure and polarized responses to the ingroup and outgroup may depend on the characteristics of groups individuals belong to (Golec de Zavala et al., 2008; Kruglanski et al., 2006). Interestingly, no research has focused on how this relationship may be affected by one of the most important aspects of intergroup relations in the real world: differences in *group status*. We argue that high-status ingroups may be better providers of certainty than low-status ingroups, leading individuals with a high need for closure to be more extreme in differentiating ingroup from outgroup when they perceive the ingroup to have greater status relative to outgroups. We begin by reviewing previous work on our key uncertainty-related variable: the need for cognitive closure.

Uncertainty and Intergroup Differentiation: The Role of Individual Differences in Need for Closure

Individual differences in the experience of uncertainty relate in important ways to intergroup differentiation. As noted above, one of the most important indices of one's orientation toward uncertainty in the current literature is the need for cognitive closure. Broadly speaking, individuals under a high need for closure tend to find uncertainty aversive, which motivates them to reduce uncertainty as quickly and decisively as possible (Kruglanski, 2004; Kruglanski & Webster, 1996; Webster & Kruglanski, 1994). Indeed, the notion of uncertainty avoidance is central to the definition of need for closure, which is commonly described as a "desire for *any* firm belief on a given topic, as opposed to confusion and uncertainty" (Jost et al., 2003, p. 348). Those high in the need for closure overcome uncertainty (1) by "seizing" quickly on available cues in order to reach conclusions and by "freezing" in a relatively unbending way on these conclusions once they are reached; and (2) by seeking out social contexts that are orderly, predictable, and familiar.

Importantly, group membership is a major source of certainty-providing knowledge. The beliefs, norms, and valued social identities consensually shared by members of a group provide people with certainty about what the world is like, what they should do in various situations, and who they are and why they are important. As a result, ingroups should be more extremely valued relative to outgroups by those who strongly seek certainty and closure. Consistent with this expectation, the need for closure tends to promote a syndrome of "group-centrism" in intergroup contexts—a disproportionate tendency to differentiate between the ingroup and the outgroup and rely on the ingroup as a reference point for judgments and behavior (Kruglanski et al., 2006; see also Hogg & Adelman, 2013).

For example, a more extreme differentiation between the ingroup and outgroup on affective and evaluative dimensions *in favor of the ingroup* enhances the subjective worth of the ingroup by reinforcing the perceived superiority of its character, aims, and values. Moreover, it provides a perceived hedge against threats from outside the group and helps group members avoid the uncertainty and risk associated with a more cooperative orientation. Accordingly, those with a high need for closure—who should especially desire the certainty provided by group membership—show more extreme ingroup biases along a variety of dimensions (e.g., Kruglanski et al., 2006; Shah et al., 1998; see also Jost, Glaser, Kruglanski, & Sulloway, 2003) and a more extreme tendency to deal with outgroups in a competitive fashion (de Grada, Kruglanski, Mannetti, & Pierro, 1999; Federico, Golec, & Dial, 2005; Golec & Federico, 2004; Golec de Zavala, 2006; Golec de Zavala et al., 2008; see also de Dreu, Koole, & Oldersma, 1999). Similarly, individuals with a high need for closure are more extreme in their identification with and attraction to ingroup versus outgroup members (Federico et al., 2005; Kruglanski et al., 2006; Kruglanski, Shah, Pierro, & Mannetti, 2002; Shah et al. 1998; see also Kruglanski & Mayseless, 1987; Kruglanski & Webster, 1991; see also Kosic, Kruglanski, Pierro, & Mannetti, 2004; Van Oudenhoven, Prins, and Buunk, 1998).

Thus, the distaste for uncertainty associated with a high need for closure sharpens the tendency to differentiate between a "good" us and a "bad" them that is so central to many forms of extremism. However, recent studies also suggest that the tendency for a high need for closure to be related to polarized responses to the ingroup and outgroup depends on the characteristics of the groups individuals belong to. For example, the need for closure more strongly predicts extreme intergroup differentiation when the ingroup is relatively homogenous in its makeup and beliefs, since a cohesive group is a stronger source of certainty (Kruglanski et al., 2002, 2006; Shah et al., 1998). Moreover, those with a high need for closure favor ingroup over outgroup they belong to groups whose norms and beliefs endorse hostile approaches to intergroup conflict; in these cases, the explicit normative support for intergroup differentiation reinforces its certainty-providing effect (Federico et al., 2005; Golec & Federico, 2004; Golec de Zavala, 2006; see also Golec de Zavala et al., 2008; see also Jost et al., 2003).

Perceived Group Status, the Need for Closure, and Intergroup Differentiation

Surprisingly, studies of the interface between the need for closure and the tendency to sharply differentiate between a "good" ingroup and a "bad" outgroup have overlooked a signal feature of most real-world intergroup contexts: namely, differences in *group status*, or the relative amount of prestige attributed to a group along valued dimensions of social comparison (Jost, Banaji, & Nosek, 2004; Tajfel & Turner, 1986). By and large, research on the consequences of the uncertainty aversion associated with the need for closure has focused on intergroup contexts in which the ingroup and outgroup were assumed to have equal status, and no studies have directly compared the relationship between the need for closure and extremity in intergroup differentiation across groups differing in status. This is a notable omission, given that most glaring examples of extremism in intergroup relations—such as a genocide—occur most frequently in the context of group hierarchy (Sidanius & Pratto, 1999).

Nevertheless, there are sound reasons to expect that the perceived status of the ingroup may moderate the relationship between the need for closure and intergroup differentiation. As we have seen, the impact of the need for closure differs as a function of ingroup characteristics. When characteristics of the ingroup—such as internal homogeneity and strong normative support for intergroup hostility—make it a "better" provider of certainty, the relationship between the need for closure and polarized views of the ingroup and outgroup is stronger (Golec de Zavala, 2006; Kruglanski et al., 2006). Similarly, we argue that groups that are relatively high in perceived status should be more valuable as sources of certainty, strengthening the tendency for those high in the need for closure to accentuate differences between the ingroup and outgroup.

But why should high-status groups be particularly valuable as certainty providers? All other things being equal, the advantages implied by an intergroup status difference make sharp differentiation in favor of the ingroup a more "realistic" response for members of high-status groups (Mullen et al., 1992; Tajfel & Turner, 1986; Sachdev & Bourhis, 1991). If a group is perceived to have relatively high status, it is easier for members to evaluate that group more positively than outgroups and justify a more extreme identification with and attraction to ingroup versus outgroup members; their position in the status hierarchy provides them with a clear basis for the superiority claims inherent in ingroup bias. Conversely, if a group is perceived to have *relatively low status*, it is more difficult for group members to "deny reality" and differentiate between groups in ways that imply ingroup superiority (Spears, Jetten, & Doosje, 2001). Consistent with these arguments, members of high-status groups show more extreme biases in the form of (1) more polarized evaluations of the ingroup and outgroups and (2) stronger attraction to ingroup members (Jost, Pelham, & Carvallo, 2002; Sachdev & Bourhis, 1991; Turner, 1978; Turner & Brown, 1978; van Knippenberg & van Oers, 1984; for reviews, see Jost et al., 2004; Mullen et al., 1992; Sidanius & Pratto, 1999; Sidanius, Pratto, van Laar, & Levin, 2004). This tendency is particularly evident in situations where the status distinction is perceived to have a legitimate basis (Jost et al., 2004; Sidanius et al., 2004; Tajfel & Turner, 1986; Turner & Brown, 1978).

In sum, the prestige attributed to high-status groups should make them a more plausible basis for sharp distinctions between a "good" ingroup and a "bad" outgroup than comparable low-status groups. If this is the case, then membership in a high-status group should be particularly valuable to those who seek certainty. In turn, this suggests that the tendency for those high in the need for closure to more extremely accentuate ingroup-outgroup differences should be more pronounced among members of groups that are perceived to be higher in status relative to an outgroup. When the ingroup is relatively high in status, membership should furnish group members with a fair degree of certainty, leading those with a high need for closure to show more extreme biases. However, when the ingroup is relatively low in status, its role as a provider of certainty may be limited, weakening the tendency for those with a high need for closure to evaluatively differentiate between ingroup and outgroup.

The goal of the studies reported here was to explore one key foundation of extremism by examining this hypothesis about the bases of the tendency to divide the world into a "good" us and a "bad" them. Study 1 focused solely on members of a high-status racial group and looked at the extent to which the perceived size of the ingroup's status advantage moderated the tendency for participants with a greater distaste for uncertainty—i.e., those high in need for closure—to adopt polarized views of the ingroup and outgroup. Study 2 experimentally manipulated the status of the ingroup to provide a more rigorous test of the moderating role of group status. In both studies, intergroup differentiation was operationalized in terms of ingroup bias in evaluations of the groups and the attribution of positive versus negative traits to the groups. In addition, Study 2 examined one other dependent measure: namely, the extent to which group members favored working with ingroup versus outgroup members.

Study 1

In Study 1, we used a survey to examine the moderating role of individual differences in the extent to which members of a high-status racial group (i.e., White Americans) perceived a relatively large status difference between the ingroup and two low-status outgroups (i.e., African Americans and Latinos). Our prediction was that certainty-oriented Whites—i.e., those high in the need for closure—would differentiate between the groups in favor of the White ingroup when they also perceived a larger status advantage for their group vis-à-vis African Americans and Latinos.

Method

Participants

The survey respondents were 204 students at a large Midwestern university. The number of racial minority students in this sample was too small to conduct a statistically powerful analysis (5 African-American students, 2 Hispanic students, 17 Asian students, and 12 students who reported their race as "other"). Therefore, we analyzed only the responses of the 164 participants who identified as White. These students were split evenly by gender (81 male and 83 female). Their mean age was 20.34 years ($SD = 2.94$).

Procedure and Measures

Participants were recruited from introductory psychology courses and given extra credit for participating in the study. After giving informed consent, participants completed a pencil-and-paper survey. Below, we describe our key variables.

Need for closure. This was measured using the 42-item Need for Cognitive Closure Scale (Webster & Kruglanski, 1994). All items were answered on a 7-point response scale ranging from 1 (*strongly disagree*) to 7 (*strongly agree*). Responses were coded such that higher scores indicated a higher need for closure and averaged ($\alpha = .83, M = 4.17, SD = .52$).

Perceived status differences. In order to operationalize perceived status differences between the White ingroup and two lower-status outgroups—i.e., African Americans and Latinos—participants were asked to rate the status of the groups "as you think most people see them." Participants rated each group on a 7-point scale ranging from 1 (*low status*) to 7 (*high status*). Two difference scores were then generated by subtracting (1) participants' ratings of African Americans from their ratings of Whites and (2) their ratings of Latinos from their ratings of Whites. Since the difference scores were highly correlated ($r = .74$), they were averaged to form a composite measure of perceived status differences. Higher scores indicate a larger status difference ($\alpha = .85$; $M = 2.83$, $SD = 1.46$).

Intergroup differentiation in evaluative ratings. Participants were also asked to indicate how positively or negatively they felt about each group on a feeling thermometer: "How positively or negatively do you feel toward the following groups?" The response scales ranged from 1 (*very negative*) to 7 (*very positive*). Difference scores were generated by subtracting (1) participants' ratings of African Americans from their ratings of Whites and (2) their ratings of Latinos from their ratings of Whites. Since the two differences were highly correlated ($r = .79$), they were averaged to form a composite measure of intergroup differentiation in evaluative ratings. Higher scores indicate a more polarized tendency to see the ingroup positively and the outgroup negatively ($\alpha = .88$; $M = .55$, $SD = 1.28$).

Intergroup differentiation in trait ratings. Participants were asked to rate each group on four dimensions: violent/not violent, unintelligent/intelligent, lazy/hardworking, and untrustworthy/trustworthy. Responses were provided on a 7-point scale, with opposing traits anchoring each end of the scale (e.g. 1 = *violent*, 7 = *not violent*). Items were recoded where needed so higher numbers indicated more positive ratings of the group, and the four items for each group were averaged to form a composite trait rating of each group ($\alpha = .73$, for Whites; $\alpha = .87$, for African Americans; $\alpha = .79$, for Latinos). Difference scores were generated by subtracting (1) participants' trait ratings of African Americans from their trait ratings of Whites and (2) their trait ratings of Latinos from their trait ratings of Whites. Since the two scores were correlated ($r = .73$), they were averaged to form a composite measure of intergroup differentiation in trait ratings. Higher scores indicate a greater tendency to see the ingroup positively and the outgroup negatively ($\alpha = .84$; $M = .12$, $SD = 1.14$).

Results

Preliminary Analyses

We began by confirming the existence of an average perceived status difference and tendency toward intergroup differentiation in favor of the ingroup on each of the dependent measures. First, confirming a perceived status gap, paired-samples *t*-tests (two-tailed) indicated that participants' status ratings of African

Table 1. Intercorrelations for Study Variables (Study 1)

Variable	1	2	3
1. Need for closure	–		
2. Composite status difference	.10	–	
3. Intergroup differentiation: Evaluative ratings	.36***	.10	–
4. Intergroup differentiation: Trait ratings	.30***	.17*	.57***

Note. All coefficients are Pearson correlations.
*p < .05; ***p < .001.

Americans ($M = 3.47$, $SD = 1.17$) and Latinos ($M = 3.07$, $SD = 1.00$) were significantly lower than their status rating of Whites ($M = 6.09$, $SD = .94$), with $t(202) = 23.10$, $p < .001$, Cohen's $d = 1.62$, for the White–African American comparison; and $t(202) = 28.72$, $p < .001$, Cohen's $d = 2.02$, for the White–Latino comparison. Second, paired-samples *t*-tests (two-tailed) indicated that participants' evaluative ratings of African Americans ($M = 4.88$, $SD = 1.23$) and Latinos ($M = 4.89$, $SD = 1.12$) were significantly lower than their rating of Whites ($M = 5.44$, $SD = 1.09$), with $t(202) = 5.72$, $p < .001$, Cohen's $d = .40$, for Whites versus African Americans; and $t(202) = 5.99$, $p < .001$, Cohen's $d = .42$, for Whites versus Latinos. Finally, with respect to trait ratings, *t*-tests (two-tailed) indicated a less consistent pattern of ingroup bias than was found with the evaluative ratings. Participants' trait ratings of African Americans ($M = 4.09$, $SD = .98$) were significantly lower than their trait rating of Whites ($M = 4.37$, $SD = .86$), $t(193) = 3.08$, $p < .01$, Cohen's $d = .22$; but their trait ratings of Latinos were not ($M = 4.40$, $SD = .92$), $t(193) = -.39$, $p > .30$, Cohen's $d = -.03$.

Intercorrelations among variables. Before turning to the main analyses, we also examined the correlations between our key variables; these are displayed in Table 1. The two differentiation measures were highly correlated ($r = .57$). Moreover, consistent with prior work, the need for closure was associated with more extreme differentiation on both measures ($r = .36$, with differentiation in evaluative ratings; $r = .30$, with differentiation in trait ratings). Finally, the composite measure of perceived status differences was significantly associated with more extreme intergroup differentiation in trait ratings ($r = .17$).

Need for Closure, Perceived Status Differences, and Intergroup Differentiation

A series of hierarchical ordinary-least squares regressions was used to examine the hypothesis that individuals with a higher need for closure would more extremely differentiate between ingroup and outgroup when they attributed a larger status advantage to the White ingroup versus the Black and Latino outgroups. In

Table 2. Need for Closure, Perceived Status Differences, and Intergroup Differentiation (Study 1)

	Intergroup differentiation: Evaluative ratings			
	Model 1		Model 2	
Predictor	b	SE	b	SE
Need for closure (NFC)	1.00***	(.16)	.95***	(.16)
Composite status difference	.04	(.06)	.05	(.06)
NFC × Composite status difference	–	–	.25*	(.11)
(Constant)	.68***	(.08)	.66***	(.08)
F (degrees of freedom)	20.42 (2, 159)***		15.57 (3, 158)***	
Adjusted R^2	.194		.214	
N	162		162	

	Intergroup differentiation: Trait ratings			
	Model 1		Model 2	
Predictor	b	SE	b	SE
Need for closure (NFC)	.78***	(.14)	.73***	(.12)
Composite status difference	.07	(.06)	.10*	(.05)
NFC × Composite status difference	–	–	.21**	(.09)
(Constant)	.19**	(.07)	.18**	(.07)
F (degrees of freedom)	17.26 (2, 152)***		13.14 (3, 151)***	
Adjusted R^2	.174		.191	
N	155		155	

Note. Entries are unstandardized OLS regression coefficients. In each model, perceived status differences and the dependent variable are a composite of difference scores comparing Whites to Blacks and Whites to Latinos.
*$p < .05$; **$p < .01$; ***$p < .001$.

these models, each differentiation measure was regressed on the need for closure and the composite status difference in a first step, while the product term for the interaction between these two independent variables was added on a second step. All independent variables were centered, and the product term was constructed from the centered variables.

The results of this analysis for evaluative ratings are summarized in the top panel of Table 2. In Model 1, which contained only the main-effect terms, the estimates indicate that the need for closure was significantly associated with intergroup differentiation in favor of the ingroup ($b = 1.00$, $p < .001$; partial $\eta^2 = .20$). Model 2 added the interaction. The estimates from this model indicate that the main effect was qualified by a significant Need for Closure × Composite Status Difference interaction ($b = .25$, $p < .05$; partial $\eta^2 = .03$). To probe this interaction, simple slopes for the relationship between the need for closure and evaluative differentiation in evaluative ratings were computed one standard deviation above and below the mean of the composite status difference measure (Aiken & West, 1991). The analyses indicated that the relationship between the need for closure and differentiation in evaluative ratings was more than twice as strong among those who saw a larger status difference between ingroup and outgroup ($b = 1.32$, $SE = .21$, $p < .001$; partial $\eta^2 = .20$) than those who saw a smaller status difference between the groups ($b = .59$, $SE = .25$, $p < .05$; partial $\eta^2 = .04$).

The results for differentiation in trait ratings—summarized in the bottom panel of Table 2—were similar. In Model 1, the need for closure was significantly associated with differentiation in favor of the ingroup ($b = .78$, $p < .001$; partial $\eta^2 = .17$). However, in Model 2, this main effect was qualified by a significant Need for Closure × Composite Status Difference interaction ($b = .21$, $p < .01$; partial $\eta^2 = .03$). Simple slope analyses similar to those carried out above indicated that the relationship between the need for closure and trait differentiation was almost three times larger among those who perceived a large status difference between the groups ($b = 1.03$, $SE = .19$, $p < .001$; partial $\eta^2 = .17$) than those who saw a smaller status difference between the groups ($b = .44$, $SE = .22$, $p < .05$; partial $\eta^2 = .03$).

Robustness Checks

As a final step, all of the above models were checked for dependent-variable outliers by computing the externally studentized residuals for the full model for each dependent variable (Cohen, Cohen, West, & Aiken, 2003). An examination of these residuals for each dependent variable revealed no large outliers (none had absolute values > 5). Moreover, further analyses for both dependent variables that excluded outliers selected using a more liberal criterion (i.e., residuals with absolute values > 3) produced identical results.

Discussion

The results of Study 1 provide consistent support for our hypothesis. While individuals with a greater aversion to uncertainty—as measured by the need for closure—generally showed a more extreme tendency to differentiate between ingroup and outgroup, this relationship was much stronger among those who saw a larger status gap between the high-status White ingroup and the low-status Black and Latino outgroups. Moreover, this relationship held across two different dependent measures. Thus, the relationship between the need for closure and the tendency to divide the social world into an evaluatively polarized "us" and "them" is contingent on group-status perceptions.

Study 2

Although the results of Study 1 are supportive, the study is not without its shortcomings. Rather than directly comparing members of *different* groups with varying levels of perceived status, we simply capitalized on individual differences among high-status group members in the extent to which they perceived a large status advantage in favor the ingroup. This is at best an indirect way of examining the moderating role of the perceived status of the ingroup. Moreover, despite the relatively low full-sample correlations between the status-difference measure and the intergroup differentiation measures in Study 1 (i.e., rs of .10 and .17), the absence of an experimental manipulation of status raises the possibility that the two sets of measures are really just different indices of the same thing—intergroup differentiation. As such, it would be helpful to subject the status variable to greater experimental control. In order to deal with these issues, Study 2 replaced Study 1's real-world groups with lab-generated groups. Specifically, we led participants to believe their performance on a cognitive task classified them as part of an ingroup of "deductive thinkers," and then randomly assigned them to receive feedback indicating this ingroup either had stronger abilities (high ingroup status) or weaker abilities (low ingroup status) than an outgroup of "inductive thinkers." We then examined the relationship between the need for closure and several indices of intergroup differentiation. We predicted that individuals with a greater aversion to uncertainty—as indicated by a high need for closure—would show more a polarized orientation to the ingroup versus the outgroup in the high-status (vs. low-status) condition.

Method

Participants

One hundred and sixty-nine undergraduates at a large Midwestern university participated in this experiment. Twelve participants who expressed suspicion about the status manipulation (see below) were excluded from the analyses, leaving us with a final sample of $N = 157$. Of these, there were 114 White students, 5 African-American students, 5 Hispanic students, 17 Asian-American students, 2 Native American students, and 14 students who reported their race as "other." The final sample was comprised disproportionately of women (106 females, 41 males, with 10 who did not report gender), with a mean age of 20.1 ($SD = 3.66$).

Procedure and Measures

Participants were recruited from introductory psychology courses and given extra credit for participating. The experimenter told students that the study was about personality difference and problem-solving abilities. Participants completed the experiment in a computer lab where MediaLab software administered all measures and manipulations.

Participants first completed the Need for Cognitive Closure Scale (Webster & Kruglanski, 1994). As in Study 1, all items were answered on a 7-point response scale ranging from 1 (*strongly disagree*) to 7 (*strongly agree*). Responses were coded such that higher scores indicated a higher need for closure and averaged to form a composite ($\alpha = .88, M = 4.21, SD = .63$). Participants then completed a 17-item measure of "reasoning styles" ostensibly designed to differentiate between deductive and inductive thinkers. Sample items included "Which word do you associate most closely with the keyword *Apple*? *Seed, tree, fruit, red*" and "Which number do you associate most closely with the number *12? 11, 6, 13, 24.*" After the computer ostensibly tabulated their score, all participants saw a screen indicating that they were deductive thinkers. At this point, participants received the status manipulation, which randomly indicated whether deductive thinkers were higher or lower status compared to inductive thinkers:

> Your results indicate that you are a DEDUCTIVE reasoner. In general, deductive reasoners perform worse (better) than inductive reasoners on tasks of cognitive ability, verbal ability, and spatial reasoning. As a result, deductive thinkers also tend to attain less (greater) occupational status in everyday life. Specifically, compared to inductive thinkers, deductive thinkers tend to earn 10% lower (higher) salaries, have significantly lower (higher) rates of acceptance to graduate and professional schools, and to demonstrate smaller (greater) rates of career advancement and promotion.

To reinforce the manipulation, participants subsequently received false feedback for their performance on 10 spatial-reasoning problems. Participants had 10 seconds to solve each problem, which progressed from easy to very difficult. Participants then received false feedback in accordance with their status condition: that they scored in the 80th percentile of undergraduates (high status), or in the 30th percentile (low status). For both conditions, the feedback stated that the participant's performance was consistent with the performance of other deductive thinkers, who tend to do better (worse) than inductive thinkers on tests measuring spatial reasoning ability. To assess whether participants believed our status manipulation, participants first read the following instructions: "There are many people who believe that members of different groups enjoy different amounts of social status in our society. We know that you may not be very familiar with the concepts of deductive and inductive thinkers, but we would like you to put forth your best guess. If you had to rate each group *as you see them,* how would you do so?" Participants then rated both inductive and deductive thinkers on a scale of 1 (low status) to 7 (high status).

For our dependent measures, *intergroup differentiation in evaluative ratings* was assessed by asking participants to indicate how positively or negatively they generally felt about the ingroup—i.e., deductive thinkers—and the outgroup—i.e., inductive thinkers—on 7-point feeling thermometer scales identical to those used in Study 1. A final measure of differentiation in evaluative ratings was generated by subtracting participants' ratings of inductive thinkers from their ratings of deductive thinkers. Higher scores indicate greater differentiation in favor of the ingroup ($M = .04$, $SD = 1.05$). Second, *intergroup differentiation in trait ratings* was assessed by asking participants to rate each group on ten trait items: unfriendly/friendly, insincere/sincere, lazy/hardworking, cold/warm, closedminded/open minded, unkind/kind, unreliable/reliable, impolite/polite, unlikeable/likeable, and uninteresting/interesting. The trait ratings were prefaced with the following text: "We know you may not be very familiar with the idea of inductive and deductive thinkers. Even if this is the case, we ask you to put forth your best guess as to what deductive and inductive thinkers would be like." Responses were provided on a 7-point scale, with the opposing traits anchoring each end of the scale (e.g., $1 = unkind$, $7 = kind$). Items were recoded where needed so that higher numbers indicated more positive ratings of the group. The 10 appropriately coded items for each group were then averaged to form a composite trait rating of each group ($\alpha = .89$, for both groups). A final measure of intergroup differentiation in trait ratings was generated by subtracting participants' trait ratings of inductive thinkers from their ratings of deductive thinkers. Higher scores indicate greater differentiation in favor of the ingroup ($M = .23$, $SD = .87$).

Finally, we told participants that we would like to solicit their feedback on some studies we were currently designing to investigate how people work in groups of majority deductive thinkers or majority inductive thinkers. We asked participants the following: "In your place of employment, would you prefer to work with a majority of inductive thinkers or to work in a group with a majority of deductive thinkers?" Participants answered on a scale ranging from 1 (*strongly prefer majority inductive thinkers*) to 7 (*strongly prefer majority deductive thinkers*). Higher scores indicate a stronger preference for working with an ingroup member ($M = 4.33$, $SD = 1.24$).

After completion of the study, the experimenter probed participants for suspicion of deception and then debriefed participants about the nature of the study. Ten participants expressed suspicion that the deductive feedback had been false. We removed these participants from subsequent analyses.

Results

Manipulation Checks and Preliminary Analyses

Manipulation checks. To assess whether participants believed our status manipulation, we subtracted ratings of inductive thinkers' status from ratings of deductive thinkers' status, forming a relative status variable in which positive numbers correspond to greater relative status of deductive over inductive thinkers. A two-sample t-test (two-tailed) revealed that participants rated deductive thinkers relatively higher than inductive thinkers in the high status condition ($M = 1.41$, $SD = 1.40$) and relatively lower than inductive thinkers in the low status condition ($M = -1.23$, $SD = 1.61$), a difference that was significant, $t(155) = 10.94$, $p < .001$, Cohen's $d = 1.75$. Moreover, a regression of the status-difference variable on the need for closure indicated no significant effect, $b = .24$, $SE = .25$, $p > .30$ partial $\eta^2 = .01$; and a regression of the status-difference variable on the need for closure, a dummy variable for status condition, and the interaction between the two revealed no significant interaction, $b = .16$, $SE = .19$, $p > .30$; partial $\eta^2 = .004$.

Basic patterns of intergroup differentiation. Collapsing across the conditions, a paired-samples t-test (two-tailed) indicated that participants' evaluative ratings of the ingroup ($M = 4.42$, $SD = 2.07$) were slightly but nonsignificantly higher than ratings of the outgroup ($M = 4.36$, $SD = .91$), $t(156) = .75$, $p > .40$, Cohen's $d = .06$. However, this result obscures starkly different patterns of differentiation within each condition. While participants in the high-status condition evaluated the ingroup ($M = 4.82$, $SD = 1.06$) more positively than the outgroup ($M = 4.48$, $SD = 1.00$), $t(78) = 3.41$, $p < .001$, Cohen's $d = .38$, those in the low-status condition displayed a marginal tendency to evaluate the outgroup ($M = 4.23$, $SD = .80$) more positively than the ingroup ($M = 4.01$, $SD = .93$), $t(77) = -1.68$, $p < .10$, Cohen's $d = -.19$. Turning to the trait ratings, a paired-samples t-test (two-tailed) indicated a pattern of intergroup differentiation in favor of the ingroup even when collapsing across conditions. Participants' trait ratings of the ingroup ($M = 4.99$, $SD = .84$) were higher than ratings of the outgroup ($M = 4.73$, $SD = .89$), $t(156) = 3.70$, $p < .001$, Cohen's $d = .30$. Subsequent analyses indicated a similar pattern of differentiation in both conditions. Participants in the high-status condition evaluated the ingroup ($M = 4.96$, $SD = .84$) more positively than the outgroup ($M = 4.72$, $SD = .93$), $t(78) = 2.36$, $p < .05$, Cohen's $d = .27$, as did those in the low-status condition ($M = 5.02$, $SD = .85$; vs. $M = 4.74$, $SD = .86$), $t(77) = 2.88$, $p < .01$, Cohen's $d = .33$. Finally, collapsing across conditions, a mean comparison t-test (one-tailed) confirmed that the mean on the work-preference measure ($M = 4.34$, $SD = .10$) was significantly greater than the neutral score of 4, $t(156) = 3.42$, $p < .001$, Cohen's $d = .27$, indicating a preference for working with the ingroup. Moreover, a two-sample t-test (two-tailed) indicated that individuals in the high-status condition showed a more extreme relative preference for working with a member of the ingroup ($M = 4.80$, $SD = 1.25$) than individuals in the low-status condition (who actually preferred working with an outgroup member; $M = 3.88$, $SD = 1.09$), $t(155) = 4.86$, $p < .001$, Cohen's $d = .78$.

Table 3. Need for Closure, Group Status, and Intergroup Differentiation (Study 2)

Predictor	Intergroup differentiation: Evaluative ratings			
	Model 1		Model 2	
	b	SE	b	SE
0	.04	(.12)	.04	(.12)
Group status	.25***	(.08)	.23**	(.08)
NFC × Group status	–	–	.33**	(.12)
(Constant)	.09	(.08)	.11	(.08)
F (degrees of freedom)	5.34 (2, 153)**		6.16 (3, 152)***	
Adjusted R^2	.053		.091	
N	156		156	

Note. Entries are unstandardized OLS regression coefficients. Results for intergroup differentiation on trait ratings are not shown; for both of the models using this dependent measure, $F < 1$.
**$p < .01$; ***$p < .001$.

Need for Closure, Group Status, and Intergroup Differentiation

The main analyses in this study were similar to those conducted in Study 1, with one major change: the continuous status difference measure from Study 1 was replaced with the dichotomous group-status variable. In a series of regression models, each dependent measure was regressed on the need for closure and group-status variable in a first step, while the product term for the interaction between these two independent variables was added on a second step. The need for closure was centered and the group status variable was effects-coded (–1 = low, 1 = high); the product term was constructed from these recoded variables.

The first two analyses looked at the effects of the need for closure and group status on the two differentiation measures. For intergroup differentiation in evaluative ratings, the results are shown in Table 3. Model 1, which contained only the main-effect terms, revealed only a significant effect of group status, such that individuals who received high status feedback showed a more extreme tendency to differentiate in favor of the ingroup ($b = .25$, $p < .001$; partial $\eta^2 = .07$); this confirms the results of the t-tests presented above. In turn, Model 2 revealed the predicted Need for Closure × Group Status interaction ($b = .33$, $p < .01$; partial $\eta^2 = .05$). To probe this interaction, simple slopes for the relationship between the need for closure and differentiation in evaluative ratings were computed for each of the two experimental groups (Aiken & West, 1991). The analyses indicated that the relationship between need for closure and differentiation in favor of the ingroup in evaluative ratings was positive and significant among individuals assigned to the high-status condition ($b = .37$, $SE = .17$, $p < .05$; partial $\eta^2 = .03$), but

Table 4. Need for Closure, Group Status, and Preference for Working With Ingroup Versus Outgroup Members (Study 2)

	Task preference			
	Model 1		Model 2	
Predictor	b	SE	b	SE
Need for closure (NFC)	.13	(.15)	.14	(.14)
Group status	.46***	(.09)	.43***	(.09)
NFC × Group status	–	–	.59***	(.14)
(Constant)	4.33***	(.09)	4.36***	(.09)
F (degrees of freedom)	12.16 (2, 154)***		14.56 (3, 153)***	
Adjusted R^2	.125		.207	
N	157		157	

Note. Entries are unstandardized OLS regression coefficients.
***$p < .001$.

negative among those assigned to the low-status condition ($b = -.29$, $SE = .17$, $p < .10$; partial $\eta^2 = .02$). In contrast, the analyses for ingroup bias in trait ratings indicated no significant effects. None of the coefficients in either model reached significance (all $ps > .20$; both $Fs < 1$); these estimates are not presented.

Finally, we examined one additional dependent variable: the extremity of participants' preference for working with an ingroup member on a hypothetical task. The results of the analyses using this variable are summarized in Table 4. As before, Model 1 revealed only a significant effect of group status, with individuals in the high-status condition showing a more extreme preference for working with an ingroup versus and outgroup member ($b = .46$, $p < .001$; partial $\eta^2 = .14$); this confirms the *t*-test results above. In turn, Model 2 revealed a significant Need for Closure × Group Status interaction ($b = .59$, $p < .001$; partial $\eta^2 = .10$). Simple slope analyses indicated that the relationship between the need for closure and preference for working with an ingroup member was positive and highly significant among individuals assigned to the high-status condition ($b = .73$, $SE = .20$, $p < .001$; partial $\eta^2 = .08$), but negative among those assigned to the low status condition ($b = -.45$, $SE = .20$, $p < .05$; partial $\eta^2 = .03$).

Robustness Checks

All models were again checked for dependent variable outliers by computing externally studentized residuals. The residuals for the full trait-differentiation and task-preference models revealed no large outliers (none had absolute values > 5). However, examination of the studentized residuals for the full evaluative-differentiation model revealed one case with a large negative residual ($d_i = -5.38$) that also split off from the others in a scatterplot. This case was deleted in the analyses presented in Table 3. Further analyses that retained the outlier produced similar results, albeit with a slightly weaker Need for Closure × Group Status interaction in the full model ($b = .23$, $SE = .13$, $p = .08$; partial $\eta^2 = .02$) and a smaller R^2 due to added error (i.e., adjusted $R^2 = .077$). Again, supplementary analyses that excluded outliers selected using a more liberal cutoff (residuals with absolute values > 3) produced results identical to those reported in above.

Discussion

In Study 2, our analyses indicated that uncertainty-averse participants—those with a high need for closure—(1) differentiated more sharply between ingroup and outgroup in evaluative ratings and (2) showed a more extreme preference for working with members of the ingroup when they were randomly assigned to receive feedback indicating that their ingroup of "deductive thinkers" had higher (vs. lower) status than an outgroup of "inductive thinkers." These findings provide additional evidence for the general hypothesis that perceptions of high relative ingroup status should strengthen the tendency for individuals with a distaste for uncertainty to differentiate between ingroup and outgroup more extremely.

General Discussion

A growing body of work suggests that individuals who experience uncertainty more aversively—such as those high in the need for closure—differentiate between ingroup and outgroup more severely, potentially making them more prone to extremism in sociopolitical domains (Kruglanski et al., 2002; see also Doosje, Loseman, & van den Bos, 2013; Hogg & Adelman, 2013). Moreover, this tendency is stronger when the ingroup possesses characteristics that make it a better provider of certainty, such as internal homogeneity and norms that strongly support intergroup hostility. Here, in an effort to further explore the roots of the tendency to accentuate the difference between "us" and "them" that is central to extreme attitudes and behaviors, we explore the role of another factor that should increase a group's ability to provide its members with certainty: *perceived group status*. Specifically, we report the results of two studies aimed at examining the hypothesis that individuals with a high need for closure should differentiation more extremely between ingroup and outgroup—in favor of the ingroup—when they perceive the ingroup to be higher in status relative to outgroups.

In our first study, we found correlational evidence that uncertainty-averse Whites accentuate evaluative differences between the ingroup and Blacks and Latinos when they perceived the ingroup to have greater relative status. To more explicitly examine the causal role of status, we experimentally manipulated perceived group status in a second study. This experiment revealed that participants high in the need for closure were also more polarized in their evaluations of the ingroup and outgroup—with a bias in favor of the ingroup—when they were assigned to the high-status group. In addition, individuals with a high need for closure who were assigned to the high ingroup status condition showed a more extreme preference for working with fellow ingroup members in an employment setting.

Thus, these two studies provide persuasive evidence that people who experience the aversion to uncertainty characteristic of a high need for closure polarize more sharply in their views of the ingroup and outgroup when they believe the ingroup to have relatively high status. In doing so, they add to a growing body of evidence for the argument that variables related to the management of uncertainty may play an important role in extremitizing intergroup attitudes and behaviors (Doosje, Loseman, & van den Bos, 2013; Esses, Medianu, & Lawson, 2013; Hogg & Adelman, 2013; Kruglanski et al., 2006). Qualifying this, however, our results also suggest that the tendency to differentiate between ingroup and outgroup in binary, Manichean fashion is not merely a function of individual differences, but an interactive function of individual differences and social structure. Hence, policies that target inequities in the social structure—or at least those that help provide equal-status in the context of intergroup contact (Allport, 1954)—might provide a way to mitigate the tendency for those high in the need for closure to differentiate more extremely between ingroup and outgroup.

Despite these contributions, we have not yet examined this issue in all possible ways. For example, our studies rely solely on explicit measures of intergroup differentiation. Nevertheless, studies using measures of the degree to which people implicitly associate groups with positive or negative attributes have also found a positive relationship between ingroup status and implicit bias (Jost et al., 2004; Rudman, Feinberg, & Fairchild, 2002). Thus, given that "group-centrism" appears to be the high-status default with respect to implicit biases as well, we would also expect individuals with a high need for closure to differentiate more extremely between ingroup and outgroup when they perceive the ingroup to have higher status. Future research should consider these implicit measures as alternative outcome variables, as well as subtle behavioral measures associated with implicit attitudes. Such subtle changes in behavior, such as physical distance or lack of eye contact, can create discomfort and make it less likely that people with different group identities will interact smoothly (Fazio & Olson, 2003). To illuminate how these tendencies play out in the real world, future research should also examine people's explicit behavior in group settings with status differences, particularly in scenarios where valued resources must actually be allocated between groups and with respect to the actual extremist preferences that should follow from extreme intergroup differentiation.

On another front, findings suggesting that the need for closure promotes conformity with dominant cultural norms (e.g., Chiu et al., 2000; Fu et al., 2007) are also relevant to further exploration the hypotheses tested in the present study. In this vein, social norms should generally favor high-status groups—and the hierarchical status quo—in societies with long-standing systems of social inequality (Jost et al., 2004). Norms of this sort should reinforce the status-based "reality constraints" governing the extent to which group members can achieve certainty by favoring the ingroup. Indeed, support for these norms should be most pronounced among members of high-status, who are most likely to benefit from the hierarchical status quo (Sidanius & Pratto, 1999); this would contribute to the asymmetrical relationship between need for closure and group-centrism that we observe here. Nevertheless, to the extent that dominant cultural norms associated with social hierarchy play a role in this process, future research will need to zero in more carefully on the moderating role of individual differences in support for dominant norms favoring inequality. For instance, we may find that status-based asymmetries in the relationship between need for closure and group-centrism are more pronounced among individuals who endorse group-based hierarchy, but less pronounced among those with a more egalitarian outlook on intergroup relations.

This is not to say that our findings have no important implications for real-world intergroup relations and for policies to promote quality intergroup interaction. We found that people high in need for closure were more likely to evaluatively differentiate between racial ingroups and outgroups; we interpreted this effect as a result of an interaction between the uncertainty aversion typical of those high in need for closure and perceptions of larger social status differences. However, it is plausible that people may also use group evaluations and trait attributions to further justify existing status inequality. In other words, there may be a cyclical effect such that beliefs about group stereotypes and perceived status differences perpetuate and reinforce each other, especially for those high in need for closure who rely on such cues to determine their attitudes. Similarly, the dependent measures employed in Study 2 also suggest the potential for further polarization in views of the ingroup and outgroup and the perpetuation of social inequality. In this experiment, we found differences in participants' preferences for future interactions with ingroup versus outgroup members. Assuming this preference for working with ingroup members translates to behavior, such an attitude would likely decrease intergroup contact. Members of high-status groups may thus self-segregate and deny themselves the opportunity to learn counter-stereotypical information about the outgroup—maintaining and even strengthening the extremity-feeding tendency to split the world into a "good" and a "bad" them. As noted above, to counter this, it may be necessary to institute policies that mitigate status differences between groups or at least the relevance of those differences in contact situations. Such implications demonstrate the importance of continuing research on the dynamics of epistemic motivation and group status. By examining the effects of the uncertainty aversion associated with a high need for closure and perceived status differences on *both* attitudes *and* behavior, we should be better able to understand the implications for real-world intergroup hostilities in which extremism often manifests itself.

References

Aiken, L. S., & West, S. G. (1991). *Multiple regression: Testing and interpreting interactions*. Newbury Park, CA: Sage.
Allport, G. (1954). *The nature of prejudice*. Menlo Park, CA: Addison-Wesley.
Chiu, C., Morris, M. W., Hong, Y., & Menon, T. (2000). Motivated cultural cognition: The impact of implicit cultural theories on dispositional attribution varies as a function of need for closure. *Journal of Personality and Social Psychology, 78*, 247–259. doi: 10.1037/0022-3514.92.2.191
Cohen, J., Cohen, P., West, S. G., & Aiken, L. S. (2003). *Applied multiple regression/correlation analysis for the behavioral sciences*. Mahwah, NJ: Lawrence Erlbaum Associates.
de Dreu, C., Koole, S. L., & Oldersma, F. L. (1999). On the seizing and freezing of negotiator inferences: Need for cognitive closure moderates the use of heuristics in negotiation. *Personality and Social Psychology Bulletin, 25*, 348–362. doi: 10.1177/0146167299025003007
de Grada, E., Kruglanski, A. W., Mannetti, L., & Pierro, A. (1999). Motivated cognition and group interaction: Need for closure affects the contents and processes of collective negotiations. *Journal of Experimental Social Psychology, 35*, 346–365. doi: 10.1006/jesp.1999.1376
Doosje, B., Loseman, A., & van den Bos, K. (2013). Determinants of radicalization of Islamic youth in the Netherlands: Personal uncertainty, perceived injustice, and perceived group threat. *Journal of Social Issues, 69*, 586–604.
Esses, V. M., Medianu, S., & Lawson, A. S. (2013). Uncertainty, threat, and the dehumanization of immigrants and refugees. *Journal of Social Issues, 69*, 518–536.
Fazio, R. H., & Olson, M. A. (2003). Implicit measures in social cognition research: Their meaning and use. *Annual Review of Psychology, 54*, 297–327. doi: 10.1146/annurev.psych.54.101601.145225
Federico, C., Golec, A., & Dial, J. (2005). The relationship between need for closure and support for military action against Iraq: Moderating effects of national attachment. *Personality and Social Psychology Bulletin, 31*, 621–632. doi: 10.1177/0146167204271588
Fu, H.-Y., Morris, M. W., Lee, S.-L., Chao, M., Chiu, C.-Y., & Hong, Y.-Y. (2007). Epistemic motives and cultural conformity: Need for closure, culture, and context as determinants of conflict judgments. *Journal of Personality and Social Psychology, 92*, 191–207. doi: 10.1037/0022-3514.92.2.191
Golec, A., & Federico, C. M. (2004). Understanding responses to political conflict: Interactive effects of the need for closure and salient conflict schemas. *Journal of Personality and Social Psychology, 87*, 750–762. doi: 10.1037/0022-3514.87.6.750
Golec de Zavala, A. (2006). Cognitive and motivational factors underlying individual responses to political conflicts. In A. Golec de Zavala & K. Skarzynska (Eds.), *Understanding social change: Political psychology in Poland* (pp. 13–32). Hauppauge, New York: Nova Publisher.
Golec de Zavala, A., Federico, C. M., Cislak, A., & Sigger, J. (2008). Need for closure and competition in intergroup conflicts: Experimental evidence for the mitigating effect of accessible conflict-schemas. *European Journal of Social Psychology, 38*, 84–105. doi: 10.1002/ejsp.438
Hogg, M. A. (2003). Intergroup relations. In J. Delamater (Ed.), *Handbook of social psychology* (pp. 479–501). New York: Kluwer Academic/Plenum.
Hogg, M. A., & Blaylock, D. L. (2012). Preface: From uncertainty to extremism. In M. A. Hogg & D. L. Blaylock (Eds.), *Extremism and the psychology of uncertainty* (pp. xv–xxv). West Sussex, UK: Wiley-Blackwell.

Hogg, M. A. (2012). Preface: From uncertainty to extremism. In M. A. Hogg & D. L. Blaylock (Eds.), *Extremism and the psychology of uncertainty* (pp. xv–xxv). West Sussex, UK: Wiley-Blackwell.

Hogg, M. A., & Adelman, J. (2013). Self-uncertainty, social identity and support for political and religious violence. *Journal of Social Issues, 69*, 436–454.

Jost, J. T., Banaji, M. R., & Nosek, B. A. (2004). A decade of system justification theory: Accumulated evidence of conscious and unconscious bolstering of the status quo. *Political Psychology, 25*, 881–919. doi: 10.1111/j.1467-9221.2004.00402.x

Jost, J. T., Glaser, J., Kruglanski, A. W., & Sulloway, F. (2003). Political conservatism as motivated social cognition. *Psychological Bulletin, 129*, 339–375. doi: 10.1037/0033-2909.129.3.339

Jost, J. T., Pelham, B. W., & Carvallo, M. (2002). Non-conscious forms of system justification: Cognitive, affective, and behavioral preferences for higher status groups. *Journal of Experimental Social Psychology, 38*, 586–602. doi: 10.1016/S0022-1031(02)00505-X

Kosic, A., Kruglanski, A. W., Pierro, A., & Mannetti, L. (2004). Social cognition of immigrants' acculturation: Effects of the need for closure and the reference group at entry. *Journal of Personality and Social Psychology, 86*, 1–18. doi: 10.1037/0022-3514.86.6.796

Kruglanski, A. W. (2004). *The psychology of closed-mindedness*. New York: Psychology Press.

Kruglanski, A. W., & Mayseless, O. (1987). Motivational effects in the social comparison of opinions. *Journal of Personality and Social Psychology, 53*, 834–842.

Kruglanski, A.W., Pierro, A., Mannetti, L., & DeGrada, E. (2006). Groups as epistemic providers: Need for closure and the unfolding of group centrism. *Psychological Review, 113*, 84–100. doi: 10.1037/0033-295X.113.1.84

Kruglanski, A. W., Shah, J. Y., Pierro, A., & Mannetti, L. (2002). When similarity breeds content: Need for closure and the allure of homogeneous and self-resembling groups. *Journal of Personality and Social Psychology, 83*, 648–662. doi: 10.1037/0022-3514.83.3.648

Kruglanski, A. W., & Webster, D. M. (1991). Group members' reactions to opinion deviates and conformists at varying degrees of proximity to decision deadline and of environmental noise. *Journal of Personality and Social Psychology, 61*, 212–225.

Kruglanski, A. W., & Webster, D. M. (1996). Motivated closing of the mind: "Seizing" and "freezing." *Psychological Review, 103*, 263–283.

Mullen, B., Brown, R., & Smith, C. (1992). Ingroup bias as a function of salience, relevance, and status: An integration. *European Journal of Social Psychology, 22*, 103–122. doi: 10.1002/ejsp.2420220202

Rudman, L. A., Feinberg, J., & Fairchild, K. (2002). Minority members' implicit attitudes: Automatic ingroup bias as a function of group status. *Social Cognition, 20*, 294–320. doi: 10.1521/soco.20.4.294.19908

Sachdev, I., & Bourhis, R. Y. (1991). Power and status differentials in minority and majority group relations. *European Journal of Social Psychology, 21*, 1–24. doi: 10.1002/ejsp.2420210102

Shah, J. Y., Kruglanski, A. W., & Thompson, E. P. (1998). Membership has its (epistemic) rewards: Need for closure effects on ingroup bias. *Journal of Personality and Social Psychology, 75*, 383–393.

Sidanius, J., & Pratto, F. (1999). *Social dominance: An intergroup theory of social hierarchy and oppression*. New York: Cambridge University Press.

Sidanius, J., Pratto, F., van Laar, C., & Levin, S. (2004). Social dominance theory: Its agenda and method. *Political Psychology, 25*, 845–880. doi: 10.1111/j.1467-9221.2004.00401.x

Spears, R., Jetten, J., & Doosje, B. (2001). The (il)legitimacy of ingroup bias: From social reality to social resistance. In J. T. Jost & B. Major (Eds.), *The psychology of legitimacy: Emerging perspectives on ideology, justice, and intergroup relations* (pp. 332–362). New York: Cambridge University Press.

Tajfel, H., & Turner, J. C. (1986). The social identity theory of intergroup behavior. In S. Worchel & W. G. Austin (Eds.), *The psychology of intergroup relations* (pp. 7–24). Chicago, IL: Nelson-Hall.

Turner, J. C. (1978). Social comparison, similarity, and ingroup favoritism. In H. Tajfel (Ed.), *Differentiation between social groups: Studies in the social psychology of intergroup relations* (pp. 235–250). San Diego, CA: Academic Press.

Turner, J. C., & Brown, R. J. (1978). Social status, cognitive alternatives and intergroup relations. In H. Tajfel (Ed.), *Differentiation between social groups: Studies in the social psychology of intergroup relations* (pp. 201–234). London: Academic Press.

van Knippenberg, A., & van Oers, M. (1984). Social identity and equity concerns in intergroup perceptions. *British Journal of Social Psychology*, *23*, 351–361. doi: 10.1111/j.2044-8309.1984.tb00651.x

Van Oudenhoven, J. P., Prins, K. S., & Buunk, B. P. (1998). Attitudes of minority and majority members towards adaptation of immigrants. *European Journal of Social Psychology*, *28*, 995–1013. doi: 10.1002/(SICI)1099-0992(1998110)28.:6<995::AID-EJSP908>3.0.CO;2-8

Webster, D. M., & Kruglanski, A. W. (1994). Individual differences in need for cognitive closure. *Journal of Personality and Social Psychology*, *67*, 1049–1062. doi: 10.1037/0022-3514.67.6.1049

Yzerbyt, V., & Demoulin, S. (2010). Intergroup relations. In S.T. Fiske, D. Gilbert, & G. Lindzey (Eds.), *Handbook of social psychology* (5th ed., Vol. 2, pp. 1024–1083). Hoboken, NJ: Wiley.

CHRISTOPHER M. FEDERICO is Associate Professor of Psychology and Political Science at the University of Minnesota, Twin Cities. He received his PhD in social psychology from the University of California, Los Angeles, in 2001. His research focuses on intergroup attitudes and the psychological bases of ideology and belief-system structure.

CORRIE V. HUNT is Senior Analyst at Hart Research Associates in Washington, DC. She received her PhD in social psychology from the University of Minnesota, Twin Cities, in 2011. Her research interests center on the interface between affect and political judgment.

EMILY L. FISHER is Assistant Professor of Psychology at Hobart and William Smith Colleges. She received her PhD in social psychology from the University of Minnesota, Twin Cities, in 2011. Her research focuses on intergroup relations, with a particular focus on the role of social capital in structuring intergroup attitudes.

Culture and Extremism

Michele J. Gelfand* and Gary LaFree
University of Maryland

Susan Fahey
Richard Stockton College of New Jersey

Emily Feinberg
Credit Suissea

Much research in the last several decades has examined the social, political, and economic factors that predict terrorism, yet to date, there has been little attention to cultural factors and their relationship to terrorism. We present findings from the Global Terrorism Database showing how numerous cultural dimensions identified in the cultural psychology literature relate to over 80,000 terrorist attacks that occurred between 1970 and 2007. Controlling for economic and religious variables, our results suggest that fatalistic beliefs, rigid gender roles, and greater tightness are related to a greater number of terrorist attacks or fatalities. While fatalism and low gender egalitarianism were related to the overall number of terrorist incidents and fatalities, cultural tightness was related the overall lethality of events, i.e., fatalities per incident. We discuss theoretical and practical implications of our findings.

Understanding, predicting, and thwarting extreme behavior, particularly as it relates to violence, is one of the most challenging issues facing humankind. On a daily basis, we witness terrorist attacks across the globe, which have devastating human and material costs. In recent years, the analysis of country-level terrorism data has increased dramatically along with the increasing availability of worldwide terrorism event data (LaFree, 2012). While recent research has linked terrorism

---

*Correspondence concerning this article should be addressed to Michele J. Gelfand, Department of Psychology, 3147c Biology/Psychology Building, University of Maryland, College Park, MD 20742 [e-mail: mjgelfand@gmail.com].

This work was supported by a Multidisciplinary University Research Initiative Grant (W911NF-08-1-0144) from the U.S. Army Research Institute, Department of Defense given to M. Gelfand.

to the macro economic and political context of countries (Dugan, LaFree, & Piquero 2005; Enders & Sandler, 2006; Fahey, LaFree, Dugan, & Piquero, in press; Greenbaum, Dugan, & LaFree, 2007; LaFree, Dugan, & Fahey, 2007; LaFree, Dugan, & Korte, 2009; Piazza, 2008; Tikusis 2009), we know of no research to date that has examined the impact of country-level cultural differences on the prevalence and severity of terrorist attacks.

The purpose of this study is to begin filling this void by examining how cultural values and norms which have been well studied in the cross-cultural psychology literature link to terrorist activity across the globe. Our analysis fits squarely into the theme of this special issue in that we are examining the impact of a set of cultural variables that function in part to reduce individual uncertainty on the occurrence of terrorism, a particularly brutal form of extremism. While we cannot make causal claims due to the correlational nature of the research, we are able to establish that cultural variables are indeed related to the risk of terrorism in predictable ways. In the next section we define terrorism and discuss relevant theories that help to explain its occurrence. We then discuss cross-cultural research on values and norms, and set forth a number of hypotheses that link research on culture to research on terrorism. We then present results from the Global Terrorism Database (GTD), maintained by the START Consortium at the University of Maryland. Our analysis links over 80,000 terrorist attacks from the GTD that occurred between 1970 and 2007 to country-level measures of culture. We conclude with theoretical and practical implications of the results for the study of violent extremism.

Terrorism as Extremism

Terrorism has been defined as "acts by nonstate actors involving the threatened or actual use of illegal force or violence to attain a political, economic, religious, or social goal through fear, coercion, or intimidation" (LaFree & Dugan, 2007, p. 183). Terrorism is radical or extreme in that it departs from the prohibition of unprovoked violence, central to most cultures and religions across history, especially of violence against unarmed civilians, uninvolved in hostile acts of any kind.

Not surprisingly, theory and research over the last several decades has focused on identifying predictors of such extreme behavior. In the early history of terrorism research in the 1960s, the radical acts of terrorists were theorized to have its basis in their extreme or psychopathic personalities. Psychiatrists and others hypothesized that terrorists suffer from unique psychopathologies and/or that they have a unique personality profile that predisposes them to violence. Extant research, however, has illustrated that such notions are not supported and that terrorists are no more likely to have psychopathic tendencies than other individuals (Horgan, 2008; Kruglanski & Fishman, 2009; Silke, 1998). Put simply, researchers agree that most terrorists fall well within the normal range of socio-emotional functioning.

More recent research has also confirmed connections between terrorism and macro political factors, including legitimacy, democratization, and failed or fragile states (for a review, see LaFree & Ackerman, 2009). For example, Ross and Gurr (1989) identified the electoral success of the Parti Quebecois, a legitimate, nonviolent political party, as one of the leading reasons that the Front de Liberation du Quebec experienced a decline in political strength. In a quantitative analysis of worldwide terrorism attacks, LaFree and Dugan (2007) found that, controlling for a wide variety of rival explanations, a common democracy measure had a strong-curvilinear relationship to terrorist attacks and fatalities. Piazza's (2007) multivariate analysis also showed that state instability is the most consistent predictor of country-level terrorist attacks. And LaFree et al. (2007) found strong support for the conclusion that by the 1990s worldwide terrorist attacks were concentrated in failed or weak states. Government policies and counter measures have also been shown to affect terrorist activity, sometimes reducing it through deterrence or target hardening, but at other times increasing it through backlash effects (for a review, see Lum, Kennedy, & Sherley, 2006).

In addition to macro-level social and political variables, research has increasingly illustrated that group processes are important to the prediction of terrorism. For example, research on social networks has highlighted the importance of network ties of kinship and friendship in the recruitment and sustainment of terrorist groups (Asal & Rethemeyer, 2008; Sageman, 2004, 2008). Beyond structural properties of groups is the idea that the group's culture—its norms, values, and beliefs—will play a critical role in terrorist activity. Atran and colleagues' (Atran, Axelrod, & Davis, 2007; Ginges & Atran, 2009) work was some of the first to highlight the importance of the group's culture, namely its sacred values, as an important lever for motivating terrorist acts. Likewise, work by Kruglanski, Chen, Dechesne, Fishman, and Orehek (2009) suggested that the terrorist group's ideology, or its "shared reality," can play a critical role in justifying violence against out-groups as laudable, heroic, and one that lends group members "significance." Although research suggests that values and norms of groups might increase the risk of terrorist activity, we know of no research to date that has examined the impact of values and norms of the *macro cultural context* within which terrorist groups operate as a predictor of the prevalence and severity of terrorist attacks. Put differently, we asked the question: are there national cultural differences in the degree to which terrorism thrives or is thwarted?

Culture

The definition of culture has long been a source of debate among anthropologists and cross-cultural psychologists (see Jahoda, 1984; Rohner 1984; Segall, 1984); a classic 1952 publication identified over 160 definitions of culture (Kroeber & Kluckhohn, 1952). Although there is variation in the definitions of culture, many point to the shared nature of culture, its ability to impart adaptive (or once adaptive) knowledge, and its transmission across time and generation (Triandis, Kurowski, & Gelfand, 1994).

While there are many dimensions on which cultures vary, we discuss a number of cultural dimensions that have potential implications for terrorism. First, *cultural fatalism* has relevance for the risk that individuals may ascribe to extreme actions in general and terrorism in particular. Second, the extent to which cultures are *tight*, or have strong norms and severe punishment for deviation of social norms, has implications for the necessity of extreme means to accomplish one's goals (e.g., address one's grievances) and the potential for extreme behavior in the context of violence. Third, *collectivism* at the national level has implications for increased group-centrism, and in contexts where there are group grievances, higher rates of self-sacrifice for the goals of the group. Fourth, high male dominance and *low gender egalitarianism* has implications for norms for aggressive behavior that creates a context conducive to terrorism. Finally, the extent to which cultures have *high power distance*, or a large differentiation between those in high versus low power positions (Hofstede, 1980; House, Hanges, Javidan, Dorfman, & Gupta, 2004), may also provide a fertile ground for terrorism in contexts where low status groups need to challenge their unequal status through extreme means.

Interestingly, one characteristic that all of these cultural dimensions have in common is that they are all related to lower complexity in thinking—a "closing of the mind"—which has been associated with extremism (see Hogg, Kruglanski, & van den Bos, 2013). Thus, by subscribing to fatalism, individuals put all of their faith in a higher authority and are absolved from taking personal responsibility for their actions; tightness is related to low tolerance for deviance and justification for strong punishments; collectivism produces a shared reality that dictates that individuals should subordinate their individual goals for group goals; strong gender roles provide specific expectations for acceptable behavior and not others; and finally, high power distance requires submitting to authorities and not challenging the status quo. We discuss predictions for each dimension in turn.

Hypotheses

Fatalism

Bernstein (1992) defined fatalism as a belief that one's destiny and life events are predetermined and that whatever happened was meant to have happened. Although people in cultures characterized by high levels of fatalism may point to a variety of external sources that exert ultimate control over their lives (i.e., god, fate, or chance), they are united by a common recognition of the role of these external factors in their lives (Caplan & Schooler, 2007). In contrast, people in less fatalistic cultures, including the United States, are more likely to endorse the belief that they maintain personal control over their outcomes and lives (see Kay & Eibach, 2013). Fatalism has been linked to harsh economic environments and extreme government regulation, which decrease individuals' perception of personal control (Moaddel & Karabenick, 2008). At the country level, fatalistic beliefs have been shown to be negatively correlated with gross domestic product (GDP) per capita, life expectancy at birth, voter turnout, environmental sustainability, and human development, and positively correlated with heart disease and suicide rates (Leung & Bond, 2004).

We hypothesized that nations that are high on fatalism have the potential for higher levels of terrorism. Most importantly, fatalism, the perceptions that one's destiny and life outcomes are predetermined, can decrease a sense of personal responsibility and increase risk-taking in a number of life domains, including those involving health and safety. Put simply, fatalism may enable risky behaviors known to have potentially adverse consequences because they can be "justified" as preordained. Compared to individuals low on fatalism, for example, those high on fatalism are less likely to engage in health and safety behaviors (Colón, 1992; Hardeman, Pierro, & Mannetti, 1997; McClure, Allen, & Walkey, 2001; Powe & Finnie, 2003), and have more deaths due to risky behaviors (e.g., traffic accidents) (Gelfand, Fulmer, Kruglanski, Abdel-Latif, Khashan et al., 2010). Extending this literature, we predicted that fatalism would lead to a reduction in individuals' perceptions of personal control, a decreased sense of personal responsibility (Aycan, Kanungo, Mendonca, Yu, Deller et al., 2000), and the use of external sources (e.g., god) as a justification for one's actions. That is, in contexts where grievances are not being addressed, extreme acts such as terrorism would occur more frequently in nations high on fatalism as compared to cultures low on fatalism.

Tightness-Looseness

Tightness-looseness reflects the degree to which societies have clear and pervasive social norms and are intolerant of deviations from norms (Gelfand, Nishii, & Raver, 2006; Pelto, 1968; Triandis, 1989). Tight societies, like those of Japan, Singapore, and Pakistan provide strong norms and monitoring systems to detect deviations, which are severely punished. As such, these societies value order, formality, discipline, and conformity (Gelfand et al., 2006, 2011; Pelto, 1968). In contrast, norms in loose societies like those of Brazil, Israel, or the United States are more ambiguous, deviations from norms are tolerated, and punishments for deviations are less severe. Gelfand et al. (2011) found that tightness is related to such factors as high population density, low percentage of arable land and food supply, high degrees of environmental threats (e.g., natural disasters, disease), high police per capita and strength of criminal justice systems (e.g., the death penalty), high degrees of autocracy, and low openness of the media.

We hypothesized that tight nations will have more vulnerability for terrorism than loose nations for a number of reasons. First, tightness is associated with higher ethnocentrism and punishment of individuals who are "different." For example, Gelfand et al. (2011) found that individuals in tight nations find socially deviant behavior much less justifiable (e.g., homosexuality, divorce, prostitution), believe that their way of life needs to be protected against foreign influence, prefer not to have immigrants as neighbors, and are more likely to believe that their culture is superior to others. This suggests that "fringe" groups will perceive more discrimination and have greater humiliation and significance loss (Kruglanski et al., 2009) in tight than in loose nations where individuals have more tolerance of differences. Second, the high degree of monitoring and constraint that characterizes tight societies would suggest that the *means* through which individuals or groups can rectify their grievances are highly circumscribed and limited, rendering more 'radical" means necessary to achieve one's goals. Indeed, Gelfand et al. (2011) found that the percentage of people participating in legitimate collective actions (e.g., signing petitions, attending demonstrations) is low in tight nations and more people report that they would never engage in such actions in comparison to loose nations. Moreover, they found that when asked how societal change generally occurs, people in tight nations were much more likely to believe that it occurs *radically*, whereas people in loose nations were more likely to believe it occurs *incrementally*. Accordingly, we predicted that tightness would be associated with greater terrorism than looseness.

Individualism-Collectivism

Extensive research has shown that individualism-collectivism is a major dimension of cultural variation. Research has shown that in collectivistic cultures, the self is construed as interdependent with others (Markus & Kitayama, 1991), people are socialized to sacrifice their own goals and maintain cooperation within the group (Triandis, 1989), and there are strong ingroup-outgroup distinctions (Triandis, McCusker, & Hui, 1990). By contrast, in individualistic cultures, the self is construed as independent of others, people are socialized to pursue their own goals over the goals of others, debate and confrontation are acceptable in ingroups, and ingroup-outgroup distinctions are much less pronounced (Markus & Kitayama, 1991; Triandis, 1989). As compared to individualistic cultures, collectivistic cultures have lower national wealth (Gelfand, Bhawuk, Nishii, & Bechtold, 2004; Hofstede, 1980), lower geographic and relational mobility (Oishi, 2010; Schug, Yuki, & Maddux, 2010), and more extended family structures (Georgas et al., 2001). Collectivism is generally found in agricultural societies wherein conformity and obedience are crucial for survival, whereas more individualism is found among hunters and in complex (e.g., information) societies (Barry, Child,

& Bacon, 1959), and in societies with an open frontier (Kitayama, Ishii, Imada, Takemura, & Ramaswamy, 2006) wherein self-reliance is crucial for survival.

We theorized that compared to more individualist nations, nations higher on collectivism will experience more terrorism. As noted, individuals in collectivistic cultures are socialized to give up their personal goals, conform to the group, and compete with outgroups (Triandis, 1995). Identification with groups also provides a way o protect against uncertainty (see Hogg & Adelman, 2013). In contexts where there is a grievance (injustice) perpetuated toward one's group (religious, national, ethnic or otherwise), a culprit portrayed as responsible for the injustice, and a means (e.g., terrorism) to address these grievances against the outgroup (Kruglanski et al., 2012), this socialization naturally makes it easier for individuals in collectivistic nations to join the fight, and commit to and sacrifice themselves for the good of the group. Indeed, previous experimental research has shown that individuals who are "fused" with their groups are more willing to sacrifice themselves for the group (Swann, Gomez, Dovidio, Hart, & Jetten, 2010). Field surveys across a number of countries in the Middle East, Indonesia, and Pakistan have also linked collectivism with support for violence when it is seen as justified (Kruglanski, Gelfand, & Gunaratna, in press). Accordingly, we predicted that compared to individualism, collectivism will be associated with higher levels of terrorism.

Gender Egalitarianism

Nations around the globe vary widely on gender egalitarianism, or "the degree to which a collective minimizes gender inequality" (House et al., 2004, p. 359). This dimension fundamentally concerns the way societies construct gender roles for men and women with at least two important implications (Hofstede, 1980; House et al., 2004). First, societies with high gender egalitarianism minimize gender differences and proscribe and prescribe similar roles for men and women; they have more women in positions of authority, less occupational sex segregation, similar levels of educational attainment for men and women, and allow women decision-making roles in everyday affairs (House et al., 2004). By contrast, societies with low gender egalitarianism proscribe very different roles for men and women; they have fewer women in positions of power, more occupational sex segregation, much lower educational attainment for women, and women have much less of a role in decision-making role in everyday affairs (House et al., 2004). Another important distinction therein relates to the extent to which societies emphasize *masculine* values, including toughness, assertiveness, success, and competition, versus *feminine* values of nurturance, tenderness, and cooperation, and solidarity (Hofstede, 1980). In cultures that are low on gender egalitarianism, men are expected to be tough and assertive, whereas in cultures high on gender egalitarianism, men and women are expected to be cooperative and nurturing (Hofstede, 1980; House et al., 2004). Gender egalitarianism practices at the national level have been found to be related to longevity and greater human development (House et al., 2004).

We theorized that nations that are low on gender egalitarianism will have a greater risk for terrorism than those that are high on gender egalitarianism. Research from the criminology literature lends some support for this prediction. In explaining different rates of crime in the United States, Miller (1958) argued that the cultures that emphasize a set of "focal concerns" that value behavior that encourages crime, including an emphasis on *toughness* (e.g., masculinity, strength); *smartness* (skill at outsmarting the other guy); and *autonomy* (resentment of authority and rules) would have more crime. Similarly, in their subculture of violence theory, Wolfgang and Ferracuti (1967) argued that elevated crime rates occur in communities wherein males' "quick resort to physical combat as a measure of daring, courage or defense of status appears to be a cultural expression" and when individuals who share this culture come into contact with others who share such norms, "physical assaults, altercations, and violent domestic quarrels that result in homicide are likely to be common (pp. 188–189)." Masculine values of toughness have also been used as an explanation for why the U.S. south has higher rates of violent crime than the North (Gastil, 1971; Hackney, 1969; Nisbett & Cohen, 1996).

More recently, Anderson's (1999) ethnographic research on violence in disadvantaged neighborhoods and the oppositional subculture known as "the code of the street" has provided an influential account of how cultural values may relate directly to differential crime rates. According to Anderson, the code of the street is an informal system that governs the use of violence. The code of the street emphasizes that one must maintain the respect of others through a violent and tough identity, and a willingness to exact retribution in the event of disrespect, or risk being "rolled on" or physically assaulted (p. 73). As Anderson noted, "an important part of the code is not to allow others to chump you, to let them know that you are 'about serious business' and not to be trifled with" (p. 130).

Cross-national studies of violent crime also support the conclusion that contexts that allow normative systems that condone aggression and violence as a response to conflict have higher crime rates (Fiala & LaFree, 1988; Gelles, 1987; Straus, 1980). For example, in an examination of homicide rates in 18 industrialized nations from 1950 to 1980, Gartner (1990) measured officially approved violence by examining the existence of the death penalty, the number of international and civil wars in which the nation participated, and total battle deaths incurred during these wars. Controlling for a variety of other variables, she found that countries with higher levels of approved violence had higher rates of homicide. While these applications have generally been aimed at explaining crime, they should also be relevant for terrorist attacks, a type of crime that frequently results in homicide (Clarke & Newman, 2006; LaFree & Dugan, 2004). Accordingly, we predicted that to the extent that societies are low on gender egalitarianism and emphasize values of assertiveness and masculinity, they will have higher terrorism rates than cultures that are high on gender egalitarianism and emphasize nurturance and femininity.

Power Distance

Power distance refers to the degree to which members of a society expect and accept inequalities (Hofstede, 1980). In high power distance cultures, such as Morocco and Nigeria, people accept large power differentials between levels of the social hierarchy. On the other hand, people in lower power distance cultures, including Denmark and the Netherlands, are less accepting of such power differentials. For example, people in high power distance cultures do not expect to have voice or to challenge authorities, whereas people in low power distance cultures expect to have voice and to challenge authorities (Hofstede, 1980; House et al., 2004). High power distance cultures often have traditions of centralized power in the hands of a monarchy or oligarchy, a small middle class, and agrarianism, while low power distance cultures are characterized by histories of representative governments, a large middle class, and more modern industry (Hofstede, 1980).

We hypothesized that terrorist activity may be higher in high versus low power distance cultures for a number of reasons. High power distance cultures have many class distinctions, have limited mobility, and resources tend to be available to only the few (i.e., high ranking individuals) as compared to low power distance cultures wherein there are fewer class distinctions, more upward mobility, and resources accessible to many (House et al., 2004). Accordingly, there may be more grievances that are found in high versus low power distance cultures. Moreover, as noted, people in high power distance cultures see subordinates and superiors as inherently separate and unequal groups, leading to greater social distance between these groups. In this respect, people in high power positions are largely unquestionable authorities who do not receive "voice" from those in lower power positions (Brockner et al., 2001; Hofstede, 1980). As such, grievances from low power parties are likely to be highly circumscribed with few available means through which they can be addressed, particularly given the highly centralized and stratified contexts that are typical in high power distance cultures. By contrast, voice and challenges to authority are much more normative in low power distance societies, providing more means to address grievances. Accordingly, we anticipated that there would be more terrorism in high versus low power distance cultures.

In sum, extant research on culture in psychology and criminology suggests some potential links between a number of cultural dimensions—fatalism, tightness, collectivism, gender egalitarianism, and power distance—and rates of terrorism. We provide the first test, to our knowledge, of the relationship between macro cultural differences and terrorism by linking established measures of culture (Aycan et al., 2000; Gelfand et al., 2011; House et al., 2004) to a number of terrorism indices, including number of incidents, number of fatalities, and the rate of fatalities per incident using the most comprehensive event database on terrorism: The GTD.

Method

The Global Terrorism Database

Because terrorism is a type of behavior that is difficult to study using police reports or victim or offender surveys, event databases have come to occupy an important role. At present, the longest running of these event databases is the GTD maintained by the START Consortium at the University of Maryland. Because the GTD is described in detail elsewhere (LaFree & Dugan, 2007, 2009), we offer only a brief explanation here. The GTD is collected by trained researchers who identify and record events from the print and electronic media. Early years of the GTD relied mostly on reports picked up by wire services (including Reuters and the Foreign Broadcast Information Service), U.S. and foreign government reports, and U.S. and foreign newspapers (including the *New York Times*, the *British Financial Times*, the *Christian Science Monitor*, the *Washington Post*, the *Washington Times*, and the *Wall Street Journal*). Over time, the GTD has been tied more directly to unclassified information available on the Internet. A major advantage of the GTD compared to other open source databases is that from its inception it has tracked domestic as well as international terrorist attacks.

Based on coding rules originally developed in the early 1970s, the analysts responsible for collecting the GTD have excluded criminal acts that have no obvious political or ideological motivation and also acts arising from open combat between opposing armed forces, both regular and irregular. Data collectors have also excluded actions taken by governments in the legitimate exercise of their authority, even when such actions are denounced by domestic or foreign critics as acts of "state terrorism." Because most terrorists seek publicity, event databases that rely on print and electronic media are likely more useful for studying terrorism than most other types of crime. Nevertheless, event data have important weaknesses, most notably media inaccuracies, conflicting information or false, multiple or no claims of responsibility, and government censorship and disinformation.

Terrorism is defined in the GTD as "the threatened or actual use of illegal force and violence by non-state actors to attain a political, economic, religious or social goal through fear, coercion or intimidation" (LaFree & Dugan, 2007, p. 184). The GTD is collected through the open-source media, including newspaper articles, news wires, foreign language aggregators, like the Foreign Broadcast Information Service, and unclassified government reports. Potential incidents are flagged for examination, and they are coded as to whether they meet the inclusion criteria.

In particular, to be included in the dataset as a terrorist incident, each incident must meet all three of these criteria: (1) "The incident must be intentional—the result of a conscious calculation on the part of a perpetrator" [this is assumed *prima facie* to be correct in cases in which it is difficult to assess the intentionality of the incident (LaFree & Dugan, 2007, p. 200, note 23)]; (2) "The incident must entail some level of violence (including violence against property) or the threat of violence"; and (3) "[T]here must be sub-national perpetrators. That is, at the time of the incident, the perpetrator group must not be exercising sovereignty (unequivocal, stable control of demarcated territory; functioning government structures)" (LaFree & Dugan, 2007, p. 188).

Thereafter, all incidents are evaluated for whether they meet the following criteria: (1) "The act must be aimed at attaining a political, economic, religious or social goal. In terms of economic goals, the exclusive pursuit of profit does not satisfy this criterion"; (2) "There must be evidence of an intention to coerce, intimidate or convey some other message to a larger audience (or audiences) than the immediate victims"; and (3) "[T]he action must be outside of the context of legitimate warfare activities; that is, the act must be outside the parameters set by international humanitarian law (particularly the admonition against deliberately targeting civilians or non-combatants)" (LaFree & Dugan, 2009, p., 188). In order to be included in the database, the incident must meet 2 out of 3 of the above criteria.

We use terrorist incidents which occurred from 1970 to 2007. We measure terrorism as *total terrorist incidents*, the *total number of fatal incidents*, and the *average number of fatalities per incident*. This allows us to capture a range of terrorism-related dependent variables. Data from 1993 were lost in an office move and we have never been able to successfully restore them. We, therefore, treat 1993 as missing.

Dimensions of Cultural Variation

We measured cultural variables using established databases. Individualism-collectivism, gender egalitarianism, and power distance were measured from House et al.'s (2004) established measures of cultural practices across 62 nations. Sample items from the *Individualism-Collectivism* practices scale included: "In this society, children take pride in the individual accomplishments of their parents" (reverse scored), "In this society, parents take pride in the individual accomplishments of their children" (reverse scored), and the measure also included items regarding whether parents live and home with their children and whether children live at home with their parents until they get married (Gelfand et al., 2004). Nations high on collectivism practices included the Philippines, Georgia,

Iran, India, and Turkey, while nations low on family collectivism practices included Denmark, Sweden, New Zealand, the Netherlands, and Switzerland.

Sample items of *gender egalitarianism* practices items included "In this society, boys are encouraged more than girls to attain a higher education" and "In this society who is more likely to serve in a position of high office" [from 1 (males) to 7 (females)]. Nations that scored the highest on gender egalitarianism practices included Hungary, Russia, Poland, Slovenia, and Denmark, while nations that scored the lowest on gender egalitarianism included South Korea, Kuwait, Egypt, Morocco, and Zambia.

Sample items from *Power Distance* practices included "In this society, followers are expected to . . . .question their leaders when in disagreement (7) or obey their leader without question (1)" (reverse scored) and "In this society power is . . . .shared throughout the society (7) or concentrated at the top (1)" (reverse scored). Nations that scored the highest on power distance practices included Morocco, Nigeria, El Salvador, Zimbabwe, and Argentina, and nations that scored lowest on power distance included Denmark, the Netherlands, Bolivia, Albania, and Israel. We also examined older scores from Hofstede (1980) values on power distance and individualism, as well as masculinity and uncertainty avoidance and did not find any relationships of these variables with terrorism. Results are available from the first author.

Tightness-looseness was measured using Gelfand et al.'s (2011) established scale across 33 nations. Sample items include: "There are many norms that people are supposed to abide by in this country," "In this country there are very clear expectations for how people should act in most situations," "In this country, if someone acts in an inappropriate way, others will strongly disapprove," and "People in this country almost always comply with social norms." Gelfand et al. (2011) found that there was wide cultural variation across the globe on tightness-looseness, with Pakistan, India, Japan, Korea, and Singapore scoring very high on tightness and the Ukraine, Israel, the Netherlands, and New Zealand scoring very low on tightness.

Fatalism was measured with Aycan et al.'s (2000) fatalism measure. Sample items include "When bad things are going to happen they just are going to happen no matter what you do to stop them," "When one is born, the success or failure one is going to have is already in one's destiny, so one might as well accept it," and "Planning only makes a person unhappy since your plans hardly every work out anyway." Data on Aycan et al.'s scale were collected across the same 33 nations as tightness (Gelfand et al., 2011). There was wide cross-cultural variation on the measure, with Pakistan, India, and Turkey being the highest on fatalism and Norway, the Netherlands, and the United States being the lowest on fatalism.

We caution that because the cultural measures we use here are cross-sectional and were measured at different times (e.g., in 1990s for GLOBE, early 2000s for tightness and fatalism; Gelfand et al., 2011), we cannot infer causality. We

Culture and Extremism

are simply examining whether there are certain cultural variables that may be correlated with the amount of terrorism, controlling for some common predictors of terrorism.

Control Variables

We measured the economic development of the nation using the GDP per capita of that nation in 2,000 U.S. dollars. These data come from the World Bank's *World Development Indicators*. We include GDP in this analysis in order to control for the economic differences between nations that may lead to differences in outcome on terrorism. We also measured religiosity as a control variable given it has been linked to terrorism (Juergensmeyer, 2003; Stern, 2003). Religiosity was measured by responses to the item regarding the importance of god in life as assessed by the World Value Survey (1995).

Results

Descriptive statistics are presented in Table 1 for all of the nations that were available for the variables being investigated. The total number of overlapping countries for all databases including the control variables, culture variables, and terrorism variables was 21. Included were a wide range of countries, including Australia, Austria, Brazil, France, Greece, Hong Kong, Hungary, India, Israel, Italy, Japan, Malaysia, Mexico, the Netherlands, New Zealand, Portugal, Singapore, Spain, Turkey, the United States, and Venezuela. From the descriptive statistics, we can see that there is a wide range of experience with terrorism incidents; the minimum number of incidents experienced by any country from 1970 to 2007 was 7 while the maximum was 4,310, and the mean was 872.33. Further, there is a great deal of variability in the number of fatalities, with a range of 1 to 13,508 and a mean of 1,271.57. Finally, the mean for the ratio of fatalities per incident was .88, and the range was .08 to 3.35, indicating that many incidents are low-fatality events. The economic and religious context of the nations also varied widely. For GDP, there was a minimum of 299.58 to a maximum of 28,363.13, with a mean of 11,597.76. For the measure of religiosity, there was a minimum of 4.61 and a maximum of 9.61, with a mean of 7.03. All of the cultural variables (fatalism, tightness, individualism-collectivism, gender egalitarianism, and power distance) also had significant variation across the countries (see Table 1).

The correlations among the variables suggest that numerous cultural variables were associated with different indices of terrorism. Number of terrorist incidents were negatively related to gender egalitarianism ($r = -.66, p < .01$) and positively related to fatalism ($r = .48, r < .05$). Number of fatalities were also negatively related to gender egalitarianism ($r = -.53, p < .05$) and positively related to fatalism ($r = .50, p < .05$). Finally, the number of fatalities per incident was

Table 1. Descriptive Statistics

	Means	SD	Incidents	Fatalities	Fatal/Incident	Religiosity	GDP	Tightness	Fatalism	Collectivism	Power distance	Gender egalitarianism
Incidents	872.33	1,154.52	1									
Fatalities	1,271.57	3,052.65	0.82**	1								
Fatal/Incident	0.88	0.99	0.44*	0.65*	1							
Religiosity	7.03	1.64	0.28	0.33	0.57*	1						
GDP	11,597.75	87,675.04	−0.23	−0.32	−0.37	−0.54*	1					
Tightness	6.25	2.73	0.28	0.41	0.55*	0.23	−0.17	1				
Fatalism	−0.43	0.43	0.48*	0.50*	0.37	0.41	−0.64*	0.44*	1			
Collectivism	5.02	0.68	0.34	0.34	0.39	0.58*	−0.66**	0.53*	0.84**	1		
Power distance	5.15	0.36	0.41	0.26	0.14	0.40	−0.56*	0.27	0.71**	0.73**	1	
Gender egalitarianism	3.38	0.29	−0.66**	−0.53*	−0.28	−0.22	−0.09	−0.23	−0.15	−0.03	−0.02	1

Note. $N = 21$; * $p < .05$; ** $p < .01$.

Table 2. Predictors of Number of Terrorist Incidents and Fatalities

	Coef	SE	z-stat	p-val	Lower CI	Upper CI
Number of incidents						
Religiosity	0.28	0.22	1.28	.200	−0.15	0.71
GDP	0.00	0.00	1.53	.126	0.00	0.00
Tightness	−0.19	0.11	−1.80	.072	−0.40	0.02
Fatalism	3.29	1.13	2.91	.004**	1.08	5.51
Collectivism	−1.45	1.05	−1.38	.167	−3.51	0.61
Power distance	1.77	0.96	1.84	.066	−0.12	3.66
Gender egalitarianism	−2.69	0.82	−3.30	.001***	−4.30	−1.10
Number fatalities						
Religiosity	0.93	0.32	2.95	.003**	0.31	1.55
GDP	0.00	0.00	1.27	.203	0.00	0.00
Tightness	−0.02	0.14	−0.14	.892	−0.29	0.25
Fatalism	3.76	1.45	2.59	.01**	0.91	6.60
Collectivism	−1.73	1.61	−1.08	.282	−4.89	1.42
Power distance	1.13	1.36	0.83	.406	−1.54	3.80
Gender egalitarianism	−2.69	1.05	−2.55	.011*	−4.75	−0.62

* $p < .05$; ** $p < .01$; *** $p < .001$.

positively related to cultural tightness ($r = .55$, $p < .05$). As these are only bivariate relationships, we next report analyses for each of our dependent variables including all of the culture variables as well as control variables.

Model 1: Number of Incidents

In this model, we predict the total count of incidents using culture, religiosity and GDP as predictors. In order to analyze the count of total terrorist incidents (as well as the count of fatalities for each country, discussed below) we utilized a negative binomial regression model. This model more appropriately handles overdispersed data, such as is usual with count data (Long, 1997). Overdispersion is a condition of count data in which the mean and the variance of the data are not equal. In addition, the NBRM provides consistent and efficient estimators and appropriately handles the standard errors in overdispersed data. The model for number of terrorist incidents was significant ($\chi^2(7) = 23.20$ $p < .01$). As can be seen in Table 2, the results show that nations high on fatalism had higher levels of terrorist incidents than nations lower on fatalism (Coeff = 3.29, $p < .01$), and nations low on gender egalitarianism have a greater number of terrorist incidents than those high on gender egalitarianism (Coeff = −2.69, $p < .001$), thus showing that cultural variables are indeed related to number of terrorist incidents from 1970 to 2007.

Table 3. Regression of Fatalities per Incident

Fatalities per incident	Unstandardized Coeff	SE	Standardized beta	t	Sig
Religiosity	.32	0.16	0.53	2.05	.06
GDP	0.00	0.00	−0.23	−0.85	.41
Tightness	.20	0.08	0.55	2.41	.03*
Fatalism	.44	0.90	0.19	0.49	.64
Collectivism	−.53	0.69	−0.36	−0.76	.46
Power distance	−.64	0.75	−0.23	−0.85	.41
Gender egalitarianism	−.10	0.74	−0.03	−0.13	.90

* $p < .05$.

Model 2: Fatalities Due to Terrorist Events

In this model, we examined the number of fatalities using culture, religiosity, and economic development as predictors. The overall model was significant ($\chi 2(7) = 26.72, p < .001$). As seen in Table 2, the results show again that nations higher on fatalism had statistically significantly greater number of fatalities than those nations lower on fatalism (Coeff = 3.76, $p < .01$). Societies with less gender egalitarianism also had a statistically significantly larger number of fatalities than nations with high gender egalitarianism (Coeff = –2.69, $p < .01$).

Model 3: Fatalities per Incident

In this model, we used multiple regression to examine the number of fatalities per incident with culture, religiosity, and economic development as predictors of fatalities per incident. The overall model was marginally significant (7, 20) = 2.71, $p = .058$. As can be seen in Table 3, the results showed that nations that are higher on cultural tightness have higher fatalities per incident than nations lower on tightness (Coeff = .55, $t = 2.41, p < .05$).

Discussion

Terrorism is a global hazard that threatens individuals, groups, and societies. On a daily basis, throughout the world, we have witnessed extreme, violent acts that threaten humans' peaceful existence. Much research in the last several decades has examined the factors that predict terrorism, focusing much attention on political, social, and psychological factors. To date, however, there has been very little attention to cultural factors and their relationship to terrorism.

In this research, we contribute to this literature by examining how the cultural context relates to the degree of terrorism that societies face. We developed theory and hypotheses linking different cultural variables that have received widespread attention in the literature to terrorism rates. The results of our analysis of the GTD, one of the most comprehensive databases on terrorism, supported a number of hypotheses. Across the different indicators of terrorism, the results showed evidence that cultural factors do matter for understanding cross-national rates in terrorism. Societies that have the belief that one's destiny and life events are predetermined (*fatalism*), have very strong norms and severe punishments for deviation from norms (*cultural tightness*), and are masculine and have very distinct gender roles (*low gender egalitarianism*) have higher terrorism rates than those that are low on these dimensions. These cultural factors predicted terrorism even when accounting for economic and religious factors. Moreover, in many of our models, these variables captured independent variance, suggesting that they each have some unique relationship with terrorism activity.

More generally, our results suggest that cultural values and norms that promote rigid thinking—fatalistic beliefs, strict gender roles, and greater tightness—are related to a greater number of terrorist attacks or fatalities. Future research should investigate the mechanisms underlying these effects. From a dynamical systems approach, it is possible that cultural systems that have a strong emphasis on certainty create a strong press for coherence which results in a *collapse of complexity*—or more simplistic Black–White thinking (Nowak & Vallacher, 1998). Indeed, the collapse of complexity has been found to be associated with conflict escalation and destructive conflict dynamics (Chung, Coleman, & Gelfand, 2011) which could provide a fertile basis for extreme behavior such as terrorism.

Interestingly, the results showed that different cultural variables were related to different measures of terrorism. While gender egalitarianism and fatalism were related to the overall number of incidents and fatalities, tightness was related to the number of fatalities per incident, a variable that can be seen as the most "extreme" or lethal of terrorism rates. It is possible that low gender egalitarianism affords a culture that permits violent behavior in general due to the enhanced masculinity and toughness, which can spark violence even when minor provocations are present (or in the case of terrorism, grievances), resulting in a greater number of incidents and fatalities. This is consistent with the criminology literature that has linked masculinity norms with homicides (Anderson, 1999; Gastil, 1971; Hackney, 1969; Nisbett & Cohen, 1996; Wolfgang & Ferracuti, 1967). Likewise, cultures that are fatalistic ultimately believe that others (i.e., god, fate, chance) control their outcomes, leaving little personal responsibility. Research has indeed shown that fatalism is associated with more deaths in the domain of safety and health (Gelfand et al., 2010; Leung & Bond, 2004). In the domain of terrorism, to the extent that there is a grievance and an ideology that justifies the grievance, fatalism may create a context that encourages more willingness to engage in violent behaviors with the justification that one's life is in others' hands, as compared to cultures low on fatalism.

By contrast, the enhanced number of fatalities per incident found in tight societies might be due to different processes that are conducive to higher impact terrorist episodes (i.e., more fatalities per incident), and more generally, the use of *extreme means* in the service of grievances. Tight nations have high degrees of monitoring and suppression, and much stronger punishments to norm violation in comparison with loose nations. Accordingly, it is possible that the means needed to air one's grievances need to be more extreme or radical. Indeed, while there are fewer legitimate forms of collective action in tight societies (e.g., signing petitions, attending demonstrations; Gelfand et al., 2011), tight cultures believe in more "radical" change than incremental change, which likely develops given the constraint pervasive in the cultural context. To be sure, these explanations are merely speculative, yet they suggest that different mechanisms may explain the relationship between different cultural dimensions and different indices of terrorism in nations.

It is interesting to point out that one cultural dimension—collectivism—had very weak direct relations with the terrorism indices. This suggests that collectivism in and of itself may not be a risk factor for terrorism at the national level. It is possible that collectivism serves as a moderator variable; that is, it is only in contexts where there is an ideology that supports the means and goals of terrorism that collectivistic values—which foster support for group over individual goals—facilitate terrorism (Kruglanski et al., 2009).

While this research begins to fill an important gap which examines cultural factors in relation to terrorism, it is clearly not without limitations. First and foremost, given the nature of the data, we do not have the ability to make any causal references regarding culture and terrorism. The cultural data available for this analysis were collected at different times during the period that we had available terrorism incident data, and thus it is impossible to determine whether cultural factors cause terrorism or vice-versa. For example, while it is theoretically possible that tightness provides a fertile breeding ground for the use of extreme means in societies, it is also possible that terrorism within nations is a threat which makes societies develop stronger norms and punishments. Second, we tested the relationship between culture and terrorism with only one set of possible operationalizations of terrorism. The GTD only represents one very broad definition of terrorism which may include incidents which other terrorism event databases may not have included. In addition, the GTD data rely primarily on open source media reports for an incident to be included in the data. This means that incidents will be excluded if reports of the incident never make it into the open source media. Accordingly, future research should examine the relationship of cultural factors to terrorism using other databases to replicate our effects. Finally, we have examined a very limited sample of countries in our test of the relationship between culture and terrorism. We were only able to analyze 21 countries that overlapped in the databases being utilized and thus, caution should be taken in generalizing the results to all countries.

Despite these limitations, the results have practical implications for public policy on terrorism and political violence. Most generally, this work supports earlier analysis (e.g., LaFree, Morris, & Dugan, 2009; LaFree, Yang, & Crenshaw, 2009) suggesting that worldwide terrorism is not evenly distributed across countries, with most countries experiencing few or no attacks and a handful experiencing most of the attacks. These results, while cross-sectional, suggest that culture may be a part of the explanation for this uneven distribution. These results also have implications for how policy makers might best respond to terrorism in different countries. For example, to the extent that these results can be replicated and extended to a broader range of countries, it may well be that they could assist policy makers in terms of determining whether a particular intervention is likely to result in a deterrent effect, and thereby reduce the future incidence of terrorism, or a backlash effect, and thereby increase attacks in the future. In general, countries exhibiting high levels of fatalism, cultural tightness and low gender egalitarianism may require special consideration when policy makers are weighing options for reducing terrorism.

References

Anderson, E. (1999). *Code of the street: Decency, violence, and the moral life of the inner city*. New York: Norton and Company.

Asal, V., & Rethemeyer, R. K. (2008). The nature of the beast: Organizational structures and the lethality of terrorist attacks. *Journal of Politics, 70*, 437–449. doi: 10.1017/S0022381608080419

Atran, S., Axelrod, R., & Davis, R. (2007). Sacred barriers to conflict resolution. *Science, 317*, 1039–1040. doi: 10.1126/science.1144241

Aycan, Z., Kanungo, R. N., Mendonca, M., Yu, K., Deller, J., Stahl, G., & Kurshid, A. (2000). Impact of culture on human resource management practices: A 10-country comparison. *Applied Psychology: An International Review, 49*, 192–221. doi: 10.1111/1464-0597.00010

Barry, H., III, Child, I. L., & Bacon, M. K. (1959). A cross-cultural survey of sex differences in socialization. *Journal of Abnormal and Social Psychology, 55*, 327–332. doi: 10.1037/h0041178

Bernstein, C. (1992). The idiot culture: Reflections of post-Watergate journalism. *The New Republic*, 22–28.

Brockner, J., Ackerman, G., Greenberg, J., Gelfand, M. J., Francesco, A. M., Chen, Z. X., & Shapiro, D. (2001). Culture and procedural justice: The influence of power distance on reactions to voice. *Journal of Experimental Social Psychology, 37*, 300–315. doi: 10.1006/jesp.2000.1451

Caplan, L. J., & Schooler, C. (2007). Socioeconomic status and financial coping strategies: The mediating role of perceived control. *Social Psychology Quarterly, 70*, 43–58. doi: 10.1177/019027250707000106

Chung, C., Coleman, P. T., & Gelfand, M. (2011). Conflict, culture, and complexity: The effects of simple versus complex rules in negotiation. Paper presented at the 24th annual conference of the International Association for Conflict Management in Istanbul, Turkey.

Clarke, R. V. G., & Newman, G. R. (2006). *Outsmarting the terrorists*. Westport, CT: Greenwood Press.

Colón, I. (1992). Race, belief in destiny, and seat belt usage: A pilot study. *American Journal of Public Health, 82*, 875–877. doi: 10.2105/AJPH.82.6.875

Dugan, L., LaFree, G., & Piquero, A. R. (2005). Testing a rational choice model of airline hijackings. *Criminology, 43*, 1031–1065. doi: 10.1111/j.1745-9125.2005.00032.x

Enders, W., & Sandler, T. (2006). *The political economy of terrorism.* Cambridge, UK: Cambridge University Press.

Fahey, S., LaFree, G., Dugan, L., & Piquero, A. R. (in press). Situational determinants of terrorist and nonterrorist aerial hijackings. *Justice Quarterly.*

Fiala, R., & LaFree, G. (1988). Cross-national determinants of child homicide. *American Sociological Review, 53*, 432–445.

Gartner, R. (1990). The victims of homicide: A temporal and cross-national comparison. *American Sociological Review, 55*, 92–106. doi: 10.2307/2095705

Gastil, R. D. (1971). Homicide and a regional culture of violence. *American Sociological Review, 36*, 412–427.

Gelfand, M. J., Bhawuk, D. P., Nishii, L., & Bechtold, D. (2004). Individualism and collectivism. In R. J. House, P. J. Hanges, M. Javidan, P. W. Dorfman, & V. Gupta (Eds.), *Culture, leadership, and organizations: The GLOBE study of 62 cultures* (pp. 437–512). Thousand Oaks, CA: Sage Publications.

Gelfand, M. J., Nishii, L., & Raver, J. (2006). On the nature and importance of cultural tightness-looseness. *Journal of Applied Psychology, 91*, 1225–1244. doi: 10.1037/0021-9010.91.6.1225

Gelfand, M. J., Fulmer, C. A., Kruglanski, A. W., Abdel-Latif, A.-H., Khashan, H., Shabka, H., & Moaddel, M. (2010). Cultures of fate: Implications for risk-taking. In C. S. Burke & M. Salazar (Chairs), *Impact of culture on collaboration and negotiation. Symposium conducted at the 3rd International Conference on Applied Human Factors and Ergonomics*, Miami, FL.

Gelfand, M. J., Raver, J. L., Nishii, L., Leslie, L. M., Lun, J., Lim, B. L., & Yamaguchi, S. (2011). Differences between tight and loose cultures: A 33-nation study. *Science, 332*, 1100–1104. doi: 10.1126/science.1197754

Gelles, R. (1987). *Family violence.* Thousand Oaks, CA: Sage.

Georgas, J., Mylonas, K., Bafiti, T., Poortinga, Y. H., Kagitcibasi, C., Kwak, K., & Kodic, Y. (2001). Functional relationships in the nuclear and extended family: A 16-culture study. *International Journal of Psychology, 36*, 289–300. doi: 10.1080/00207590143000045

Ginges, J., & Atran, S. (2009). Non-instrumental reasoning over sacred values: An Indonesian field experiment. In D. M. Bartels, C. W. Bauman, L. J. Skitka, & D. L. Medin (Eds.), *Psychology of learning and motivation, Vol. 50: Moral judgment and decision making.* San Diego, CA: Academic Press.

Greenbaum, R., Dugan, L., & LaFree, G. (2007). The impact of terrorism on Italian employment and business activity. *Urban Studies, 44*, 1093–1108. doi: 10.1080/00420980701255999

Hackney, S. (1969). Southern violence. In H. D. Graham & T. R. Gurr (Eds.), *The history of violence in America* (pp. 505–527). New York: Praeger.

Hardeman, W., Pierro, A., & Mannetti, L. (1997). Determinants of intentions to practice safe sex among 16–25 year-olds. *Journal of Community and Applied Social Psychology, 7*, 345–360. doi: 10.1002/(SICI)1099-1298(199712)7:5<345::AID-CASP431>3.0.CO;2-F

Hofstede, G. (1980). *Culture's consequences.* London: Sage.

Hogg, M. A., & Adelman, J. (2013). Uncertainty-identity theory: Extreme groups, radical behavior, and authoritarian leadership. *Journal of Social Issues, 69*, 436–454.

Hogg, M. A., Kruglanski, A., & van de Bos, K. (2013). Uncertainty and the roots of extremism. *Journal of Social Issues, 69*, 407–418.

Horgan, J. (2008). From profiles to pathways and roots to routes: Perspectives from psychology on radicalization into terrorism. *Annals of American Association of Political and Social Sciences, 618*, 80–94. doi: 10.1177/0002716208317539

House, R. J., Hanges, P. J., Javidan, M., Dorfman, P. W., & Gupta, V. (2004). *Leadership, culture, and organizations: The GLOBE study of 62 societies.* Thousand Oaks, CA: Sage Publications.

Jahoda, G. (1984). Do we need a concept of culture? *Journal of Cross-Cultural Psychology, 15*, 139–151. doi: 10.1177/0022002184015002003

Juergensmeyer, M. (2003). *Terror in the mind of God: The global rise of religious violence.* Berkeley, CA: University of California Press.

Kay, A. C., & Eibach, R. P. (2013). Compensatory control and its implications for ideological extremism. *Journal of Social Issues, 69*, 564–585.
Kitayama, S., Ishii, K., Imada, T., Takemura, K., & Ramaswamy, J. (2006). Voluntary settlement and the spirit of independence: Evidence from Japan's Northern frontier. *Journal of Personality and Social Psychology, 91*, 369–384. doi: 10.1037/0022-3514.91.3.369
Kroeber, A. L., & Kluckhohn, C. (1952). *Culture: A critical review of concepts and definitions.* Cambridge, MA: Harvard University Peabody Museum.
Kruglanski, A. W., Chen, X., Dechesne, M., Fishman, S., & Orehek, E. (2009). Fully committed: Suicide bombers' motivation and the quest for personal significance. *Political Psychology, 30*, 331–557. doi: 10.1111/j.1467-9221.2009.00698.x
Kruglanski, A. W., & Fishman, S. (2009). Psychological factors in terrorism and counterterrorism: Individual, group, and organizational levels of analysis. *Social Issues and Policy Review, 3*, 1–44. doi: 10.1111/j.1751-2409.2009.01009.x
Kruglanski, A. W., Gelfand, M. J., & Gunaratna, R. (2012). Terrorism as means to an end: How political violence bestows significance. In P. R. Shaver & M. Mikulincer (Eds), *Meaning, mortality, and choice: The social psychology of meaning, mortality and choice.* Washington, DC, US: American Psychological Association.
LaFree, G., & Ackerman, G. (2009). The empirical study of terrorism: Social and legal research. *Annual Review of Law and Social Science, 5*, 347–374.
LaFree, G. (2012). Generating terrorism event databases: Results from the global terrorism database, 1970 to 2008. In C. Lum & L. W. Kennedy (Eds.), *Evidence-based counterterrorism policy* (pp. 41–64). New York: Springer.
LaFree, G., & Dugan, L. (2004). How does studying terrorism compare to studying crime? In M. DeFlem (Ed.), *Criminology and terrorism* (pp. 53–74). New York: Elsevier.
LaFree, G., & Dugan, L. (2007). Introducing the global terrorism database. *Terrorism and Political Violence, 19*, 181–204 doi: 10.1080/09546550701246817
LaFree, G., & Dugan, L. (2009). Tracking global terrorism trends, 1970–2004. In D. Weisburd, T. E. Feucht, I. Hakimi, L. F. Mock, & S. Perry (Eds.), *To protect and to serve: Policing in an age of terrorism* (pp. 43–80). New York: Springer.
LaFree, G., Dugan, L., & Fahey, S. (2007). Global terrorism and failed states. In J. J. Hewitt, J. Wilkenfeld, & T. R. Gurr (Eds.), *Peace and conflict.* Boulder, CO: Paradigm Publishers.
LaFree, G., Dugan, L., & Korte, R. (2009). The impact of British counter terrorist strategies on political violence in Northern Ireland: Comparing deterrence and backlash models. *Criminology, 47*, 501–530. doi: 10.1111/j.1745-9125.2009.00138.x
LaFree, G., Morris, N., & Dugan, L. (2009). Cross-national patterns of terrorism: Comparing trajectories for total, attributed and fatal attacks, 1970 to 2006. *British Journal of Criminology, 50*, 622–649. doi: 10.1093/bjc/azp066
LaFree, G., Yang, S. M., & Crenshaw, M. (2009). Trajectories of terrorism: Attack patterns of foreign groups that have targeted the United States, 1970 to 2004. *Criminology and Public Policy, 8*, 445–473. doi: 10.1111/j.1745-9133.2009.00570.x
Leung, K., & Bond, M. H. (2004). Social axioms: A model for social beliefs in multi-cultural perspective. *Advances in Experimental Social Psychology, 36*, 119–197. doi: 10.1016/S0065-2601(04)36003-X
Long, J. S. (1997). *Regression models for categorical and limited dependent variables.* Thousand Oaks, CA: Sage Publications.
Lum, C., Leslie, W. K., & Sherley, A. J. (2006). Are counterterrorism strategies effective? The results of the Campbell Systematic Review on counter-terrorism strategy. *Fletcher Forum of World Affairs, 26*, 17–29.
Markus, H., & Kitayama, S. (1991). Culture and self: Implications for cognition, emotion, and motivation. *Psychological Review, 98*, 224–253. doi: 10.1037/0033-295X.98.2.224
McClure, J., Allen, M. W., & Walkey, F. (2001), Countering fatalism: Causal information in news reports. *Basic and Applied Social Psychology, 23*, 109–121. doi: 10.1207/153248301300148863
Miller, W. (1958). Lower-class culture as a generating milieu of gang delinquency. *Journal of Social Issues, 14*, 5–19. doi: 10.1111/j.1540-4560.1958.tb01413.x

Moaddel, M., & Karabenick, S. (2008) Religious fundamentalism among young Muslims in Egypt and Saudi Arabia. *Social Forces, 86*, 1675–1710. doi: 10.1353/sof.0.0059

Nisbett, R. E., & Cohen, D. (1996). *Culture of honor: The psychology of violence in the South.* Boulder, CO: Westview Press.

Nowak, A., & Vallacher, R. R. (1998). *Dynamical social psychology.* New York: Guilford Press.

Oishi, S. (2010). The psychology of residential mobility: Implications for the self, social relationships, and well-being. *Perspectives on Psychological Science, 5*, 5–21. doi: 10.1177/1745691609356781

Pelto, P. J. (1968). The differences between "tight" and "loose" societies. *Transaction, 5*, 37–40. doi: 10.1007/BF03180447

Piazza, J. (2007). Draining the swamp: Democracy promotion, state failure, and terrorism in 19 Middle Eastern countries. *Studies in Conflict and Terrorism, 30*, 521–539.

Piazza, J. A. (2008). Incubators of terror: Do failed and failing states promote terrorism? *International Studies Quarterly, 52*, 469–488. doi: 10.1111/j.1468-2478.2008.00511.x

Powe, B. D., & Finnie, R. (2003). Cancer fatalism: The state of science. *Cancer Nursing, 26*, 454–467.

Rohner, R. P. (1984). Toward a conception of culture for cross-cultural psychology. *Journal of Cross-Cultural Psychology, 15*, 111–138. doi: 10.1177/0022002184015002002

Ross, J. I., & Gurr, T. R. (1989). Why terrorism subsides: A comparative study of Canada and the United States, *Comparative Politics, 21*, 405–426.

Sageman, M. (2004). *Understanding terror networks.* Philadelphia, PA: University of Pennsylvania Press.

Sageman, M. (2008). *Leaderless Jihad: Terror networks in the 21st century.* Philadelphia, PA: University of Pennsylvania Press.

Schug, J., Yuki, M., & Maddux, W. W. (2010). Relational mobility explains between- and within-culture differences in self-disclosure toward close friends. *Psychological Science, 21*, 1471–1478. doi: 10.1177/0956797610382786

Segall, M. H. (1984). More than we need to know about culture, but are afraid not to ask. *Journal of Cross-Cultural Psychology, 15*, 153–162. doi: 10.1177/0022002184015002004

Silke, A. (1998). Cheshire-Cat Logic: The recurring theme of terrorist abnormality in psychological research. *Psychology, Crime and Law, 4*, 51–69. doi: 10.1080/10683169808401747

Stern, J. (2003). *Terror in the name of God: Why religious militants kill.* New York: Harper-Collins.

Straus, M. (1980). A sociological perspective on the prevention of wife-beating. In M. Straus & G. Hotaling (Eds.), *Social Causes of Husband-Wife Violence* (pp. 211–32) Minneapolis: University of Minnesota Press.

Swann, W. B. Jr., Gomez, A., Dovidio, J. S., Hart, S., & Jetten, I. (2010). Dying and killing for one's group: Identity fusion moderates responses to intergroup versions of the trolley problem. *Psychological Science, 21*, 1176–1183. doi: 10.1177/0956797610376656

Tikusis, P. (2009). On the relationship between weak states and terrorism. *Behavioral Sciences of Terrorism and Political Aggression, 1*, 66–78. doi: 10.1080/19434470802482175

Triandis, H. C. (1989). The self and social behavior in differing social contexts. *Psychological Review, 96*, 506–520. doi: 10.1037/0033-295X.96.3.506

Triandis, H. C. (1995). *Individualism and collectivism.* Boulder, CO: Westview.

Triandis, H. C., Kurowski, L., & Gelfand, M. J. (1994). Workplace diversity. In H. C. Triandis, M. Dunnette, & L. Hough (Eds.), *Handbook of industrial and organizational psychology* (Vol. 4, pp. 769–827). Palo Alto, CA: Consulting Psychologists Press.

Triandis, H. C., McCusker, C., & Hui, C. H. (1990). Multimethod probes of individualism and collectivism. *Journal of Personality and Social Psychology, 59*, 1006–1020. doi: 10.1037/0022-3514.59.5.1006

Wolfgang, M., & Ferracuti, F. (1967). *The subculture of violence.* Thousand Oaks, CA: Sage Publications.

World Bank. (2009). World development indicators. Data downloaded 07/20/2009. http://web.worldbank.org/WBSITE/EXTERNAL/DATASTATISTICS/0,,contentMDK:20398986~menuPK:64133163~pagePK:64133150~piPK:64133175~theSitePK:239419,00.html.

World Value Survey, Official Data File. V.3. World Values Survey Association (Online database, www.worldvaluessurvey.org) (1995). When Wave 3 data were unavailable, we used data from subsequent wave.

MICHELE GELFAND is Professor of Psychology and Distinguished University Scholar Teacher at the University of Maryland, College Park. She received her PhD from the University of Illinois, Urbana-Champaign. Her work explores cultural influences on conflict, negotiation, justice, and revenge; workplace diversity and discrimination; and theory and methods in cross-cultural psychology. She has published in such journals as *Science*, the *Journal of Applied Psychology*, *Journal of Personality and Social Psychology*, *Academy of Management Review*, *Annual Review of Psychology*, and *Psychological Science*, among other journals. She is the founding Co-Editor of the *Advances in Culture and Psychology* (Oxford University Press).

GARY LAFREE is Director of the National Consortium for the Study of Terrorism and Responses to Terrorism (START) at the University of Maryland, as well as professor in the Department of Criminology and Criminal Justice. He received his PhD in Sociology from Indiana University. Dr. LaFree served as President of the American Society of Criminology (ASC) in 2005–6006 and has also served as the President of the ASC's Division on International Criminology (1991–1993). Much of Dr. LaFree's current research is related to the development and analysis of the Global Terrorism Database, a major project being supported by START.

SUSAN FAHEY is Assistant Professor of Criminal Justice and Coordinator of Criminal Justice Internships at the Richard Stockton College of New Jersey. She attained her MA and PhD in Criminology and Criminal Justice from the University of Maryland, College Park, and she studied terrorism at the National Consortium for the Study of Terrorism and Responses to Terrorism (START) using the Global Terrorism Database (GTD). Her research and teaching interests focus on terrorism, political instability, criminological theory, and transnational crime and justice.

EMILY FEINBERG is a PhD Candidate at the University of Maryland. Her research focuses on expatriate management and leadership development, including cross-cultural training. She is currently the program manager for firm-wide management and leadership development at Credit Suisse in New York.

Uncertainty, Threat, and the Role of the Media in Promoting the Dehumanization of Immigrants and Refugees

Victoria M. Esses* and Stelian Medianu
University of Western Ontario

Andrea S. Lawson
Mount Sinai Hospital, Toronto

Immigration policies and the treatment of immigrants and refugees are contentious issues involving uncertainty and unease. The media may take advantage of this uncertainty to create a crisis mentality in which immigrants and refugees are portrayed as "enemies at the gate" who are attempting to invade Western nations. Although it has been suggested that such depictions promote the dehumanization of immigrants and refugees, there has been little direct evidence for this claim. Our program of research addresses this gap by examining the effects of common media portrayals of immigrants and refugees on dehumanization and its consequences. These portrayals include depictions that suggest that immigrants spread infectious diseases, that refugee claimants are often bogus, and that terrorists may gain entry to western nations disguised as refugees. We conclude by discussing the implications of the findings for understanding how uncertainty may lead to dehumanization, and for establishing government policies and practices that counteract such effects.

Migration and issues surrounding immigrants and refugees are defining features of the 21st century. More people live outside their country of birth today than in any other period of human history, and these levels are expected to continue to rise in the future (International Organization for Migration, 2011). In this

---

*Correspondence concerning this article should be addressed to Victoria Esses, Department of Psychology, University of Western Ontario, London, Ontario, Canada N6A 5C2 [e-mail: vesses@uwo.ca].

Preparation of this article was supported by Social Sciences and Humanities Research Council of Canada grants to the first author.

context, it is important to consider why perceptions of immigrants and refugees tend to be volatile, easily susceptible to perceived threat, and can result in the dehumanization of these groups.

In most Western nations today, immigration policies and the treatment of immigrants and refugees are contentious issues involving uncertainty and unease (Artiles & Molina, 2011; Brader, Valentino, & Suhay, 2008; Esses, Brochu, & Dickson, 2011). There is considerable uncertainty about the costs and benefits of allowing immigrants to take up residence in one's country, and about the obligation of host nations to provide protection for those seeking asylum. Questions that arise include how many immigrants should be accepted each year, the extent to which immigrants and refugees present threats to members of host nations, whether refugee claimants are legitimately in need of asylum, and the types of assistance that should be provided to immigrants and refugees.

Little direct information is available to the public to answer these questions and, as a result, the media and political elites may take advantage of this uncertainty to create a crisis mentality in which immigrants and refugees are portrayed as "enemies at the gate," who are attempting to invade Western nations (El Rafaie, 2001; Henry & Tator, 2002; Lynn & Lea, 2003). Such depictions grab the public's attention, alerting them to potential physical, economic, and cultural threats. In this way, uncertainty can be used to media and political advantage, allowing the transformation of relatively mundane episodes into newsworthy events that can be sold to the public and can serve as support for relatively extreme political platforms. The resultant dehumanization of immigrants and refugees may appeal to members of the public, serving to justify the status quo, strengthening ingroup–outgroup boundaries, and defending against threats to the ingroup's position in society (see also Haslam, 2006; Leyens, Demoulin, Vaes, Gaunt, & Paladino, 2007).

In this article, we begin by describing the portrayal of immigrants and refugees by the media, highlighting how uncertainty is often transformed into crisis and threat. We then introduce the concept of dehumanization, and discuss relevant research on dehumanization and its consequences. The main body of this article next presents research from our laboratory in which we have examined the role of media portrayals in promoting the dehumanization of immigrants and refugees, and the consequences for support for relevant policies and programs. The media portrayals used in our research include depictions in which the purported link between immigrants and disease is made salient, depictions in which the ambiguity surrounding the arrival of refugee claimants is translated into portrayals of these individuals as queue-jumpers who are illegitimately seeking entry into host nations, and depictions of refugee claimants as potential terrorists. These portrayals are contained in editorial cartoons and in news articles in which we manipulate information about immigrants and refugees. Our measures of dehumanization include explicit and implicit denial of the humanity of these groups. The consequences we examine include support for immigration and refugee levels and policies. Following our description of this research, we discuss the implications of the findings for understanding the functions that the dehumanization of immigrants and refugees may serve (see also Esses, Veenvliet, Hodson, & Mihic, 2008), and strategies that may be used to counteract such effects.

The Problematization of Immigrants and Refugees by the Media

The media play a large role in framing public policy and discourse about immigrants and refugees. In addition to disseminating policy messages, the media also construct and promote particular positions on these issues (Fleras & Kunz, 2001). Over the course of the past 10 to 15 years, portrayals of immigrants and refugees in many Western countries have become increasingly negative, with the media focusing on the threats that immigrants and refugees pose to members of host societies. For example, Chavez (2001) analyzed magazine covers from major American publications (e.g., *Time, Newsweek*) between 1965 and 1999, and found that a sense of threat and alarm about the perceived negative impact of immigration on the country has risen markedly, with a particular focus on immigrants as invaders. Similarly, Cisneros' (2008) analysis of American television news for 4 months in 2005 indicated that immigrants are represented visually and metaphorically as dangerous and destructive pollutants that must be controlled in order to prevent contamination.

A report on immigrants in the Norwegian media in 2009 found similar effects, with 71% of stories on immigration or integration found to be problem-focused (Islam in Europe, 2010). Extending this work to government media releases, Klocker and Dunn (2003) analyzed media representations of asylum-seekers in Australia between August 2001 and January 2002, focusing on both federal government media releases and newspaper articles. They found that 90% of the descriptive terms used by the federal government to describe asylum-seekers during this time were negative, with the asylum-seekers described as illegitimate, illegal, and threatening. The print media also tended to describe asylum-seekers negatively, with 76% of the descriptive terms used being negative, and a similar focus on threat (e.g., terrorists, criminals).

Although attitudes toward immigrants in Canada tend to be more positive than in many other Western nations (see, for example, German Marshall Fund of the United States, 2010), media depictions, particularly of refugees, tend to similarly focus on problems and threats to Canadians. For example, Mahtani and Mountz (2002) suggest that the arrival of four boats of asylum-seekers from China to the west coast of British Columbia, Canada in 1999 were framed by the media as a crisis, despite the relatively small number of individuals involved. Mahtani and Mountz (2002) propose that these portrayals were specifically designed to promote anxiety and panic through the use of metaphors about immigration, including the description of immigration as an invasion and as flooding the country, and the description of the asylum-seekers as bogus, as carriers of threatening diseases, and as potential terrorists. Mahtani and Mountz (2002) conclude that, as a result, "what is generally 'soft' support for policy levels quickly becomes negative following the catalyst of a negatively portrayed immigration event" (p. 5). In other words, positive attitudes toward immigration in Canada are based on a weak foundation, and negative portrayals by the media can rapidly degrade these attitudes.

In analyzing the coverage of immigration more generally between 1998 and 2000, as published in the National Post, a Canadian national newspaper known to be quite anti-immigrant, Henry and Tator (2002, p. 111) found that "the overwhelming majority of the articles, features, and editorials are opposed to current immigration policies and practices and critical of the values and norms of immigrants and refugees." Of interest, only 10 of 61 articles on immigration could be classified as positive. Henry and Tator (2002, p. 111) suggest that the National Post treats any issue dealing with immigration as a "discursive event / crisis," irrespective of the evidence. Recurring themes highlighted by Henry and Tator (2002) are (1) that "bogus refugees," particularly those who arrive by boat, are flooding into Canada and trying to take advantage of our lax refugee policy; (2) that the lax refugee policy allows many terrorists to enter Canada and obtain refugee status; and (3) that immigrants do not receive appropriate screening at our borders and thus are bringing in diseases that threaten the health of Canadians.

Hier and Greenberg (2002, p. 139) have suggested that these types of depictions, and the problematization of immigration by the media more generally, may be seen as responses to collective insecurity and uncertainties about citizenship and national identity "stemming from globalization and ideological realignments associated with the rise of neoliberalism." They propose that by manufacturing a crisis around immigration and refugee policy, a problem is identified that can be decisively solved, reducing anxiety in the process. Though this may provide some benefit for members of the host population, the results of this problematization can be severe for those who are targeted, including dehumanization that can serve to justify inhumane treatment.

It is likely that the media both reflect the tendency for the problematization of immigration to occur as a response to uncertainty, and exacerbate this tendency. Uncertainty—both uncertainty about national identity as discussed by Hier and Greenberg (2002) and uncertainty inherent in bringing in unknown immigrants—leads individuals to look to the groups to which they belong for uncertainty reduction (see Hogg, 2000; Hogg & Adelman, 2013; Kruglanski, Pierro, Mannetti, & De Grada, 2006). The group-centrism that results leads to intolerance of "otherness" and outgroup derogation (Kruglanski et al., 2006; see also Federico, Hunt, & Fisher, 2013; McGregor, Zanna, Holmes, & Spencer, 2001). In addition, uncertainty surrounding immigration is especially likely to be viewed as a threat when one feels one does not have the resources to deal with it (see Blascovich & Tomaka, 1996), promoting the variety of negative reactions resulting from perceived threats from immigrants (e.g., Esses, Hodson, & Dovidio, 2003). These perceived threats may include both tangible threats to physical and economic well-being and potential cultural threats to society.

The media may then reinforce these perceptions, providing one-sided negative portrayals of immigrants and refugees that serve to further reduce uncertainty. Crises sell news, whereas positive stories are less newsworthy (see Shoemaker & Vos, 2009; Soroka & McAdams, 2010), so that negative media portrayals of immigrants and refugees both reduce uncertainty and take advantage of the public's preference for negative news content to sell stories. What may result is extreme negative reactions to immigrants and refugees, including their dehumanization. Dehumanization may be considered the ultimate form of intolerance of "otherness," in which immigrants and refugees are not even permitted entry into the human ingroup.

Indeed, we argue that what many negative media portrayals of immigrants and refugees have in common is their tendency to promote the dehumanization of these groups. Such dehumanization can serve to reduce uncertainty, providing definitive answers as to how immigrants and refugees should be viewed and how they should be treated. We turn next to a discussion of dehumanization, its measurement, and its consequences.

Dehumanization

Dehumanization involves the denial of full humanness to others, and their exclusion from the human species (e.g., Bar-Tal, 2000; Haslam, 2006; Haslam, Loughnan, & Kashima, 2008). This is an extreme reaction to members of other groups, removing them from considerations that surround our treatment of other humans (Opotow, 1995). In an integrative review of the psychological literature on dehumanization, Haslam et al. (2008) suggest that an important way in which others may be denied full humanness is in an animalistic sense in which they are seen as not having risen above their animal origins; that is, they are seen as less than human. Further, they suggest that this dehumanization is characterized by a perception that the dehumanized lack such characteristics as refinement, civility, morality, self-control, and cognitive sophistication.

Previous attempts to assess dehumanization have focused on several of these specific dimensions. Leyens and colleagues (Delgado, Rodríguez-Pérez, Vaes, Leyens, & Betancor, 2009; Leyens et al., 2000) suggest that one way of dehumanizing (in their terms, infrahumanizing) outgroups is to deny that they experience complex, secondary emotions. That is, the infrahumanized may experience primary emotions (e.g., pleasure, fear), just as animals may, but not the secondary emotions generally attributed only to humans (e.g., hope, remorse). This infrahumanization predicts rejection of Muslim immigrants in Europe (Leyens et al., 2007).

Another indication of dehumanization has been proposed by Schwartz and his colleagues. According to Schwartz and Struch (1989), people infer a group's humanity by looking at the extent to which their values reflect that they have "transcended their basic animal nature and developed their human sensitivities and moral sensibilities" (Schwartz & Struch, 1989, p. 155). "Prosocial" values (e.g., equality, helpful, forgiving) are an example of such values because they "reflect a conscious desire to promote the welfare of others" (Schwartz & Struch, 1989, p. 155). If people perceive that a group lacks prosocial values, then they will judge that group to be less human and thus less worthy of humane treatment. Consequently, to assess dehumanization, Schwartz and his colleagues have utilized measures of the perceived values of a group (Schwartz, Struch, & Bilsky, 1990; Struch & Schwartz, 1989).

Esses and colleagues examined the dehumanization of refugees along this moral dimension (Esses et al., 2008). In addition to assessing dehumanization using the value attributions suggested by Schwartz and colleagues (1990), they included an assessment of the enemy/barbarian image (Alexander, Brewer, & Herrmann, 1999), which centrally includes perceptions of a group as immoral. They also developed a new measure to assess the extent to which refugees are seen as trying to violate procedures and cheat the system, which is a view that is certainly prevalent in the media (see also Louis, Duck, Terry, Schuller, & Lalonde, 2007). The three measures were highly intercorrelated, suggesting that, as desired, they are tapping into an underlying perception of immorality and lack of human sensibility. Importantly, however, the latent variable underlying these measures was distinct from overall negative attitudes toward refugees (Esses et al., 2008), so that it is not merely tapping general negativity toward a group.

An important issue in the area of dehumanization has been understanding why some individuals are particularly likely to dehumanize members of other groups, particularly low status, seemingly victimized groups, such as refugees. One possibility is that some people dehumanize other groups because they want to protect their privileged positions and keep other groups, such as refugees, in their place. By perceiving refugees as not completely part of the human ingroup, individuals may justify the status quo, believing that refugees deserve their negative outcomes (Opotow, 1995; Schwartz & Struch, 1989). As a result, existing systems and the status quo are maintained and perpetuated (Jost & van der Toorn, 2012).

Based on this reasoning, we would expect that Social Dominance Orientation would be a strong predictor of the dehumanization of refugees (see Cohrs & Stelzl, 2010, for a meta-analysis of the relation between Social Dominance Orientation and anti-immigrant attitudes). Individuals who are higher in Social Dominance Orientation support group hierarchies and inequality in society, view the world as a competitive place in which only the toughest survive, and express a willingness to discriminate against other groups in order to attain or maintain group dominance (e.g., Duckitt, 2006; Sidanius & Pratto, 1999). These individuals are described as holding hierarchy-enhancing legitimizing beliefs that provide moral and intellectual justification for an unequal distribution of resources (e.g., Roccato & Ricolfi, 2005). Thus, higher social dominance oriented individuals may dehumanize refugees in order to maintain group dominance and protect resources. By dehumanizing refugees, they may legitimize their own entitlement to resources and justify the plight of refugees (see also Louis et al., 2007). Our research has demonstrated that higher social dominance oriented individuals are indeed especially likely to dehumanize refugees (Esses et al., 2008; see also Louis et al., 2007), supporting the assertion that dehumanization may serve as a legitimizing myth supporting the plight of refugees.

The dehumanization of refugees may lead to specific negative emotional reactions to members of the group. In particular, theorizing and prior research on dehumanization, particularly dehumanization in terms of animalization, indicates that it may lead to contempt and lack of admiration for a group (Haslam, 2006). Similarly, research on the stereotype content model indicates that groups that are dehumanized through perceptions that they are low in competence and warmth elicit feelings of contempt, as well as some pity (Fiske, Cuddy, Glick, & Xu, 2002; Harris & Fiske, 2006). We would expect, then, that to the extent that refugees are dehumanized, they will elicit feelings of contempt and lack of admiration. Consistent with this prediction, research on the dehumanization of refugees has demonstrated that dehumanization predicts contempt and lack of admiration toward the group (Esses et al., 2008; see also Verkuyten, 2004), as well as support for exclusion of refugees from one's country.

We turn now to a description of the experiments we have conducted over the past few years that have sought to determine the causal connection between media depictions of immigrants and refugees, and resultant dehumanization of these groups.

Media Portrayals and the Dehumanization of Immigrants and Refugees

Although it has been proposed that negative media portrayals of immigrants and refugees are likely to lead to dehumanization of these groups (e.g., Henry & Tator, 2002), there has been little direct evidence for this assertion. In order to determine the causal relation between negative media depictions of immigrants and refugees and the dehumanization of these groups, we have conducted a number of experiments to examine the potential consequences of media depictions that focus on the threats that immigrants and refugees pose to members of host societies. We focus here on several of the threats that are particularly prevalent in the media both in Canada and in a number of other Western countries: (1) immigrants are sources and spreaders of infectious diseases, (2) refugee claimants are bogus queue-jumpers who are trying to take advantage of lax refugee policies to gain entry to western nations, and (3) terrorists are trying to gain entry to western nations as refugee claimants.

Immigrants are Sources and Spreaders of Infectious Diseases

A common charge laid against immigrants by the Canadian media is that they are bringing in infectious diseases that threaten the health of Canadians. Indeed, a well-known anti-immigrant website that operated for a number of years had a section devoted to presenting published news articles that highlighted the association of immigrants with disease. We reasoned that such an association might be especially likely to lead to the dehumanization of immigrants because vermin are typically associated with the spreading of disease. To examine this issue, we conducted an experiment using editorial cartoons designed specifically for this purpose (Lawson & Esses, 2008).

Participants in this research were asked to read an online article reviewing a biography of the actor Steve Martin, and to answer some questions about it. On the bottom right-hand side of the page, and thus viewed incidentally, was an editorial cartoon. This cartoon showed an immigrant arriving at an Immigration Canada booth carrying several suitcases and a number of documents. In one condition the large suitcase that the immigrant was carrying displayed labels for various diseases (e.g., AIDS, SARS), whereas in the other condition, no labels were present. Following questions about the online article that was the purported focus of the study, we asked participants to complete a set of additional items, including questions about immigrants. These included items assessing memory for the editorial cartoon, perceptions of immigrants as sources and spreaders of disease, value dehumanization (Schwartz et al., 1990), enemy/barbarian image (Alexander et al., 1999), emotions toward immigrants (Fiske et al., 2002), and attitudes toward immigrants and immigration (Esses, Dovidio, Jackson, & Armstrong, 2001).

Of interest, participants' memory of the content of the editorial cartoon was poor, with many reporting that they had not seen the cartoon. Nonetheless, as shown in Table 1, the content of the cartoon had significant effects. Participants who viewed the cartoon with the disease labels were significantly more likely to indicate that immigrants are a source and spreader of disease. They were also significantly more likely to dehumanize immigrants on both measures of dehumanization, and to express contempt and lack of admiration toward them. Finally, the disease labels led to less favorable attitudes toward immigrants and immigration overall.

In order to determine the relations among the variables involved in these effects, we conducted structural equation modeling, testing a variety of alternative models. As shown in Figure 1, the model that fit the data best indicated that the disease label manipulation led to stronger perceptions of immigrants as sources and spreaders of disease, which resulted in the dehumanization of immigrants. In

Table 1. Effect of the Editorial Cartoon with Disease Labels on Perceptions of Immigrants as Sources of Disease, Dehumanization, Emotions, and Attitudes toward Immigrants and Immigration

	No disease labels	Disease labels
Immigrants as sources/spreaders of disease (1 to 7)*	2.75	3.25
Value dehumanization (0 to 4)**	0.21	0.57
Dehumanization: Enemy/barbarian image (1 to 7)*	2.57	2.97
Contempt (−3 to +3)*	−1.69	−1.31
Lack of admiration (−3 to +3)*	−0.31	0.08
Attitudes toward immigrants and immigration (1 to 7)†	1.72	1.26

Note. **$p < .01$, *$p < .05$, †$p < .09$.

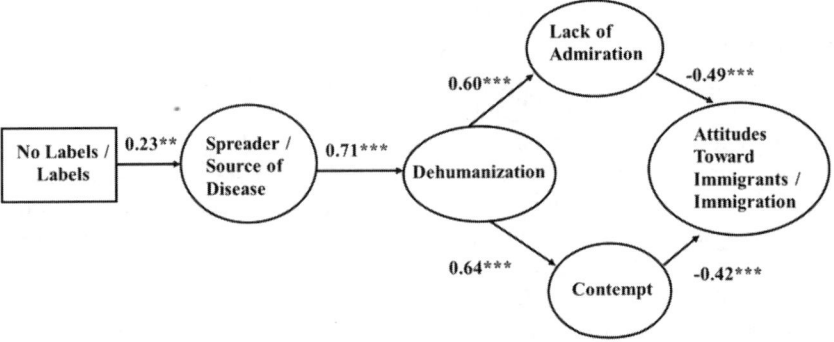

Fig. 1. Structural equation model of the paths from viewing the different editorial cartoons to dehumanization and its consequences.
Note. $\chi^2/df = 1.81$; CFI $= .97$; RMSEA $= .076$; ***$p < .001$, **$p < .01$.

turn, dehumanization led to feelings of contempt and lack of admiration toward immigrants, which resulted in negative attitudes toward immigrants and toward Canada's immigration policy.

The results of this study support the claim that media depictions of immigrants as a threat to members of the host nation can lead to their dehumanization. The findings are striking in that participants were not asked to look at the editorial cartoon, and many reported that they did not see it, yet the editorial cartoon that made a link between immigrants and disease led to the dehumanization of immigrants, and resultant emotional and attitudinal consequences of this dehumanization.

In this case, the purported threat involved was quite severe—infectious diseases—and we might question whether similar effects would be obtained with threats that are less likely to be viewed as life-threatening. Thus, we turn next to a study that examined what might be considered a milder threat—the claim that many refugee claimants are bogus queue-jumpers taking advantage of lax refugee policies in order to gain entry to western countries.

Table 2. Effect of the Bogus Refugees Article on Dehumanization, Emotions, and Attitudes toward Refugees and Refugee Policy

	Neutral	Bogus queue-jumpers
Dehumanization: Enemy/barbarian image (1 to 7)*	2.34	3.05
Contempt (1 to 7)*	1.85	2.57
Lack of admiration (1 to 7)**	3.41	4.52
Attitudes toward refugees and refugee policy (−4 to +4)***	1.88	0.17

Note. ***$p < .001$, **$p < .01$, *$p < .05$.

Refugee Claimants are Bogus Queue-Jumpers

Media depictions of asylum seekers often portray them as bogus queue-jumpers who are attempting to gain entry to western countries through illicit means (e.g., Klocker & Dunn, 2003; Mahtani & Mountz, 2002). What effect do these claims have on perceptions of refugees? To find out, we asked participants in this study to read an editorial about current affairs in Canada and to answer some questions about it (Esses, Veenvliet, & Medianu, 2011). We randomly assigned participants to read one of two newspaper editorials on refugees to Canada. In the experimental condition, participants read a real editorial that had appeared in a Canadian newspaper in 2001. This article described Canada's costly refugee program, and depicted refugee claimants as immoral cheaters (e.g., "Refugees are not people who have been displaced and are brought into Canada for humanitarian reasons. Only a few are in that category. Most are smuggled in or are queue-jumpers who lie their way into the country by pretending they cannot go home and get all the entitlements they need immediately... These people come here by plane, have passports when they board then flush them down the toilet and declare refugee status, even when they are from rich countries"; Francis, 2001). In the control condition, we adapted this editorial so that it described Canada's costly refugee program but did not describe refugee claimants as immoral cheaters (e.g., "These people come here by plane, but have nowhere further to go once they arrive. They sign up for social assistance until they can get themselves settled and look for work.") Following questions about the editorial to maintain the cover story, we asked participants to complete a set of additional items, including items assessing the dehumanization of refugees using the measure of enemy/barbarian image (Alexander et al., 1999), emotions toward refugees (Fiske et al., 2002), and attitudes toward refugees and Canada's refugee policy (Esses et al., 2001).

Participants' perceptions of the editorials themselves did not differ, indicating that they found them quite easy to understand and relatively convincing. In terms of the main dependent measures, as shown in Table 2, we found that that the editorial presented in the experimental condition (the *real* editorial) significantly increased the dehumanization of refugees, and contempt and lack of admiration toward them. In addition, the editorial depicting refugees as bogus queue-jumpers also led to significantly less favorable attitudes toward refugees and toward Canada's refugee policy. Thus, dehumanization resulted from this presumed threat to the integrity of the refugee system, with a media claim that refugee claimants are often fake leading to the dehumanization of refugees in general. In the study to be described next, we build on this finding, examining the effect of the framing of a recent event—the arrival of a boat carrying Tamil asylum-seekers to the west coast of British Columbia, Canada in 2010. In addition, we focus on implicit dehumanization, and the association of refugees with animals.

Refugee Claimants are Bogus and are Harboring Terrorists

In August 2010, a ship was intercepted off of the west coast of British Columbia containing 492 Tamil passengers claiming refugee status. The asylum-seekers were immediately detained by the Canadian government and the media depictions of these individuals included claims that they were bogus refugees trying to take advantage of Canada's lax system, and that they included members of the Tamil Tigers, labeled as a terrorist organization in Canada (see di Tomasso, 2012). The sense of crisis and threat promoted by the media seemed to far exceed the seriousness of the incident, given the number of individuals involved, who constituted approximately 2% of the total number of asylum claims registered in Canada that year (Canadian Council for Refugees, 2011).

In order to examine the effect of the media depictions used to describe the Tamil asylum-seekers, we created new editorials in which we described a fictitious group of asylum seekers ("Sandirians") arriving off of the east coast of Canada (Medianu, Sutter, Esses, & Gawronski, 2013). These editorials were made to look like real editorials from a major Canadian newspaper. The purpose of using a description of a fictitious group in the editorials was to prevent bias due to participants' possible preconceptions about Tamil asylum-seekers. In these editorials, descriptions of the Sandirians either highlighted that they were bogus refugee claimants trying to take advantage of Canada's lax refugee system to get into the country illegally; highlighted that many were members of a terrorist organization who could be bringing violence to Canada; or contained neutral descriptions of the Sandirians and of refugees in general.

After reading one of the three editorials, participants were asked to complete a sequential priming task in order to determine whether the editorials had influenced participants' mental associations between refugees and animals. The procedure consisted of participants being briefly presented with one of three primes on a computer screen: the word Canadian, the word Refugee, or no prime. Immediately following this, participants were presented with a human or an animal picture. Because previous research has shown that task instructions can have important effects on priming (e.g., De Houwer, Hermans, Rothermund, & Wentura, 2002), we asked participants to complete one of two categorization tasks. Half of the participants were asked to categorize the pictures as humans versus animals. The other half of the participants were asked to evaluate the pictures as positive versus negative.

The *human pictures* included pictures showing the upper body and face of either a white man or a white woman, and included four positive and four negative pictures. The positive pictures included the emotions of happiness and pride. The negative pictures included the emotions of sadness and anger. The *animal pictures* similarly included four positive and four negative pictures. The positive pictures included a baby seal, a butterfly, a dragonfly, and a ladybug. The negative pictures included a rat, a cockroach, worms, and a fly.

The basic assumption behind this study is that when mental concepts are closely related to each other, the activation of one of the concepts will automatically lead to the activation of its related concepts (Wittenbrink & Schwartz, 2007). Thus, our measure of dehumanization was the degree of mental association between refugees and animals, in comparison to the association between refugees and humans. If reading the bogus or terrorist editorials led to a stronger mental association between refugees and animals, then the presentation of the word refugee would facilitate participants' reaction to the animal pictures more than to the human pictures, whereas this would not be the case for the presentation of the word Canadian. As shown in Figure 2, the results supported this prediction. In both the bogus refugee and terrorist conditions, participants dehumanized refugees more than they dehumanized Canadians, whereas in the neutral condition, this was not the case. Furthermore, this implicit dehumanization of refugees occurred irrespective of the task at hand. Thus, the media depiction of the Sandirian refugees as bogus queue-jumpers or as terrorists increased implicit dehumanization, that is, it increased participants' implicit association between refugees and animals.

This study extends the findings of the first two studies in several ways. First, it shows that effects of threat are evident on implicit measures of dehumanization, as well as on the explicit measures used in the first two studies. The measure of implicit dehumanization specifically involves the association of the group with animals, focusing on this aspect of dehumanization. In addition, this study demonstrates the effect of an additional type of threat that has recently come to be associated with immigrants and refugees by the media—the threat that they may be terrorists. Finally, and of importance, this study demonstrates that the description of a single group of asylum-seekers can have severe effects on perceptions of refugees in general.

Implications and Conclusion

These studies suggest that the uncertainty surrounding immigration, paired with the media's proclivity to focus on negative rather than positive news stories,

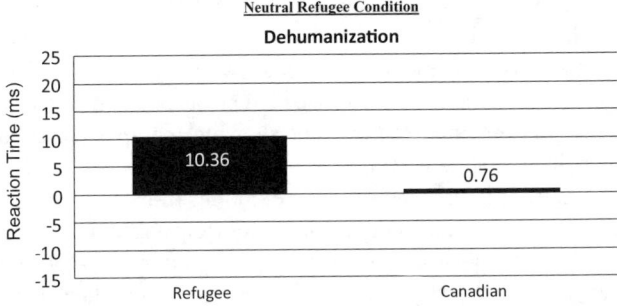

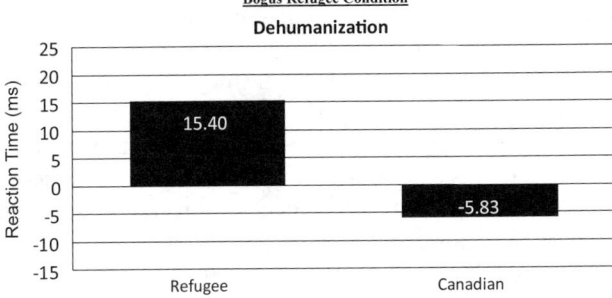

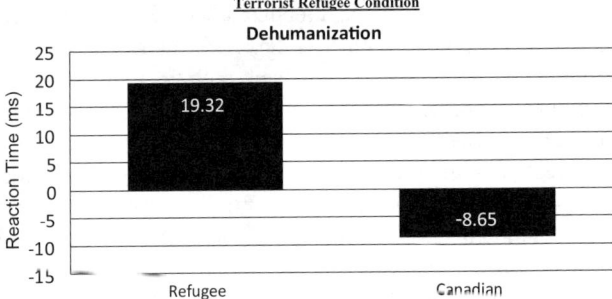

Fig. 2. Implicit dehumanization after reading the neutral, bogus, or terrorist refugee media article.
Neutral Refugee Condition
Note. Higher values indicate more dehumanization. Participants did not dehumanize refugees more than they dehumanized Canadians, $t(19) = .95$, $p = .35$.
Bogus Refugee Condition
Note. Participants dehumanized refugees more than they dehumanized Canadians, $t(15) = -2.45$, $p < .05$.
Terrorist Refugee Condition
Note. Participants dehumanized refugees more than they dehumanized Canadians, $t(13) = -2.94$, $p < .05$.

can lead to extreme negative reactions to immigrants and refugees—their removal from the human race through dehumanization. In turn, through the removal of the constraints imposed by humanity and kindness considerations, extreme behaviors toward members of these groups may be released. These behaviors may be justified on the grounds that they are required in order to protect the ingroup from the "threats" that immigrants and refugees are seen to pose. Thus, the media may not only promote dehumanization of immigrants and refugees through depictions that highlight potential threats to the host society, but provide ready justifications for the dehumanization and consequent outcomes.

The consistent finding that media portrayals of immigrants and refugees that highlight potential threats to members of the host society cause the dehumanization of these groups provides insight into the function that this dehumanization may serve. In particular, this dehumanization may help to reduce uncertainty as to how to view and treat immigrants and refugees, particularly for individuals with little direct contact with members of these groups, and justify their exclusion and mistreatment. By perceiving immigrants and refugees as not completely part of the human ingroup, one can more easily believe that they deserve negative outcomes and that perceptions of the national ingroup do not need to shift to accommodate their inclusion. In this way, threat is reduced and the status quo is maintained (see also Esses et al., 2008).

To test some of these assumptions, and the links among uncertainty, threat, and dehumanization, future research might explore whether susceptibility to negative portrayals of immigrants and refugees are especially likely among individuals who are in a state of high uncertainty. This uncertainty may be external to the issue of immigration, manipulated in an independent context, or directly relevant to immigration, manipulated through information that highlights the uncertainty surrounding the arrival of newcomers. If the predicted relation between uncertainty and susceptibility to negative messages about immigrants and refugees is supported, future research would also do well to test strategies for reducing these negative effects, potentially through manipulations that directly reduce uncertainty. In this way, dehumanization can be minimized. This is a worthy goal, given the dire consequences that may result from negative media portrayals and the dehumanization that we have shown to occur.

Returning to the example of the portrayal of Tamil asylum-seekers arriving in British Columbia in 2010, it seems likely that negative media portrayals served to fan the flames of distrust and anxiety, with dire consequences. An Angus Reid Poll conducted quite soon after the incident found that 63% of Canadians agreed with the statement that "the ship should have been turned back and not allowed to reach Canada" (Angus Reid, 2010). This was considered a substantial hardening of attitudes. In addition, in response to perceptions of the Tamils as bogus and as potential criminals, a new Bill was introduced by the ruling Conservative party to reform Canada's refugee system and crack down on bogus refugee claimants.

This Bill was described by the Minister of Public Safety as, "cracking down on those criminals who would abuse our generous immigration system and endanger the safety and security of Canadian communities" (Toews, 2010). Though the Bill was toned down somewhat before passing, its provisions currently include the ability of the Minister of Public Safety to designate certain groups of asylum-seekers as "irregular arrivals," who will not receive the same protections as other refugee claimants. For example, they can be held in detention for up to a year with limited review, and even if found to be valid refugees will have to wait 5 years before they can apply for permanent resident status, preventing them from sponsoring family members during that time (Citizenship and Immigration Canada, 2012).

The findings thus have important implications at both the level of public policy and the behavior of those who produce the media for public consumption. Many Western nations need immigrants to fill labor needs and to support their population base, and these nations have an obligation to protect refugees, as signatories to the 1951 Geneva Refugee Convention and its 1967 Protocol (Esses, Medianu, Hamilton, & Lapshina, in press). Media depictions highlighting threat, and the resultant dehumanization of immigrants and refugees, directly undermine these goals. Dehumanization results not only in negative emotions toward the groups, but negative attitudes toward immigrants and refugees. Dehumanization also produces lack of support for government policies that guide the admittance of immigrants and refugees, and calls for reducing the number of immigrants and refugees admitted each year. Thus, in order to promote the benefits of immigration, and support harmonious relations between immigrants and members of host societies, it is essential that media portrayals of immigrants and refugees not serve the function of transforming uncertainty into crisis.

To support the media in this regard, governments need to do a better job of communicating with the media about immigration, providing information that reduces uncertainty and countering the potential perceptions of threat that are currently prevalent in public discourse. This should include communication not only in response to events that have the potential to be anxiety-provoking and are used by the media to sell news—such as the arrival of groups of asylum-seekers—but also proactive information on positive immigrant outcomes and contributions (Mahtani & Mountz, 2002). Such information can be provided in government press releases, as well as being prominently displayed on government websites. These actions may aid in the prevention of extreme negative reactions to immigrants and refugees, while reducing uncertainty. A corresponding reduction in dehumanization will benefit not only immigrants and refugees, but also members of host societies who have much to gain by embracing those who come to their shores seeking a new life.

References

Alexander, M. G., Brewer, M. B., & Herrmann, R. K. (1999). Images and affect: A functional analysis of out-group stereotypes. *Journal of Personality and Social Psychology, 77*, 78–93. doi:10.1037/0022-3514.77.1.78

Angus Reid. (2010). *Almost half of Canadians believe Tamil migrants should be deported.* Retrieved June 1, 2012, from http://www.angus-reid.com/polls/43181/almost-half-of-canadians-believe-tamil-migrants-should-be-deported/

Artiles, A. M., & Molina, O. (2011). Crisis, economic uncertainty and union members' attitudes toward immigrants in Europe. *European Review of Labour and Research, 17*, 453–469. doi:10.1177/1024258911419752

Bar-Tal, D. (2000). *Shared beliefs in a society.* Thousand Oaks, CA: Sage. doi: 10.1002/casp.701

Blascovich, J., & Tomaka, J. (1996). The biopsychosocial model of arousal regulation. In M. Zanna (Ed.), *Advances in experimental social psychology* (Vol. 28, pp. 1–51). New York: Academic Press. doi: 10.1016/S0065-2601(08)60235-X

Brader, T., Valentino, N. A., & Suhay, E. (2008). What triggers public opposition to immigration? Anxiety, group cues, and immigration threat. *American Journal of Political Science, 52*, 959–978. doi:10.1111/j.1540-5907.2008.00353.x

Canadian Council for Refugees. (2011). *Myths and facts 2011.* Retrieved June 1, 2012, from http://ccrweb.ca/en/myths-and-facts-2011

Chavez, L. R. (2001). *Covering immigration: Popular images and the politics of a nation.* Berkeley, CA: University of California Press.

Cisneros, J. D. (2008). Contaminated communities: The metaphor of "immigrant as pollutant" in media representations of immigration. *Rhetoric and Public Affairs, 11*, 569–601. doi:10.1353/rap.0.0068

Citizenship and Immigration Canada (2012). *Protecting Canada's immigration system.* Retrieved August 7, 2012, from http://www.cic.gc.ca/english/refugees/reform.asp

Cohrs, C. J., & Stelzl, M. (2010). How ideological attitudes predict host society members' attitudes toward immigrants: Exploring cross-national differences. *Journal of Social Issues, 66*, 673–694. doi: 10.1111/j.1540-4560.2010.01670.x

De Houwer, J., Hermans, D., Rothermund, K., & Wentura, D. (2002). Affective priming of semantic categorization responses. *Cognition and Emotion, 16*, 643–666. doi:10.1080/02699930143000419

Delgado, N., Rodríguez-Pérez, A., Vaes, J., Leyens, J-P., & Betancor, V. (2009). Priming effects of violence on infrahumanization. *Group Processes & Intergroup Relations, 12*, 699–714. doi:10.1177/1368430209344607

Di Tomasso, L. (2012). More equal than others: The discursive construction of migrant children and families in Canada. *International Journal of Child, Youth and Family Studies, 2 & 3*, 331–348.

Duckitt, J. (2006). Differential effects of right wing authoritarianism and social dominance orientation on outgroup attitudes and their mediation by threat from and competitiveness to outgroups. *Personality and Social Psychology Bulletin, 32*, 684–696. doi:10.1177/0146167205284282

El Refaie, E. (2001). Metaphors we discriminate by: Naturalized themes in Austrian newspaper articles about asylum seekers. *Journal of Sociolinguistics, 5*, 352–371. doi:10.1111/1467-9481.00154

Esses, V. M., Brochu, P. M., & Dickson, K. R. (2011). Economic costs, economic benefits, and attitudes toward immigrants and immigration. *Analyses of Social Issues and Public Policy, 12*, 133–137. doi: 10.1111/j.1530-2415.2011.01269.x

Esses, V. M., Dovidio, J. F., Jackson, L. M., & Armstrong, T. L. (2001). The immigration dilemma: The role of perceived group competition, ethnic prejudice, and national identity. In V. M. Esses, J. F. Dovidio, & K. L. Dion (Eds.), *Immigrants and immigration. Journal of Social Issues, 57*, 389–412. doi: 10.1111/0022-4537.00220

Esses, V. M., Hodson, G., & Dovidio, J. F. (2003). Public attitudes toward immigrants and immigration: Determinants and policy implications. In C. M. Beach, A. G. Green, & J. G. Reitz (Eds.), *Canadian immigration policy for the 21st century* (pp. 507–535). Montreal, Canada: McGill Queen's Press.

Esses, V. M., Medianu, S., Hamilton, L., & Lapshina, N. (in press). Psychological perspectives on immigration and acculturation. In P. Shaver & M. Mikulincer (Eds.), *Handbook of personality and social psychology* (Vol. 2). American Psychological Association.

Esses, V. M., Veenvliet, S., Hodson, G., & Mihic, L. (2008). Justice, morality, and the dehumanization of refugees. *Social Justice Research, 21*, 4–25. doi: 10.1007/s11211-007-0058-4

Esses, V. M., Veenvliet, S., & Medianu, S. (2011). The dehumanization of refugees: Determinants and consequences. In S. Wiley, G. Philogene, & T. A. Revenson (Eds.), *Social categories in everyday experience* (pp. 133–150). Washington: APA Books. doi: 10.1037/13488-007

Federico, C. M., Hunt, C. V., & Fisher, E. L. (2013). Uncertainty and status-based asymmetries in the distinction between the "good" us and the "bad" them: Evidence that group status strengthens the relationship between the need for cognitive closure and extremity in intergroup differentiation. *Journal of Social Issues, 69*, 473–494.

Fiske, S. T., Cuddy, A. J. C., Glick, P., & Xu, J. (2002). A model of (often mixed) stereotype content: Competence and warmth respectively follow from perceived status and competition. *Journal of Personality and Social Psychology, 82*, 878–902. doi: 10.1037/0022-3514.82.6.878

Fleras, A., & Kunz, J. L. (2001). *Media and minorities: Representing diversity in multicultural Canada*. Toronto: Thompson.

Francis, D. (2001, May 15). Cities fight for fair refugee policies. *National Post*. Retrieved November 1, 2005, from www.dianefrancis.com/

German Marshall Fund of the United States. (2010). *Transatlantic trends: Immigration 2010*. Retrieved January 4, 2012, from http://trends.gmfus.org/immigration/doc/TTI2010_English_Key.pdf

Harris, L. T., & Fiske, S. T. (2006). Dehumanizing the lowest of the low: Neuro-imaging responses to extreme outgroups. *Psychological Science, 17*, 847–853. doi: 10.1111/j.1467-9280.2006.01793.x

Haslam, N. (2006). Dehumanization: An integrative review. *Personality and Social Psychology Review, 10*, 252–264. doi: 10.1207/s15327957pspr1003_4

Haslam, N., Loughnan, S., & Kashima, Y. (2008). Attributing and denying humanness to others. *European Review of Social Psychology, 19*, 55–85. doi: 10.1080/10463280801981645

Henry, F., & Tator, C. (2002). *Discourses of domination: Racial bias in the Canadian English-language press*. Toronto: University of Toronto Press.

Hier, S. P., & Greenberg, J. L. (2002). Constructing a discursive crisis: Risk, problematization and illegal Chinese in Canada. *Ethnic and Racial Studies, 25*, 490–531. doi: 10.1080/01419870020036701

Hogg, M. A. (2000). Subjective uncertainty reduction through self-categorization: A motivation theory of social identity processes. *European Review of Social Psychology, 11*, 223–255. doi: 10.1080/14792772043000040

Hogg, M. A., & Adelman, J. (2013). Uncertainty-identity theory: Extreme groups, radical behavior, and authoritarian leadership. *Journal of Social Issues, 69*, 436–454.

International Organization for Migration (2011). *About migration*. Retrieved January 15, 2011, from http://www.iom.int/jahia/Jahia/about-migration/lang/en

Islam in Europe. (2010). *Norway: Immigrants, Muslims portrayed negatively in the media*. Retrieved May 20, 2012, from http://islamineurope.blogspot.ca/2010/02/norway-immigrants-muslims-portrayed.html

Jost, J. T., & van der Toorn, J. (2012). System justification theory. In P. A. M. van Lange, A. W. Kruglanski, & E. T. Higgins (Eds.), *Handbook of theories of social psychology*. (Vol. 2, pp. 313–343). London: Sage.

Klocker, N., & Dunn, K. M. (2003). Who's driving the asylum debate? Newspaper and government representations of asylum seekers. *Media International Australia, 109*, 71–93.

Kruglanski, A. W., Pierro, A., Mannetti, L., & De Grada, E. (2006). Groups as epistemic providers: Need for closure and the unfolding of group-centrism. *Psychological Review, 113*, 84–100. doi: 10.1037/0033-295X.113.1.84

Lawson, A. S., & Esses, V. M. (2008, June). The competitive consequences of the association of immigrants with disease. *Paper presented at the bi-annual meeting of the Society for the Psychological Study of Social Issues*, Chicago, IL.

Leyens, J.-P., Demoulin, S., Vaes, J., Gaunt, R., & Paladino, M. P. (2007). Infra-humanization: The wall of group differences. *Social Issues and Policy Review, 1*, 139–172. doi: 10.1111/j.1751-2409.2007.00006.x

Leyens, J.-P., Paladino, P. M., Rodriguez-Torres, R., Vaes, J., Demoulin, S., Rodriguez-Perez, A., & Gaunt, R. (2000). The emotional side of prejudice: The attribution of secondary emotions to ingroups and outgroups. *Personality and Social Psychology Review, 4*, 186–197. doi: 10.1207/S15327957PSPR0402_06

Louis, W. R., Duck, J., Terry, D. J., Schuller, R., & Lalonde, R. (2007). Why do citizens want to keep refugees out? Threats, fairness, and hostile norms in the treatment of asylum seekers. *European Journal of Social Psychology, 37*, 53–73. doi: 10.1002/ejsp.329

Lynn, N., & Lea, S. (2003). A phantom menace and the new apartheid: The social construction of asylum-seekers in the United Kingdom. *Discourse and Society, 14*, 425–452. doi:10.1177/0957926503014004002

Mahtani, M., & Mountz, A. (2002). Immigration to British Columbia: Media representation and public opinion. *Metropolis Working Paper*. Retrieved June 1, 2012, from http://riim.metropolis.net/assets/uploads/files/wp/2002/WP02-15.pdf

McGregor, I., Zanna, M. P., Holmes, J. G., & Spencer, S. J. (2001). Compensatory conviction in the face of personal uncertainty: Going to extremes and being oneself. *Journal of Personality and Social Psychology, 80*, 472–488. doi: 10.1037/0022-3514.80.3.472

Medianu, S., Sutter, A., Esses, V. M., & Gawronski, B. (2013). *The role of the media in the automatic dehumanization of refugees*. Manuscript submitted for publication.

Opotow, S. (1995). Drawing the line: Social categorization, moral exclusion, and the scope of justice. In B. B. Bunker & J. Z. Rubin (Eds.), *Conflict, cooperation, and justice: Essays inspired by the work of Morton Deutsch* (pp. 347–379). San Francisco, CA: Jossey-Bass.

Roccato, M., & Ricolfi, L. (2005). On the correlation between right-wing authoritarianism and social dominance orientation. *Basic and Applied Social Psychology, 27*, 187–200. doi: 10.1207/s15324834basp2703_1

Schwartz, S. H., & Struch, N. (1989). Values, stereotypes, and intergroup antagonism. In D. Bar-Tal, C. G. Grauman, A. W. Kruglanski, & W. Stroebe (Eds.), *Stereotypes and prejudice: Changing conceptions* (pp. 151–167). New York: Springer-Verlag.

Schwartz, S. H., Struch, N., & Bilsky, W. (1990). Values and intergroup social motives: A study of Israeli and German students. *Social Psychology Quarterly, 53*, 185–198. doi: 10.2307/2786958

Shoemaker, P. J., & Vos, T. P. (2009). *Gatekeeping theory*. New York: Routledge.

Sidanius, J., & Pratto, F. (1999). *Social dominance: An intergroup theory of social hierarchy and oppression*. New York: Cambridge University Press.

Soroka, S., & McAdams, S. (2010). *An experimental study of the differential effects of positive versus negative news content*. Paper presented at the Elections, Public Opinion and Parties Annual Conference, Colchester, UK.

Struch, N., & Schwartz, S. H. (1989). Intergroup aggression: Its predictors and distinctness from in-group bias. *Journal of Personality and Social Psychology, 56*, 364–373. doi: 10.1037/0022-3514.56.3.364

Toews, V. (2010). Human smuggling and the abuse of Canada's refugee system. *Public Safety Canada*. Retrieved May 12, 2012, from http://www.publicsafety.gc.ca/media/sp/2010/sp20101021-eng.aspx

Verkuyten, M. (2004). Emotional reactions to and support for immigrant policies: Attributed responsibilities to categories of asylum seekers. *Social Justice Research, 17*, 293–314. doi: 10.1023/B:SORE.0000041295.83611.dc

Wittenbrink, B., & Schwarz, N. (Eds.). (2007). *Implicit measures of attitudes*. New York: Guilford Press.

VICTORIA M. ESSES is Professor of Psychology and Director of the Centre for Research on Migration and Ethnic Relations at the University of Western Ontario. She is Principal Investigator of the Pathways to Prosperity Partnership, a national, multidisciplinary network dedicated to promoting the settlement and integration of immigrants in Canada. In 2010, she was awarded the Harold Crabtree Foundation Award in Public Policy Research for her work in this area.

STELIAN MEDIANU is a PhD student in the Social Psychology program and the Collaborative Graduate Program in Migration and Ethnic Relations at the University of Western Ontario. His research interests are in the area of intergroup relations, dehumanization, attitude change, and mass media effects, with a particular emphasis on immigrants and refugees.

ANDREA S. LAWSON, PhD, is the Research Coordinator for the Psychiatry Department at Mount Sinai Hospital, Toronto. Current research interests include access to health care for vulnerable populations, the impact of stigma on health care seeking/discontinuation, and the relationship between early childhood experiences and health care utilization.

Anxious Uncertainty and Reactive Approach Motivation (RAM) for Religious, Idealistic, and Lifestyle Extremes

Ian McGregor*
York University, Canada

Mike Prentice
University of Missouri

Kyle Nash
York University, Canada

Reactive Approach Motivation (RAM) theory proposes that the personal uncertainty arising from motivational conflict causes anxiety, and that anxiety draws people to extremes because extremes activate approach-motivated states that automatically downregulate anxiety. Five new studies consolidate existing evidence for the RAM view of uncertainty-related threats and reactive extremism. In Studies 1–3, religious, idealistic, and RAM reactions after agentic, communal, and mortality threats were most extreme when threat-relevant goals had been implicitly primed to create motivational conflict. In Study 4 uncertainty predicted extreme reactions only if goal conflict had been experimentally manipulated. In Study 5 personal uncertainty uniquely predicted lifestyle extremes among undergraduates whose educational goals were conflicted by a labor disruption at their university. Results converge on the conclusion that uncertainty-related threats cause defensively extreme RAM reactions only if they arouse personal uncertainty about active goals. Results suggest that policies and programs to support the prosocial and/or

---

*Correspondence concerning this article should be addressed to Ian McGregor, Department of Psychology, York University, 4700 Keele Street, Toronto, Ontario M3J 1P3, Canada [e-mail: ianmc@yorku.ca].

This research was supported by grants from the Social Sciences and Humanities Research Council of Canada. We are grateful to So-Jin Kang and Susan Clark for data collection in Study 5.

nonextreme goals, ideals, and identifications of at-risk people would reduce their motivation for antisocial extremism.

Why do people go to extremes? Reactive Approach Motivation (RAM) theory proposes that eagerly engaging in religious, idealistic, or behavioral extremes provides an efficient and potent antidote to the experience of anxiety (McGregor, 2006; McGregor, Nash, Mann, & Phills, 2010). Anxiety arises when goal pursuit is impeded by conflict, frustration, or uncertainty (Gray & McNaughton, 2000; Hirsh, Mar, & Peterson, 2012). Religious, idealistic, and behavioral extremes are rewarding because they help people engage clearly approach-motivated states that automatically mute anxiety (McGregor, Nash, & Prentice, 2010; Nash, Inzlicht, & McGregor, 2012; Nash, McGregor, & Prentice, 2011). The RAM view is consistent with theories of terror management (Greenberg, Solomon, & Pyszczynski, 1997), lay epistemics (Kruglanski, 1989), uncertainty management (Hogg, 2012; McGregor, 2006; Van den Bos, 2009), compensatory control (Kay & Eibach, 2013), and meaning maintenance (Heine, Proulx, & Vohs, 2006; Proulx, Inzlicht, & Harmon-Jones, 2012; Proulx & Major, 2013). The contribution of RAM theory is that it parsimoniously explicates a neural and motivational process capable of integrating competing theoretical perspectives about the motivation for extremism without having to posit super-ordinate motivational constructs beyond the basic anxiety and approach-motivation systems that humans share with pigeons and fish.

The RAM view is guided by research on the Behavioral Inhibition System (BIS)—a motivational system humans share with other vertebrate animals. The BIS regulates motivational processes when goal progress is threatened by awareness of goal conflict or impedance, or by bewildering, novel, or obstructed terrain (Gray & McNaughton, 2000; Hirsh et al., 2012; Proulx et al., 2012). Under such conditions the BIS initiates an aroused and anxious vigilance that persists until a tenable alternative goal or means for the original goal resumes unconflicted engagement. Once clear engagement is resumed motivated attention again becomes constrained to task-relevant thoughts and perceptions, and inconsistent and distracting stimuli become automatically suppressed to facilitate goal completion (Harmon-Jones, Amodio, & Harmon-Jones, 2009; McGregor, 2006). With the resumption of clear, approach-motivated engagement, BIS-regulated anxiety is correspondingly relieved (Nash et al., 2012). This basic process can enable conflicted and bewildered organisms to pragmatically shift to alternative means in less fraught terrain in service of the original end (Kruglanski et al., 2002), but it is also conducive to palliative engagement in any alternative, unrelated goal that would be rewarding to the extent that it could be eagerly pursued without conflict.

Extreme absorption in idealistic or ideological goals may be a particularly attractive strategy for achieving such relief from anxious personal uncertainty. Ideational and behavioral extremes are similarly processed for humans. The same approach-motivation-related neural processes occur when adults think about the ideals that guide their lives (Amodio, Shah, Sigelman, Brazy, & Harmon-Jones, 2004) as when sugar is placed on a baby's tongue (Fox & Davidson, 1986). As different as they may seem the difference between the pursuit of ideals and sweets, from a goal-regulation perspective, is only in their level of abstraction. Ideals are abstract goals that can be promoted with the same kind of determination and eager absorption as concrete goals. Indeed, there is evidence that ideological goals may be particularly intuitive as vehicles for RAM relief from anxiety, perhaps because they tend to be pure and uncomplicated by ambivalent complexities and compromises (see Klein & Kruglanski, 2013). Idealistic goals seem to be the spontaneous lever people use to activate the sanguine relief of RAM (McGregor, Galliot, Vasquez, & Nash, 2007; McGregor, Nash, Mann, & Phills, 2010; McGregor, Nash, & Prentice, 2010; Nash et al., 2011).

In the present article, we review existing evidence for the front end (motivational conflict), middle (personal uncertainty/anxiety), and back end (approach motivation for extremes) of RAM theory. We then report results of five new experiments that further consolidate evidence for a RAM understanding of socially consequential forms of defensive extremism.

The Front End of RAM Theory: The Role of Motivational Conflict

Following Gray and McNaughton (2000) our starting premise is that the essential psychological trigger for personal uncertainty and anxiety is motivational conflict (see Hirsh et al., 2012). We recently published four studies demonstrating it is specifically motivational conflict imposed by uncertainty threats that arouses anxious-uncertainty, reactive ideology, and approach motivation. Those four studies demonstrated that achievement and relationship threats caused anxious, ideological, and approach-motivated reactions only when they conflicted with implicitly primed goals germane to the subsequent threats (Nash et al., 2011).

In the first study participants were randomly assigned to complete a scrambled sentence task that implicitly primed either achievement or relationship goals. They were then confronted with randomly assigned achievement or relationship threats. Participants felt significantly more anxious about each kind of threat when it was preceded by a relevant goal prime. In the second study the same combination of goal primes (this time primed with crossword puzzles) and same-domain uncertainty threats caused self-reported RAM in participants' personal goals in life. In the third study, an academic dilemma caused behavioral neuroscience evidence of RAM when preceded by the (crossword) achievement goal prime but not a neutral prime. In the fourth study, a relationship uncertainty threat caused ideological conviction when the relationship threat was preceded by the (scrambled sentence) relationship goal prime but not by the achievement goal prime. Moreover, this effect was eliminated among participants who had a randomly assigned chance to misattribute their anxiety to a mundane source.

Studies 1–3 in the present research extend these past goal-priming findings in several ways. Study 1 demonstrates for the first time that the same kind of implicitly primed achievement-goal conflicts can cause religious extremism. Study 2 demonstrates for the first time that implicitly primed goal conflict causes idealistically extreme reactions regardless of whether the prime precedes or follows the threat. Study 3 uses the same goal-priming logic to show that extreme reactions to mortality salience may also arise from motivational conflict.

As with agentic and communal threats, mortality salience threats have been linked to anxious uncertainty. In one study a randomly assigned mortality salience (vs. neutral) threat significantly heightened self-reported felt uncertainty as assessed by the items "bothered," "uneasy," "uncomfortable," "aroused," "excited," "anxious," but not general positive or negative affect (McGregor, Zanna, Holmes, & Spencer, 2001, Study 3). Moreover, personal uncertainty and mortality salience threats often have similar effects on a variety of defensive outcomes (Heine et al., 2006; McGregor, 2006; McGregor et al., 2001; Proulx et al., 2012; Van den Bos, Poortvliet, Maas, Miedema, & Van den Ham, 2005), and mortality salience effects on angry reaction are particularly strong among participants for whom mortality salience reminds them of uncertainty (Van den Bos, 2005, Study 3, Footnote 8; for an explanation of why mortality salience and other threats should be so fundamentally linked to personal uncertainty, see Hirsh et al., 2012; McGregor, 2006; Proulx et al., 2012). Detection of the anxious uncertainty elicited by mortality salience is often shrouded in research studies by the routine use of inadequate manipulation checks that are insensitive to the specific kind of affect related to uncertainty. Detection of uncertainty-related distress is also often hampered by routine assessment of affect immediately after mortality salience when both uncertainty and mortality concerns are momentarily suppressed (McGregor, Prentice, & Nash, 2009).

Personal uncertainty salience manipulations cause the same kinds of defensive reactions as mortality salience when they remind participants of important goal-relevant uncertainties more akin to insecurities than merely informational uncertainties. Original research on personal uncertainty demonstrated this by either plunging participants into thoughts about their real life goal dilemmas (McGregor et al., 2001) or requiring them to reflect on personal insecurities (Van den Bos, 2001)—in both cases participants reacted with the same kinds of extremism as after mortality salience (see also McGregor Prentice, & Nash, 2009; Van den Bos, 2009; Van den Bos et al., 2005).

Imprecise Dutch–English language translation has sometimes obscured this now well-established link between mortality salience and personal uncertainty (Pyszczynski, Greenberg, Solomon, & Maxfield, 2006). The Dutch word for uncertainty used in Dutch uncertainty-salience manipulations implies a grapply kind of personally insecure uncertainty. Dutch research that asks participants to describe their uncertain feelings is therefore asking participants to describe important personal uncertainties (akin to Hogg & Adelman, 2013). Mortality salience researchers have often failed to replicate the well-established personal uncertainty effect on outcomes related to extremism because they translate the Dutch manipulation of "personally uncertain" as merely the word, "uncertain." Mere informational uncertainty is too trivial to arouse anxiety and cause extreme reactions (see Van den Bos, 2009, for discussion of distinction between informational and personal uncertainty, and McGregor Prentice, & Nash, 2009 for empirical evidence for the translation effect).

The Middle of RAM Theory: Experienced Personal Uncertainty and Anxiety

There is reason to believe that anxious personal uncertainty may mediate the effects of various psychological threats on ideological and RAM reactions. Indeed, most of the threats that cause ideological and worldview defenses, including mortality salience, have been theoretically and empirically linked with personal uncertainty or anxiety (Nash et al., 2011; Proulx et al., 2012; Van den Bos et al., 2005). In our past research we have found that the mortality, dilemma, achievement, and relationship related uncertainty threats (the ones used in the present research) that have caused extreme ideological and RAM reactions also cause specific increases in self-reported personal uncertainty (but not general positive or negative affect; McGregor & Marigold, 2003; McGregor, Nash, & Inzlicht, 2009; McGregor, Nash, Mann, & Phills, 2010; McGregor, Nash, & Prentice, 2010; McGregor et al., 2001, Studies 1 and 2). Moreover, allowing participants to misattribute their uncertainty and anxiety to an external source eliminates ideological reactions to goal conflict (Nash et al., 2011) and to various other uncertainty-related threats that usually cause ideologically extreme reactions (reviewed in Nash et al., 2011). Still, evidence for the mediating role of personal uncertainty in idealistic and RAM reactions remains indirect. Accordingly, Studies 4 and 5 presented below provide more direct evidence for the unique role of personal uncertainty in idealistic and behavioral RAM reactions to goal conflict. Study 4 investigates whether self-reported personal uncertainty most strongly predicts extreme reactions when in the context of goal conflict, and Study 5 tests whether personal uncertainty specifically mediates behavioral lifestyle extremes in the context of real-life goal impedance.

The Back End of RAM Theory: Defensive Extremes are Approach-Motivated

There are now hundreds of published experiments demonstrating that a wide range of uncertainty-related perceptual, self, existential, and goal threats are capable of causing compensatory extremes in domains not closely linked to the domains of the threats (reviewed in Nash et al., 2011). There is also theoretical and empirical reason to believe that the extremism may be mediated by approach motivation (Hirsh et al., 2012; Marigold, McGregor, & Zanna, 2010; McGregor, 2006; Nash et al., 2011). Achievement and relationship threats, for example, have caused increased brain activity, perceptual bias, and implicit associations indicative of a reactive shift to generalized approach motivation (McGregor, Nash, Mann, & Phills, 2010). Relationship and mortality salience threats also cause research participants to shift toward pursuing more approach-motivated personal goals in life—a shift completely mediated by the extent to which those goals are idealistic and ideological (McGregor et al., 2007; McGregor, Nash, Mann, & Phills, 2010). Responses to achievement, relationship, and mortality threats are also often hostile, and anger is closely tied to approach motivation (Carver & Harmon-Jones, 2009). Moreover, approach-motivated personality traits consistently moderate idealistic, ideological, and approach-motivated reactions to agentic, communal, and mortality threats (McGregor et al., 2007; McGregor & Marigold, 2003; McGregor, Nail, Marigold, & Kang, 2005; McGregor, Nash, & Inzlicht, 2009; McGregor, Nash, & Prentice, 2010; Schmeichel et al., 2009). Study 5 of the present research fortifies the approach-motivation interpretation of defensive extremism by demonstrating that the personal uncertainty from a real-life goal disruption predicts a behavioral correlate of approach motivation—disinhibited, risky, and extreme lifestyle choices (Keltner, Gruenfeld, & Anderson, 2003; Smillie & Jackson, 2006; Smillie et al., 2006, Suhr & Tsanadis, 2007).

Study 1: Achievement Goal Conflict and Religious Idealism

Past research has found that an achievement uncertainty manipulation (requiring undergraduate psychology students to summarize an incomprehensible passage from a graduate structural equation modeling textbook) reliably causes a reactive surge in domain-nonspecific extremity, conviction, idealism, and approach motivation. Specifically, it has caused extremity and conviction for social issue opinions about capital punishment, abortion, and terrorism (McGregor et al., 2005; McGregor & Jordan, 2007); tenacious and idealistic devotion to personal goals (Nash et al., 2011) devotion and willingness to kill and die for idealistic religious beliefs (McGregor, Haji, Nash, & Teper, 2008; McGregor, Nash, & Prentice, 2010); electroencephalographic and behavioral neuroscience evidence of brain activity characteristic of approach motivation (McGregor, Nash, & Inzlicht, 2009; McGregor, Nash, Mann, & Phills, 2010; Nash, McGregor, & Inzlicht, 2010); and implicit associations of self with approach-related words and dissociations with avoidance-related words (McGregor, Nash, Mann, & Phills, 2010).

Other results suggest that such idealistic and eager reactions are specifically caused by motivational conflict. In two studies, the statistics-related achievement uncertainty manipulation only caused anxiety and RAM if an implicit achievement goal had first been primed, but not when a relationship goal had been primed (Nash et al., 2011). The present study accordingly tested for the first time whether extreme religious idealism after the same statistics-related achievement uncertainty manipulation might similarly depend on whether an implicit achievement goal had been primed. If so, extremes of religious idealism could more confidently be understood as being exacerbated by basic goal conflict.

Participants and Procedure

Sixty-two undergraduates (48 female) at a Canadian university participated for credit in their introductory psychology course. Four were excluded for incorrectly completing the materials, leaving 58 participants (45 females) for analyses (age, $M = 19.72$). Participants were preselected based on their identification with a religious belief system: Christian = 57%, Muslim = 22%, Hindu = 10%, Jewish = 3%, Buddhist = 2%, Other = 5%. Ethnic identifications of participants were: White = 40%, South Asian = 26%, Asian = 10%, Black = 7%, Arab = 5%, Latin American 3%, Other = 7%, Declined to Answer = 2%. In this diverse sample, 40% of the participants were born in a country other than Canada. More generally, in this student population 78% report identifying with one of the religious belief systems versus 22% identifying as agnostic or atheist. The religious, ethnic, and international diversity of this sample is typical of this student population in which approximately 80% of the students have one or both parents born in a country other than Canada (Studies 2–5 were drawn from this same population). Data were collected online in a single session and the materials were presented as a series of unrelated personality tasks and opinion questionnaires.

Materials

Goal primes. Participants completed a scrambled sentence task that implicitly primes goals (Bargh, Gollwitzer, Lee-Chai, Barndollar, & Troetschel, 2001). The task requires unscrambling of 16 sets of five words to form grammatical sentences. Participants were randomly assigned to either an achievement goal-prime or neutral prime condition. In the achievement goal-prime condition, eight of the sentences contained achievement related words (e.g., *strive, excellence*).

Achievement uncertainty manipulation. All participants were then randomly assigned to either the statistics achievement uncertainty condition from McGregor et al. (2005), described above, or a similar no-threat control condition in which participants summarized a simple passage underlining the utility of statistics in daily life.

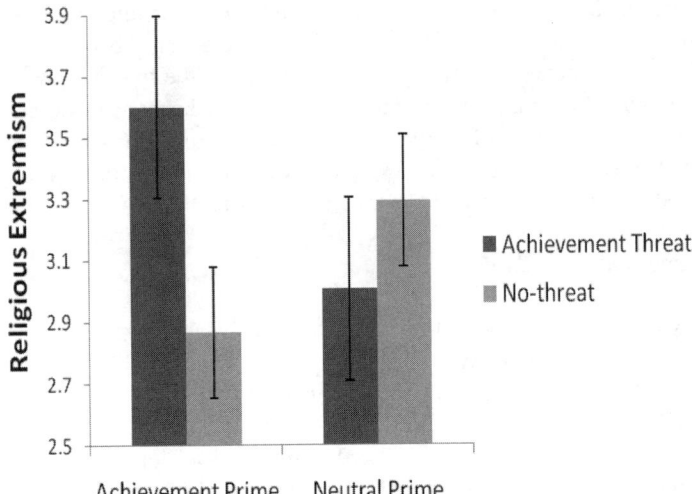

Fig. 1. Idealistic religious extremism as a function of goal prime and threat in Study 1.

Delay period and dependent measure of religious extremism. The delay task in this study instructed participants to let their minds wander for three minutes and record the topics that came to mind. Three minutes has been sufficient to allow for RAM and defensive extremes to emerge in past research (e.g., McGregor, Nash, Mann, & Phills, 2010). Participants then completed a 17-item religious extremism scale adapted from previous research (see McGregor, Nash, & Prentice, 2010, for 16 of the items). Participants rated their agreement on a 1–5 scale (from 1 = *strongly disagree* to 5 = *strongly agree*) with statements such as "My religious beliefs are grounded in objective truth," and "I would support a war that defended my religious beliefs." In this study we added a new item to explicitly tap willingness to engage in divinely inspired radical action, "If I was sincerely convinced that God wanted me to do something extreme, I would do it." The 17 items were averaged for an overall religious extremism score, $\alpha = .95$.

Results and Discussion

A 2 (Goal Prime: Achievement Prime vs. Neutral Prime) × 2 (Uncertainty Threat: Achievement Uncertainty vs. Low-Uncertainty) between-subjects ANOVA revealed a significant Goal Prime × Uncertainty Threat interaction effect, $F(1, 54) = 5.73$, $p < .05$, $\eta_p^2 = .10$ (see Figure 1). Planned pairwise comparisons revealed that Religious Extremism was higher in the Achievement Prime × Achievement Uncertainty condition ($M = 3.58$, $SD = .85$) than in either the Achievement Prime × Low-Uncertainty condition ($M = 2.85$, $SD = .64$),

$F(1, 54) = 5.68, p < .05, \eta_p^2 = .10$ or in the Neutral Prime × Achievement Uncertainty condition ($M = 2.93, SD = .80$), $F(1, 54) = 5.16, p < .05, \eta_p^2 = .09$. Although the sample size was too small to assess effects within specific religious affiliations, other research with larger samples indicates that religious RAM is a generic response across religious groups (McGregor, Nash, & Prentice, 2010; Schumann, McGregor, Nash, & Ross, 2013). Study 1 demonstrates that the uncertainty generated by frustrating an active achievement goal causes extreme religious idealism. This finding is consistent with past research showing that threats caused the most religiously extreme reactions among participants whose goals in life were not going well (McGregor, Nash, & Prentice, 2010).

Study 2: Relationship Goal Conflict and Personal Goal Conviction

Study 2 conceptually replicates and theoretically extends the results of Study 1 and the results presented in Nash et al. (2011). Specifically, in Study 2 the randomly assigned relevant or irrelevant goal primes were placed *after* the threats. We reasoned that priming a goal in the same domain as a previously threatened goal should arouse just as much goal conflict as priming a goal in the same domain as a subsequently threatened goal does. This is an important point because one possible critique of our goal priming work to date, in which goal primes have always preceded uncertainty threats, could be that the threat-irrelevant goal-primes somehow shield participants from fully experiencing the subsequent uncertainty threat. If so, then it would be premature to conclude, as we have elsewhere, that uncertainty-threat manipulations are consequential only to the extent that they raise the prospect of goal impedance. Positioning the goal prime after the threat ensures that all participants process the uncertainty-threat materials to the same extent, but that the uncertainty-threat becomes consequential only when it arouses motivational conflict.

Study 2 crossed randomly assigned achievement versus relationship goal primes with randomly assigned relationship uncertainty versus low uncertainty materials. In past research, the relationship uncertainty materials used in Study 2 caused compensatory conviction for opinions about capital punishment and abortion (McGregor & Marigold, 2003), implicit associations of self with approach and dissociations of self with avoidance motivation terms (McGregor, Nash, Mann, & Phills, 2010), and extreme religious devotion, including willingness to kill and die for one's religious belief system (McGregor, Nash, & Prentice, 2010). Other relationship uncertainty threats in our research have also caused ideological extremism about social issues and religious affiliations (McGregor et al., 2005; McGregor et al., 2008), and approach motivation and idealism in personal goals (McGregor, Nash, Mann, & Phills, 2010). Moreover, the exact relationship uncertainty manipulation used in Study 2 has caused the most self-reported anxious uncertainty, the most reactive approach motivation, and also the most compensatory conviction about an ideologically charged social issue (capital punishment) when *preceded* by a relationship goal prime (Nash et al., 2011).

The design for Study 2 was a between subjects 2 (Uncertainty Threat: Relationship Uncertainty vs. Low-Uncertainty Control) × 2 (Goal Prime: Achievement Prime vs. Belongingness Prime). The dependent variable focused on idealistic extremes in participants' personal goals. Contemplating ideals, a key component of an approach motivation mindset (Higgins, 1997), has been associated with approach-related EEG activity (Amodio et al., 2004). Further, idealistic and approach-motivated personal project dimensions are closely linked (McGregor et al., 2007; McGregor, Nash, Mann, & Phills, 2010). In Study 2 we accordingly predicted that priming a relationship goal after the relationship uncertainty manipulation would cause reactive approach for ideals in participants' personal projects.

Participants and Procedure

Undergraduates ($n = 112$) completed all study materials online in exchange for partial credit in an introductory psychology course (age, $M = 19.40$). Six who incorrectly completed the goal priming/threat materials were excluded from the analyses leaving 106 participants (83 female). Study materials were described to participants as pretest measures of personality and goals.

Materials

Relationship uncertainty manipulation. Participants were randomly assigned to complete either the relationship uncertainty or low-uncertainty materials from McGregor and Marigold (2003). In the relationship uncertainty condition participants nominated a close personal relationship that was currently not going very well, described the problems, and imagined the possibilities that the relationship would remain troubled or even get worse. In the low uncertainty condition participants nominated a friend's relationship that was not going very well and responded to the same questions about it.

Goal prime conditions. After completing the threat materials, participants were then randomly assigned to complete either the scrambled sentence achievement goal prime used in Study 1, or a matched relationship goal prime (with words such as *caring*). This task was completed immediately after the threat manipulation and served a dual role as the delay period.

Reactive idealistic approach. Participants then completed a personal projects analysis (Little, 1983) module in which they listed four central goals in their lives and rated them on eight dimensions. Along with the two approach dimensions from Nash et al. (2011), we included six dimensions related to tenacious and idealistic approach (from McGregor et al., 2007), including Determination (How firmly determined are you to complete it, even if it requires sacrifices?); Outcome (How likely are you to make this goal go as planned?); Value-Congruence (To what extent does it reflect the most important values that guide your life?); Conviction (How certain do you feel that this is a goal that you want to engage in?); Self-Identity (To what extent does it reflect the kind of person you really are, at your core?); and Control (To what extent do you feel in control of how this goal turns out?). Consistent with previous research (McGregor et al., 2007), a principal components analysis of the personal project dimension scores was unifactorial, explaining 61.4% of the variance, with all dimension loadings > .65. A reliability analysis of the eight dimension scores revealed good internal consistency, $\alpha = .91$. Thus, we created a unit-weighted dependent variable labeled Reactive Idealistic Approach.

Results and Discussion

We conducted a 2 (Uncertainty Threat: Relationship Uncertainty vs. Low Uncertainty) × 2 (Goal Prime: Achievement Prime vs. Relationship Prime) between-subjects ANOVA with Reactive Idealistic Approach as the dependent variable. There was a significant Uncertainty Threat × Goal Prime interaction effect, $F(1, 102) = 5.39, p < .05, \eta_p^2 = .05$. Planned pairwise comparisons revealed that Reactive Idealistic Approach was higher in the Relationship Uncertainty–Relationship Prime condition ($M = 5.83, SD = .65$) than in either the Low Uncertainty—Relationship Prime condition ($M = 5.39, SD = .67$), $F(1, 102) = 5.24, p < .05, \eta_p^2 = .05$ or in the Relationship Uncertainty–Achievement Prime condition ($M = 5.35, SD = .57$), $F(1, 102) = 6.82, p < .05, \eta_p^2 = .06$ (see Figure 2). Study 2 thus demonstrates that an uncertainty-related goal-conflict can cause an extreme reaction regardless of whether the goal prime precedes (Study 1) or follows (Study 2) the uncertainty threat.

Study 3: Priming Goals before Mortality Salience

Studies 1 and 2 demonstrate that people respond to uncertainty-related goal conflicts with reactive approach of religious, idealistic, and tenacious extremes. Mortality salience has caused very similar outcomes in research conducted over the past 25 years (see Burke, Martens, & Faucher, 2010 for a recent meta-analysis). Moreover, in our own research mortality salience has caused participants to surge toward ideals and personal meanings in the same way that other personal uncertainty threats have (McGregor et al., 2001; McGregor Prentice, & Nash, 2009; Schmeichel et al., 2009). Mortality salience has also caused participants to

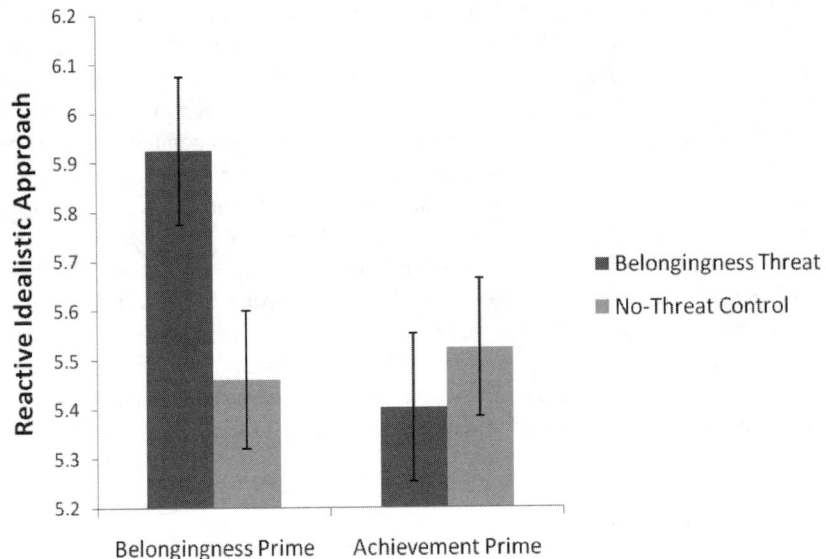

Fig. 2. Reactive idealistic approach as a function of goal prime and threat in Study 2.

exaggerate idealistic approach motivation in their personal goals on a dependent measure very close to the one used in Study 2 above (McGregor et al., 2007). According to our RAM view, mortality salience is such a powerful psychological threat because it is the ultimate source of goal conflict (death casts an uncertain shadow on all temporal goals—achievement and belongingness alike).

We tested this goal conflict account of mortality salience effects by randomly assigning participants to achievement goal, relationship goal, or neutral primes before they all completed the two-question mortality salience manipulation most frequently used in terror management theory research (Greenberg et al., 1997). They then completed a dependent measure that assessed the extent to which their personal goals were relatively more approach than avoidance motivated. Using a relative measure of approach motivation helps rule out the possibility that the results of Study 2 could reflect heightened motivation of any kind. We predicted greater RAM reactions after mortality salience in the goal prime conditions.

Participants and Procedure

Ninety-five undergraduates (58 female) participated for course credit (age, $M = 19.70$). Two participants were excluded from all analyses for incorrectly completing the materials, leaving 93 participants (57 female). The aim of the study was obscured as in Studies 1 and 2.

Materials

Goal prime. Participants were randomly assigned to either an achievement goal prime, relationship goal prime, or neutral prime condition. Goal-relevant words embedded in the achievement and belongingness priming tasks were similar to those of Studies 1 and 2. In the neutral priming condition, participants received a word-search puzzle with target words unrelated to normative goal constructs (e.g., *ranch*, and *hat*; Bargh et al., 2001).

Mortality salience. All participants then completed mortality salience materials. They were given 2 minutes for each of two questions that asked them (i) to describe the emotions that the thought of their own death arouses in them, and (ii) to describe their thoughts about what will happen to their bodies as they physically die (see Rosenblatt et al., 1989).

Delay period and relative approach motivation. Participants then completed the mind wander delay task used in Study 1 and a dependent measure of Relative Approach Motivation derived from participants' ratings of their four most self-characteristic personal projects on the two approach and two avoidance personal project dimensions from Nash et al. (2011, Study 2). The personal project approach and avoidance indices had satisfactory reliability αs of .73 and .78, respectively.

Results and Discussion

Following Nash et al. (2011) and Gable (2006), we created a difference score representing clear approach motivation by subtracting the avoidance average from the approach average to create the Relative Approach Motivation score. This score was then entered into a one-way ANOVA with the Goal Prime conditions as the between-group variable. The results revealed a significant ominibus $F(2, 90) = 3.22, p < .05, \eta^2_p = .07$. As predicted, planned comparisons revealed significantly lower Relative Approach Motivation in the Neutral Prime condition ($M = .26$, $SD = .92$) than in either the Achievement Prime condition ($M = .82, SD = 1.04$), $F(1, 90) = 4.58, p < .05, \eta^2_p = .05$ or the Belongingness Prime condition ($M = .86, SD = 1.05$), $F(1, 90) = 5.24, p < .05, \eta^2_p = .05$. The Achievement and Relationship Prime conditions did not differ ($F < 2$; see Figure 3). These results are consistent with the RAM view that mortality salience is particularly effective at inflaming defensive extremes because it undermines both agentic and communal goals alike.

Studies 1–3 support the front (motivational conflict) end of the RAM model. The most pronounced idealistic and tenacious RAM occurs when threat-relevant goals are primed. The results of Studies 1–3 also provide additional evidence

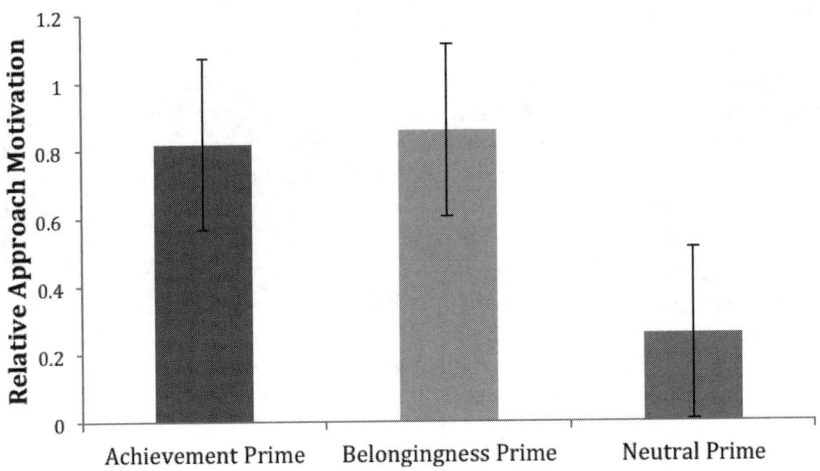

Fig. 3. Relative approach motivation after mortality salience as a function of goal prime in Study 3.

for the back (approach-motivation) end of the RAM model. If they undermine relevant goals, achievement, relationship, and mortality threats predict reactive approach-motivation for personal goals in life.

Study 4

Studies 4 and 5 probe the middle of the RAM model and focus on the mediating role of subjectively experienced personal uncertainty. Despite ample evidence of links between various threats and subjective personal uncertainty (Arndt & Goldenberg, 2002; Elliot & Devine, 1994; Nash et al., 2011; Van den Bos et al., 2005; Van Harreveld et al., 2009), evidence for mediation of the link between threat and defense by personal uncertainty has been elusive. Three issues likely account for difficulty in demonstrating the mediating role of personal uncertainty.

First, if the purpose of habitual defensive reactions is to block the experience of anxious uncertainty, then participants' self-reports might be unreliable. Indeed, threat researchers across theoretical orientations have repeatedly demonstrated that immediately after threat experiences, proximal defenses elevate positive affect and inhibit awareness of distressing thoughts and feelings (e.g., DeWall & Baumeister, 2007; Dodgson & Wood, 1998; Pyszczynski, Greenberg, & Solomon, 1999; Wichman et al., 2008). In our own research, we have accordingly been most successful in detecting effects of our threats on manipulation checks of personal uncertainty and anxiety after substantial delays. After 5 minutes participants seem able to report unpleasant feelings associated with prior threats (e.g., McGregor et al., 2001; Nash et al., 2011).

Second, the Positive and Negative Affect Scales (PANAS; Watson, Clark, & Tellegen, 1988) are typically used to measure negative affect after threats, but they are not well suited to detecting feelings related to personal uncertainty and anxiety. Based on the RAM premise of specific links between motivational conflict, personal uncertainty, and anxiety, we use a 19-item personal uncertainty scale to specifically assess anxious and uncertain feelings. Uncertainty-related threats have specifically increased personal uncertainty on this scale, but had no effect on positive or negative PANAS scales or on state self-esteem (McGregor et al., 2001; McGregor & Marigold, 2003). Other, shorter manipulation checks of personal uncertainty, focusing on adjectives such as *bothered*, *uneasy*, and *uncomfortable* (Elliot & Devine, 1994), or *uncertain*, *anxious*, and *frustrated* have also been affected by the uncertainty threats like those in Studies 1 and 2 in the present research (McGregor et al., 2001; McGregor, Nash, & Inzlicht, 2009; McGregor, Nash, Mann, & Phills, 2010; Nash et al., 2011).

A third limitation of past research attempting to demonstrate that personal uncertainty mediates the effects of threats on reactive defenses is that scales targeting feelings related to uncertainty often fail to differentiate between informational uncertainty and personal uncertainty. People are willing to report feeling confused, uncertain, and ambivalent about circumstances or scenarios that are not closely linked to the self or important personal goals. For example, many of us might readily admit to feeling highly confused and uncertain about quantum physics or the life-cycle of a newt, but as these domains of knowledge have little bearing on our salient goals in life, such informational uncertainties do not cause defensive reactions (Van den Bos, 2009; empirical demonstration by McGregor, Prentice, & Nash, 2009). Indeed, informational uncertainty tends to have the opposite effect. It spurs scrutiny and vigilant analysis of specific, concrete information at hand, which *decreases* heuristic and idealistic judgments (e.g., Weary, Jacobson, Edwards, & Tobin, 2001). Moreover, in nonthreatening circumstances, low informational uncertainty increases personal confidence and reliance on heuristic and ego-centric judgments (e.g., Petty, Briñol, & Tormala, 2002). It is this kind of informational uncertainty that participants in no-threat control conditions are likely inclined to report on self-report uncertainty scales.

In contrast, in uncertainty threat conditions, when uncertainty is experienced in contexts that are consequential for important personal goals, there is a reverse tendency for the (now personal) uncertainty to defensively boost ego-centric, heuristic, and ideological judgments (McGregor, Prentice, & Nash, 2009; Van den Bos et al., 2005). Under these conditions of more threatening personal uncertainty, self-reports on uncertainty-affect scales will reflect the more insecurity-related kinds of uncertainty that should be correlated with defensive reactions. Accordingly, with these different interpretations of uncertainty in the control and experimental conditions, experimental designs that experimentally manipulate personal uncertainty and then assess uncertainty-related affect on a self-report scale are not well equipped to detect statistical mediation (Spencer, Zanna, & Fong, 2005).

In such circumstances, a better test of the role of personal uncertainty would be a statistical test of *moderation*. A statistical test of moderation would assess the significance of differences between the uncertainty-extremism slopes in personal uncertainty (i.e., personal goal relevant) versus merely informational uncertainty circumstances. A positive slope would be expected in the personal-goal-relevant, and a negative slope would be expected in the personal-goal-irrelevant condition (see Haas & Cunningham, in press, for a similar application of this technique). Study 4 accordingly tests the moderational hypothesis that self-reported uncertainty should differentially predict ideological extremes in randomly assigned personal-goal-relevant (i.e., personal uncertainty) versus personal-goal-irrelevant (i.e., informational uncertainty) uncertain circumstances.

Participants and Procedures

Fifty-six female and 17 male undergraduates participated for course credit (age, $M = 20.18$). They first completed randomly assigned personal uncertainty versus informational uncertainty materials. They then completed ten minutes worth of neutral filler materials that provided the substantial delay after the threat. After the delay participants completed the Felt Uncertainty scale, the negative affect subscale of the PANAS (Watson et al., 1988), and then the dependent measure of ideological conviction.

Materials

Personal uncertainty manipulation. In the personal uncertainty condition participants answered several questions about the conflicting goals and values associated with a current difficult dilemma in their lives. They were instructed that the dilemma should be complex and should take the form of "Should I . . . or not?" After naming the dilemma they further summarized the conflicting personal values associated with the dilemma's conflicting sides, and then speculated about consequences of acting in either direction. In the informational uncertainty condition participants instead answered similar questions about a friends' dilemma (materials from McGregor et al., 2001).

Felt uncertainty and negative affect. The Felt Uncertainty scale contains 19 items drawn from the dissonance, ambivalence, and self-discrepancy literatures that target conflict-related discomfort: *mixed, uneasy, torn, bothered, preoccupied, confused, unsure of self or goals, contradictory, distractible, unclear, of two minds, muddled, restless, confused about identity, jumbled, uncomfortable, conflicted, indecisive, and chaotic*, $\alpha = .89$. The personal uncertainty manipulation described

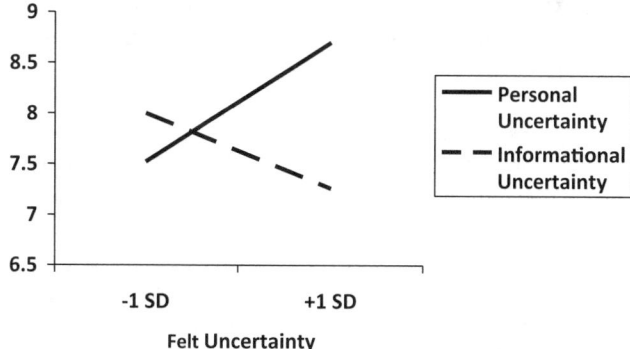

Fig. 4. Effect of experimentally manipulated personal uncertainty on extreme opinion conviction in Study 4.

above has significantly increased scores on this measure in past research (McGregor et al., 2001). This measure has never before been tested, however, as a possible moderator of extreme reactions to uncertainty threats. For comparison, the Negative Affect Scale (of the PANAS; Watson et al., 1988) assessed general and negative affect, $\alpha = .75$. On both measures participants rated each adjective or phrase on a scale from 1 (not at all) to 5 (extremely) with respect to how they felt at the moment.

Ideological conviction. Participants rated extremity of conviction for their opinions about capital punishment and abortion (as in McGregor & Marigold, 2003). For each issue, participants viewed a list of 14 diverse opinion statements from across the ideological spectrum, selected the single opinion they agreed with most, and then rated it on four questions that asked about firmness, strength, certainty, and willingness to defend the position in an argument. These four items across the two issues were averaged for an 8-item Conviction index, $\alpha = .90$.

Results and Discussion

For the main analysis we regressed Conviction on effect-coded Personal Uncertainty (Own Dilemma vs. Friend's Dilemma), mean-centered Felt Uncertainty, and the Personal Uncertainty × Felt Uncertainty interaction term (following the procedure advocated by Aiken & West, 1991). Results shown in Figure 4 depict the Personal Uncertainty × Felt Uncertainty interaction effect, $Beta = .31$, $t(69) = 2.78$, $p < .01$, with most extreme Conviction among participants in the Own Dilemma condition who reported the highest Felt Uncertainty. In contrast, Negative Affect did not significantly interact with the Personal Uncertainty manipulation to predict Conviction ($|t| < 1$; main effect of negative affect also nonsignificant). Moreover, when Negative Affect and its interactions with the Personal Uncertainty manipulation were included in the regression equation, the Personal Uncertainty × Felt Uncertainty interaction remained significant, $t(67) = 3.99, p < .001$.

Simple effect analyses (conducted with the experimental variable dummy coded, as recommended by Aiken & West, 1991) within the Personal Uncertainty × Felt Uncertainty interaction revealed predicted values such that in the Own Dilemma (i.e., personal uncertainty) condition there was significantly more extreme Conviction among participants who reported feeling relatively high Felt Uncertainty ($y' = 8.70$) than among those who reported relatively low Felt Uncertainty ($y' = 7.52$), $Beta = .39, t(69) = 2.55, p = .01$. In contrast, in the Friend's Dilemma (i.e., informational uncertainty) condition there was a nonsignificant relation between Felt Uncertainty and Conviction extremity in the opposite direction, $Beta = -.25, t(69) = 1.45, p = .15$. Looking at the simple effects from another angle, among participants who reported feeling relatively high Felt Uncertainty there was significantly more extreme Conviction in the Own Dilemma condition ($y' = 8.70$) than in Friend's Dilemma condition ($y' = 7.26$), $Beta = .48, t(69) = 2.94, p < .01$. In contrast, however, among participants who reported feeling relatively low Felt Uncertainty here was no difference in extremity of Conviction between conditions, $Beta = -.16, t(69) = 1.01, p = .32$.

These results indicate that under circumstances of personal uncertainty (i.e., related to self-relevant, motivational conflict), felt uncertainty is the specific kind of negative affect that uniquely predicts ideological extremes. It is important to note that participants had viewed a list of 14 diverse opinions about the ideologically charged social issues just before rating conviction for them. Even with full awareness of diverse social opinions participants still endorsed extreme conviction ratings of almost 9 out of a possible score of 10.

Study 5

Study 5 was designed to conceptually replicate the results of Study 4 with a more behavioral form of lifestyle RAM. Lifestyle RAM should be associated with disinhibited and extreme outcomes because approach motivation and related constructs are associated with disinhibition, impulsivity, and risk-taking (Galinsky, Gruenfeld, & Magee, 2003; Knoch et al., 2006; Smillie & Jackson, 2006; Smillie et al., 2006; Suhr & Tsanadis, 2007; Zuckerman & Kuhlman, 2000; see also Hirsh et al., 2012). We used lifestyle RAM as the dependent variable in a retrospective correlational study about feelings and actions during a major goal impedance in real life—a prolonged labor dispute that disrupted university students' academic goals and put their school year in jeopardy. For the measure of lifestyle RAM, we assessed self-reported increases in eating, appearance change, use of alcohol, tobacco, and drugs, and relationship conflict and change.

Participants and Procedures

Data were retrospectively collected from students at the end of an academic year (in March) that had been disrupted by a strike for 11 weeks from November to January. Picket lines had obstructed undergraduates from getting to their classes and many classes had been cancelled. It had been uncertain how long the strike would persist, and whether the academic year might be lost completely. Affected undergraduates (254 women, 104 men) between the ages of 18 and 22 (age, $M = 20.17$) completed a web survey that assessed recollections of uncertainty, negative affect, and the extent to which, during the strike, they had initiated changes in their appearance, eating, smoking, drinking, drug-taking, relationship conflict, and relationship status.

Materials

Felt uncertainty and negative affect. Participants rated the feelings they recalled having during the strike on the measures from Study 4 of Felt Uncertainty, $\alpha = .86$, and Negative Affect, $\alpha = 80$.

Lifestyle RAM. Participants' reported the extent to which, compared to their normal tendency, they changed their appearance (e.g., piercings, tattoos, hairstyles), ate more food, drank more alcohol, smoked more tobacco, used more illicit drugs, fought more in their relationships, and considered or made radical changes in their relationships. They made their ratings on a scale from $1 = less\ than\ usual$, $2 = same\ as\ usual$, $3 = a\ little\ more\ than\ usual$, $4 = more\ than\ usual$, to $5 = a\ lot\ more\ than\ usual$. Ratings were averaged to create a composite index of Lifestyle RAM, $\alpha = .67$.

Participants could also choose a "not applicable" response if a particular item was not relevant to them. Not applicable responses were given by 17 participants for the eating item, 69 for the alcohol item, 182 for the smoking item, 170 for the drug-taking item, 2 for the relationship conflict item, and 1 for the relationship change item. Ratings across applicable scores were averaged to create a composite, cross-domain index of Lifestyle RAM. A subset of 188 participants considered all domains applicable and rated all items. Our primary analysis focused on this subset.

Covariates included to assess third-variable explanations. Participants indicated their gender and answered (1) three questions related to the extent to which they felt bored during the strike, (2) two questions related to the extent to which they remained presently distressed about the strike, (3) two questions about how much social contact relative to usual they had with friends and relationship partners during the strike, (4) two questions about loss of respect for their university due to the strike, and (5) face-valid, single item measures of dispositional Neuroticism, Extraversion, Openness, Agreeableness, and Conscientiousness.

Results and Discussion

The Lifestyle RAM, Felt Uncertainty, and Negative Affect scales had respective item means of 2.54, 3.51, and 3.61 out of 5. For the primary analysis, we regressed Lifestyle RAM on Felt Uncertainty and Negative Affect, along with the covariates.

Felt Uncertainty (and none of the covariates) significantly predicted Lifestyle RAM, $Beta = .27$, $t(173) = 2.53$, $p = .01$. Negative Affect did not, $Beta = .06$, $t(173) = 2.57$, $p = .57$. When this analysis was conducted on all participants, including those who rated some of the domains as not applicable, there was still a significant relation of Lifestyle RAM with Felt Uncertainty, $Beta = .15$, $t(384) = 1.96$, $p = .05$, but not with Negative Affect, $Beta = .02$, $t(384) < 1$. The specific effects for felt uncertainty but not for negative affect are consistent with the finding in Study 4 that felt uncertainty is specifically linked to RAM.

It should also be noted that the markers of lifestyle RAM in Study 5 were not intended to comprehensively represent all possible manifestations of RAM. For example, had we measured prosocial, public, or even trait-scale disinhibitions we would likely have detected an increase in them as well (as in Cavallo, Fitzsimmons, & Holmes, 2009; Galinsky et al., 2003; Van den Bos et al., 2009; Van den Bos et al., 2011). The relation between felt uncertainty and lifestyle RAM did not likely result from participants guessing the hypothesis and venting their frustration about the strike by exaggerating the extent to which it caused them to do unusual things. Such demand characteristics would presumably not be specific to felt uncertainty (they would also show up for negative affect). The results were also not due to third-variable confounds arising from boredom, residual distress, more frequent social contact, loss of institutional respect, or the dispositional covariates that we measured. None of the covariates significantly predicted lifestyle RAM.

General Discussion

The results of Studies 1–5 are consistent with the RAM view that uncertainty arising from motivational conflict spurs religious, idealistic, and behavioral extremes in order to mobilize sanguine, approach motivated states. In Studies 1–3 experimentally induced personal uncertainty about active goals caused various forms of RAM, and in Study 4 experimentally manipulated personal uncertainty interacted with felt-uncertainty to cause extreme conviction for opinions about capital punishment and abortion, even when negative affect was statistically controlled. Study 5, conducted in the context of a major goal disruption, found similarly specific links between retrospectively reported felt-uncertainty, and lifestyle RAM.

The finding in Study 5 that lifestyle RAM was specifically predicted by uncertainty, just as ideological conviction was in Study 4, provides additional support for the goal-regulation account of reactive extremism and may help explain the appeal of the radical action agendas of extremist groups (Hogg & Adelman, 2013). Until now, the RAM account has been based primarily on evidence of extreme ideals, ideologies, and intentions after experimentally induced threats. The Study 5 findings provide converging goal-(dys)regulation evidence for more concrete forms of RAM. Together with other RAM findings, Study 5 is consistent with the observation that the extremes aroused by personal uncertainty do not need to be aggressive or interpersonally hostile (Proulx & Major, 2013). For relief from anxiety, any extreme will presumably do.

The results of Studies 1–5 consolidate more comprehensive support for the claim that uncertainty-related achievement, relationship, and mortality threats cause religious, ideological, and behavioral extremes to the extent that they confront people with motivational conflicts. The present research relied on self-report measures of approach motivation and anxiety, however. Future research should assess neural measures of RAM (e.g., left frontal asymmetry) and anxiety (e.g., magnitude of startle reactions) after manipulation of various forms of threat and during measurement of various forms of extremism. Doing so could more clearly reveal that extremes mediated by basic approach-motivated brain states function to relieve anxiety. This approach might be a particularly fruitful strategy for determining the extent to which the RAM view is consistent with meaning-making, compensatory control, and group-based interpretations of extremism (Hogg & Adelman, 2013; Kay & Eibach, 2013; Proulx & Major, 2013).

From the RAM perspective, external control threats and perceptual anomalies would signal that the terrain might not be conducive to goal pursuit, and anxiety would result. Restoration of external control, perceptual clarity, or group membership would relieve the eliciting anxiety by restoring the green-light for approach motivation either directly by one's own actions or vicariously through identification with potent groups. Future research should implicitly prime goals before external control or perceptual anomaly threats to see if compensatory reactions to these external uncertainty threats (i.e., discrepancies and randomness) are also amplified by goal pursuit. If so, meaning maintenance and compensatory control theories would fit compatibly with the goal-regulation assumptions of RAM theory.

Future research should also explore the potential for directing RAM reactions toward prosocial "extremes," even in the context of religious extremism. Uncertainty and religion are ubiquitous and if RAM reactions to uncertainty are as primitive and reflexive as we propose then managing extremism could benefit from efforts to orient and direct as well as mute religiously extreme reactions. Compensatory control research (Shepherd, Kay, Landau, & Keefer, 2011) suggests the domain of compensatory reactions is constrained by primes that are salient in the threatening environment. Other research indicates that salient prosocial and religious norms can also prime people to react prosocially after uncertainty-related threats (Gailliot et al., 2008; Schumann et al., 2013). These findings suggest that counter-extremism efforts should focus on redirecting as well as muting extremism. Still, to the extent that RAM theory exposes the motivational foundation for uncertainty threat and defense processes, populations at risk for extremism might benefit from policies and programs that facilitate progress in basic achievement and relationship goals in life (Sheldon, Ryan, Deci, & Kasser, 2004). Indeed, in a previous study we found most reactive religious extremism among participants whose personal goals in life were frustrated (McGregor, Nash, & Prentice, 2010; see also Martin, 1999).

Social justice is a basic form of goal facilitation that could help mute the motivation for extremism (Fiske, 2013). People who are low in power are especially sensitive to the extent to which their goals are supported by just and reliable social systems (Laurin, Fitzsimons, & Kay, 2011). Fair treatment of new immigrants might go a long way to making them feel able to accomplish their goals in a welcoming society, and be therefore less inclined toward extremism as a lever for active and idealistic RAM (cf. Doosje, Loseman, & Van den Bos, 2013; Esses, Medianu, & Lawson, 2013).

Finally, RAM theory may help explain why expressing ones guiding values in life eliminates diverse defensive reactions and worldview extremes after various threats (e.g., McGregor et al., 2001; Schmeichel & Martens, 2005; Sherman & Cohen, 2006). Value affirmations may supplant defenses by preemptively activating approach motivation for the values (which, from a goal regulation perspective, are abstract goals that people promote/approach). Policies aimed at relieving motivation for extremism should accordingly support opportunities for prosocial value expression. One natural way to facilitate value expression might be to encourage identification and engagement with the values of prosocial groups and causes (e.g., ethnic, religious; cf. Hogg, 2012). Group affirmations can provide powerful immunity against the anxieties arising from more concrete goal conflicts (McGregor et al., 2005, Study 4; and perhaps especially groups with an empowered action agenda, see Hogg & Adelman, 2013). Indeed, giving participants the chance to write about meaningful ethnic and religious group memberships has eliminated outgroup derogation reactions to uncertainty just as effectively as affirming personal worth and values (McGregor, Haji, & Kang, 2008; see also Doosje et al., 2013 for a negative relation between ingroup identification and extremism). In at-risk populations, however, care would have to be taken to discourage jingoistic in-group superiority and status comparisons that could inflame extremism (Doosje et al., 2013).

References

Aiken, L. S., & West, S. G. (1991). *Multiple regression: Testing and interpreting interactions.* Thousand Oaks, CA: Sage.

Amodio, D. M., Shah, J. Y., Sigelman, H., Brazy, P. C., & Harmon-Jones, E. (2004). Implicit regulatory focus associated with asymmetrical frontal cortical activity. *Journal of Experimental Social Psychology, 40,* 225–232. doi: 10.1016/S0022-1031(03)00100-8

Arndt, J., & Goldenberg, J. L. (2002). From threat to sweat: The role of physiological arousal in the motivation to maintain self-esteem. In A. Tesser, D. A. Stapel, and J. V. Wood (Eds.), *Self and motivation: Emerging psychological perspectives* (pp. 43–70). Washington, DC: American Psychological Association. doi: 10.1037/10448-002

Bargh, J. A., Gollwitzer, P. M., Lee-Chai, A., Barndollar, K., & Troetschel, R. (2001). The automated will: Nonconscious activation and pursuit of behavioral goals. *Journal of Personality and Social Psychology, 81,* 1014–1027. doi: 10.1037/0022-3514.81.6.1014

Burke, B. L., Martens, A., & Faucher, E. H. (2010). Two decades of terror management research: A meta-analysis of mortality salience research. *Personality and Social Psychology Review, 14,* 155–195. doi: 10.1177/1088868309352321

Carver, C. S., & Harmon-Jones, E. (2009). Anger is an approach-related affect: Evidence and implications. *Psychological Bulletin, 135,* 183–204. doi: 10.1177/1088868309352321

Cavallo, J. V., Fitzsimons, G. M., & Holmes, J. G. (2009). Taking chances in the face of threat: Romantic risk regulation and approach motivation. *Personality and Social Psychological Bulletin, 35,* 737–751. doi: 10.1177/0146167209332742

DeWall, C. N., & Baumeister, R. F. (2007). From terror to joy: Automatic tuning to positive affective information following mortality salience. *Psychological Science, 18,* 984–990. doi: 10.1111/j.1467-9280.2007.02013.x

Dodgson, P. G., & Wood, J. V. (1998). Self-Esteem and the cognitive accessibility of strengths and weaknesses after failure. *Journal of Personality and Social Psychology, 75,* 178–197. doi: 10.1037/0022-3514.75.1.178

Doosje, B., Loseman, A. & Van den Bos, K. (2013). Determinants of radicalization of Islamic youth in the Netherlands: Personal uncertainty, perceived injustice, and perceived group threat. *Journal of Social Issues, 69,* 586–604.

Elliot, A. J., & Devine, P. G. (1994). On the motivational nature of cognitive dissonance: Dissonance as psychological discomfort. *Journal of Personality and Social Psychology, 67,* 382–394. doi: 10.1037/0022-3514.67.3.382

Esses, V. M., Medianu, S., & Lawson, A. S. (2013). Uncertainty, threat, and the role of the media in promoting the dehumanization of immigrants and refugees. *Journal of Social Issues, 69,* 518–536.

Fiske, S. T. (2013). A millennial challenge: Extremism in uncertain times. *Journal of Social Issues, 69,* 605–613.

Fox, N. A., & Davidson, R. J. (1986). Taste elicited changes in facial signs of emotion and the asymmetry of brain electrical activity in human newborns. *Neuropsychologia, 24,* 417–422. doi: 10.1016/0028-3932(86)90028-X

Gable, S. L. (2006). Approach and avoidance social motives and goals. *Journal of Personality, 74,* 175–222. doi: 10.1111/j.1467-6494.2005.00373.x

Gailliot, M. T., Stillman, T. F., Schmeichel, B. J., Maner, J. K., & Plant, A. (2008). Mortality salience increases adherence to salient norms and values. *Personality and Social Psychology Bulletin, 34,* 993–1003.

Galinsky, A. D., Gruenfeld, D. H., & Magee, J. C. (2003). From power to action. *Journal of Personality and Social Psychology, 85,* 453–466. doi: 10.1037/0022-3514.85.3.453

Gray, J. A., & McNaughton, N. (2000). *The neuropsychology of anxiety: An enquiry into the functions of the septo-hippocampal system.* New York: Oxford University Press.

Greenberg, J., Solomon, S., & Pyszczynski, T. (1997). Terror management theory of self-esteem and cultural worldviews: Empirical assessments and conceptual refinements. In M. P. Zanna (Ed.), *Advances in experimental social psychology* (pp. 61–139). San Diego, CA: Academic Press. doi: 10.1016/S0065-2601(08)60016-7

Haas, I. J., & Cunningham, W. A. (2013). The uncertainty paradox: Perceived threat moderates the effect of uncertainty on political tolerance. *Political Psychology*. doi: 10.1111/pops.12035

Harmon-Jones, E., Amodio, D. M., & Harmon-Jones, C. (2009). Action-based model of dissonance: A review, integration, and expansion of conceptions of cognitive conflict. In M. P. Zanna (Ed.) *Advances in experimental social psychology* (Vol. 41, pp. 119–166). Burlington, MA: Academic Press. doi: 10.1016/S0065-2601(08)00403-6

Heine, S. J., Proulx, T., & Vohs, K. D. (2006). The meaning maintenance model: On the coherence of social motivations. *Personality and Social Psychology Review*, *10*, 88–110. doi: 10.1207/s15327957pspr1002_1

Higgins, E. T. (1997). Beyond pleasure and pain. *American Psychologist*, *52*, 1280–1300. doi: 10.1037/0003-066X.52.12.1280

Hirsh, J. B., Mar, R. A., & Peterson, J. B. (2012). Psychological entropy: A framework for understanding uncertainty-related anxiety. *Psychological Review*, *119*, 304–320. doi: 10.1037/a0026767

Hogg, M. A. (2012). Uncertainty-identity theory. In P. A. M. Van Lange, A. W. Kruglanski, & E. T. Higgins (Eds.), *Handbook of theories of social psychology* (pp. 62–80). Thousand Oaks, CA: Sage. doi: 10.1016/S0065-2601(06)39002-8

Hogg, M. A., & Adelman, J. (2013). Uncertainty-identity theory: Extreme groups, radical behavior, and authoritarian leadership. *Journal of Social Issues*, *69*, 436–454.

Kay, A. C., & Eibach, R. P. (2013). Compensatory control and its implications for ideological extremism. *Journal of Social Issues*, *69*, 564–585.

Keltner, D., Gruenfeld, D. H., & Anderson, C. (2003). Power, approach, and inhibition. *Psychological Review*, *110*, 265–284. doi: 10.1037/0033-295X.110.2.265

Klein, K. M., & Kruglanski, A. W. (2013). Commitment and extremism: A goal systemic analysis. *Journal of Social Issues*, *69*, 419–435.

Knoch, D., Gianotti, L. R. R., Pascual-Leone, A., Treyer, V., Regard, M., Hohmann, M., & Brugger, P. (2006). Disruption of right prefrontal cortex by low-frequency repetitive transcranial magnetic stimulation induces risk-taking behavior. *Journal of Neuroscience*, *26*, 6469–6472. doi: 10.1523/JNEUROSCI.0804-06.2006

Kruglanski, A. W. (1989). *Lay epistemics and human knowledge: Cognitive and motivational bases*. New York: Plenum Press.

Kruglanski, A. W., Shah, J. Y., Fishbach, A., Friedman, R., Chun, W. Y., & Sleeth-Keppler, D. (2002). A theory of goal systems. In M. P. Zanna (Ed.), *Advances in experimental social psychology* (Vol. 34, pp. 331–378). San Diego, CA: Academic Press. doi.org/10.1016/S0065-2601(02)80008-9

Laurin, K., Fitzsimons, G. M., & Kay, A. C. (2011). Social disadvantage and the self-regulatory function of justice beliefs. *Journal of Personality and Social Psychology*, *100*, 149. doi: 10.1037/a0021343

Little, B. R. (1983). Personal projects: A rationale and method for investigation. *Environment and Behavior*, *15*, 273–309. doi: 10.1177/0013916583153002

Marigold, D. C., McGregor, I., & Zanna, M. P. (2010). Defensive conviction as emotion regulation: Goal mechanisms and relationship implications. In R. M. Arkin, K. C. Oleson, & P. J. Carroll (Eds.). *The uncertain self: A handbook of perspectives from social and personality psychology* (pp. 232–248). Mahwah, NJ: Lawrence Erlbaum Associates.

Martin, L. L. (1999). I-D compensation theory: Some implications of trying to satisfy immediate-return needs in a delayed-return culture. *Psychological Inquiry*, *10*, 195–209.

McGregor, I. (2006). Offensive defensiveness: Toward an integrative neuroscience of compensatory zeal after mortality salience, personal uncertainty, and other poignant self-threats. *Psychological Inquiry*, *17*, 299–308. doi: 10.1080/10478400701366977

McGregor, I., Gailliot, M. T., Vasquez, N. A., & Nash, K. A. (2007). Ideological and personal zeal reactions to threat among people with high self-esteem: Motivated promotion focus. *Personality and Social Psychology Bulletin*, *33*, 1587–1599. doi: 10.1177/0146167207306280

McGregor, I., Haji, R., & Kang, S-J. (2008). Can ingroup affirmation relieve outgroup derogation? *Journal of Experimental Social Psychology*, *44*, 1395–1401. doi: 10.1016/j.jesp.2008.06.001

McGregor, I., Haji, R., Nash, K. A., & Teper, R. (2008). Religious zeal and the uncertain self. *Basic and Applied Social Psychology*, *30*, 183–188. doi: 10.1080/01973530802209251

McGregor, I., & Jordan, C. H. (2007). The mask of zeal: Low implicit self-esteem, threat, and defensive extremism. *Self and Identity, 6*, 223–237. doi: 10.1080/15298860601115351

McGregor, I., & Marigold, D. C. (2003). Defensive zeal and the uncertain self: What makes you so sure? *Journal of Personality and Social Psychology, 85*, 838–852. doi: 10.1037/0022-3514.85.5.838

McGregor, I., Nail, P. R., Marigold, D. C., & Kang, S.-J. (2005). Defensive pride and consensus: Strength in imaginary numbers. *Journal of Personality and Social Psychology, 89*, 978–996. doi: 10.1037/0022-3514.89.6.978

McGregor, I. Nash, K. A., Mann, N., & Phills, C. (2010). Anxious uncertainty and reactive approach motivation (RAM). *Journal of Personality and Social Psychology, 99*, 133–147. doi: 10.1037/a0019701

McGregor, I., Nash, K., & Inzlicht, M. (2009). Threat, high self-esteem, and reactive approach motivation: Electroencephalographic evidence. *Journal of Experimental Social Psychology, 45*, 1003–1007. doi: 10.1016/j.jesp.2009.04.011

McGregor, I., Nash, K., & Prentice, M. (2010). Reactive approach motivation (RAM) for religion. *Journal of Personality and Social Psychology, 99*, 148–161. doi: 10.1037/a0019702

McGregor, I., Prentice, M., & Nash, K. (2009). Personal uncertainty management by reactive approach motivation. *Psychological Inquiry, 20*, 225–229. doi: 10.1080/10478400903333460

McGregor, I., Zanna, M. P., Holmes, J. G., & Spencer, S. J. (2001). Compensatory conviction in the face of personal uncertainty: Going to extremes and being oneself. *Journal of Personality and Social Psychology, 80*, 472–488. doi: 10.1037/0022-3514.80.3.472

Nash, K., Inzlicht, M., & McGregor, I. (2012). Approach-related left prefrontal EEG asymmetry predicts muted error-related negativity. *Biological Psychology, 91*, 96–102. doi: 10.1016/j.biopsycho.2012.05.005

Nash, K., McGregor, I., & Inzlicht, M. (2010). Line bisection as a neural marker of approach motivation. *Psychophysiology, 47*, 979–998. doi: 10.1111/j.1469-8986.2010.00999.x

Nash, K., McGregor, I., & Prentice, M. (2011). Threat and defense as goal regulation: From implicit goal conflict to anxious uncertainty, reactive approach motivation, and ideological extremism. *Journal of Personality and Social Psychology, 101*, 1291–1301. doi: 10.1037/a0025944

Petty, R. E., Briñol, P., & Tormala, Z. L. (2002). Thought confidence as a determinant of persuasion: The self–validation hypothesis. *Journal of Personality and Social Psychology, 82*, 722–741. doi: 10.1037/0022-3514.82.5.722

Proulx, T., Inzlicht, M., & Harmon-Jones, E. (2012). Understanding all inconsistency compensation as a palliative response to violated expectations. *Trends in Cognitive Sciences, 16*, 285–291. doi: 10.1016/j.tics.2012.04.002

Proulx, T., & Major, B. (2013). A raw deal: Heightened liberalism following exposure to anomalous playing cards. *Journal of Social Issues, 69*, 455–472.

Pyszczynski, T., Greenberg, J., & Solomon, S. (1999). A dual-process model of defense against conscious and unconscious death-related thoughts: An extension of terror management theory. *Psychological Review, 106*, 835–845. doi: 10.1037/0033-295X.106.4.835

Pyszczynski, T., Greenberg, J., Solomon, S., & Maxfield, M. A. (2006). On the unique psychological import of death: Theme and variations. *Psychological Inquiry, 17*, 328–356. doi:10.1080/10478400701369542

Rosenblatt, A., Greenberg, J., Solomon, S., Pyszczynski, T., & Lyon, D. (1989). Evidence for terror management theory: I. The effects of mortality salience on reactions to those who violate or uphold cultural values. *Journal of Personality and Social Psychology, 57*, 681–690. doi: 10.1037/0022-3514.58.2.308

Schmeichel, B. J., Gailliot, M. T., Filardo, E-A., McGregor, I., Gitter, S., & Baumeister, R. F. (2009). Terror management theory and self-esteem revisited: The roles of implicit and explicit self-esteem in mortality salience effects. *Journal of Personality and Social Psychology, 96*, 1077–1087. doi: 10.1037/a0015091

Schmeichel, B. J., & Martens, A. (2005). Self-affirmation and mortality salience: Affirming values reduces worldview defense and death-thought accessibility. *Personality and Social Psychology Bulletin, 31*, 658–667. doi: 10.1177/0146167204271567

Schumann, K., McGregor, I., Nash, K., & Ross, M. (2013). *Religious magnanimity: When do diverse religious belief systems inspire forbearance?* Unpublished Manuscript, Palo Alto, CA: Stanford University.

Sheldon, K. M., Ryan, R., Deci, E., & Kasser, T. (2004). The independent effects of goal contents and motives on well-being: It's both what you pursue and why you pursue it. *Personality and Social Psychology Bulletin, 30*, 475–486. doi: 10.1177/0146167203261883

Shepherd, S., Kay, A. C., Landau, M. J., & Keefer, L. A. (2011). Evidence for the specificity of control motivations in worldview defense: Distinguishing compensatory control from uncertainty management and terror management processes. *Journal of Experimental Social Psychology, 47*, 949–958. doi: 10.1016/j.jesp.2011.03.026

Sherman, D. K., & Cohen, G. L. (2006). The psychology of self-defense: Self-affirmation theory. In M. P. Zanna (Ed.), *Advances in experimental social psychology* (Vol. 38, pp. 183–242). San Diego, CA: Academic Press.

Smillie, L., & Jackson, C. (2006). Functional impulsivity and reinforcement sensitivity theory. *Journal of Personality, 74*, 47–83. doi: 10.1111/j.1467-6494.2005.00369.x

Smillie, L. D., Jackson, C. J., & Dalgleish, L. I. (2006). Conceptual distinctions among Carver and White's (1994) BAS scales: A reward-reactivity versus trait impulsivity perspective. *Personality and Individual Differences, 40*, 1039–1105. doi: 10.1016/j.paid.2005.10.012

Spencer, S. J., Zanna, M. P., & Fong, G. T. (2005). Establishing a causal chain: Why experiments are often more effective than mediational analyses in examining psychological processes. *Journal of Personality and Social Psychology, 89*, 845–851. doi: 10.1037/0022-3514.89.6.845

Suhr, J. A., & Tsanadis, J. (2007). Affect and personality correlates of the Iowa Gambling Task. *Personality and Individual Differences, 43*, 27–36. doi: 10.1016/j.paid.2006.11.004

Van den Bos, K. (2001). Uncertainty management: The influence of uncertainty salience on reactions to perceived procedural fairness. *Journal of Personality and Social Psychology, 80*, 931–941.

Van den Bos, K. (2009). Making sense of life: The existential self trying to deal with personal uncertainty. *Psychological Inquiry, 20*, 197–217. doi: 10.1080/10478400903333411

Van den Bos, K., Muller, P. A., & Van Bussel, A. A. L. (2009). Helping to overcome intervention inertia in bystander's dilemmas: Behavioral disinhibition can improve the greater good. *Journal of Experimental Social Psychology, 45*, 873–878. doi: 10.1016/j.jesp.2009.03.014

Van den Bos, K., Poortvliet, P. M., Maas, M., Miedema, J., & Van den Ham, E.-J. (2005). An enquiry concerning the principles of cultural norms and values: The impact of uncertainty and mortality salience on reactions to violations and bolstering of cultural worldviews. *Journal of Experimental Social Psychology, 41*, 91–113. doi: 10.1016/j.jesp.2004.06.001

Van den Bos, K., Van Lange, P. A. M., Lind, E. A., Venhoeven, L. A., Beudeker, D. A., Cramwinckel, F. M., Smulders, L., & Van der Laan, J. (2011). On the benign qualities of behavioral disinhibition: Because of the prosocial nature of people, behavioral disinhibition can weaken pleasure with getting more than you deserve. *Journal of Personality and Social Psychology, 101*, 791–811. doi: 10.1037/a0023556

Van Harreveld, F., Rutjens, B. T., Rotteveel, M., Nordgren, L. F., & Van der Pligt, J. (2009). Ambivalence and decisional conflict as a cause of psychological discomfort: Feeling tense before jumping off the fence. *Journal of Experimental Social Psychology, 45*, 167–173. doi: 10.1016/j.jesp.2008.08.015

Watson, D., Clark, L. A., & Tellegen, A. (1988). Development and validation of brief measures of positive and negative affect: The PANAS scales. *Journal of Personality and Social Psychology, 54*, 1063–1070. doi: 10.1037/0022-3514.54.6.1063

Weary, G., Jacobson, J. A., Edwards, J. A., & Tobin, S. J. (2001). Chronic and temporarily activated causal uncertainty beliefs and stereotype usage. *Journal of Personality and Social Psychology, 81*, 206–219. doi: 10.1037/0022-3514.81.2.206

Wichman, A. L., Brunner, R. P., & Weary, G. (2008). Immediate and delayed effects of causal uncertainty inductions on uncertainty accessibility. *Journal of Experimental Social Psychology, 44*, 1106–1113. doi: 10.1016/j.jesp.2007.12.002

Zuckerman, M., & Kuhlman, D. M. (2000). Personality and risk-taking: Common biosocial factors. *Journal of Personality, 68*, 999–1029. doi: 10.1111/1467-6494.00124

IAN MCGREGOR received his MA in Personality Psychology from Carleton University and his PhD in Social Psychology from the University of Waterloo. He is currently a Professor of Psychology in the Faculty of Health at York University in Canada. His research is funded by the Social Sciences and Humanities Research Council of Canada and he is an editorial board member for the *Journal of Personality and Social Psychology*, the *Journal of Experimental Social Psychology*, *Social Psychological and Personality Science*, and the *European Journal of Social Psychology*.

MIKE PRENTICE earned his MA in Social-Personality Psychology with supervision from Ian McGregor at York University, and is now a psychology instructor at Knox College and a PhD student at the University of Missouri. Mike's eclectic interests and areas of methodological expertise span a wide range of topics in psychology, including existential, developmental, personality, social, and neural.

KYLE NASH earned his MA and PhD at York University under the supervision of Ian McGregor. His dissertation focused on motivational and neural mechanics of anxiety, reactive approach-motivation, and risk-taking. In 2012 he began a postdoctoral position in the Psychology Department at the University of Basel, in Switzerland, to further investigate neural processes related to self-regulation and risk-taking.

Compensatory Control and Its Implications for Ideological Extremism

Aaron C. Kay[*]
Duke University

Richard P. Eibach
University of Waterloo

This article outlines and reviews evidence for a model of compensatory control designed to account for the motivated belief in personal and external sources of control. In doing so, we attempt to shed light on the content and strength of ideologies, including extreme libertarian, nationalist, socialist, and religious fundamentalist ideologies. We suggest that although these ideologies differ in their content they commonly function to provide people with a sense of control over otherwise random events. We propose that extreme ideologies of personal control (e.g., libertarianism) and external control (e.g., socialism, religious fundamentalism) are equifinal means of meeting a universal need to believe that things, in general, are under control—that is, that events do not unfold randomly or haphazardly. We use this model to explain how the adoption and strength of ideologies of personal and external control may vary across temporal and sociocultural contexts.

Introduction

In the Spring of 2009, the Tea Party, a new conservative populist movement within the United States, emerged in response to economic and sociopolitical uncertainties evoked by the global economic recession. Although the Tea Party is not an official political party at the federal level, it has had a significant political impact through its influence on the Republican Party, which is the major conservative party within the United States. Since its emergence onto the political

---

[*]Correspondence concerning this article should be addressed to Aaron C. Kay, Duke University, Fuqua School of Business, 100 Fuqua Drive, Durham, NC 27708. Tel: (919) 660-3737 [e-mail: aaron.kay@duke.edu].

scene the Tea Party has exhibited a number of extremist tendencies, including strong aversion to political compromise, efforts to replace moderate conservative officeholders with more extreme candidates, efforts to abolish longstanding institutions such as the U.S. Federal Reserve, and labeling centrist political opponents "socialists" or "fascists." Perhaps the most salient example of the movement's relative extremism was the threat by Congressional Tea Party caucus members to oppose legislation that would prevent the U.S. government from going into default with its creditors unless the government agreed to enact deeper cuts in Federal spending. The Tea Party movement has thus shifted American politics in a more extreme rightward direction on both economic and social issues. Indeed, members of the Tea Party Caucus are significantly more conservative than the average Congressional Republican, and in public opinion surveys the average Tea Party supporter is significantly more conservative on a number of issues than the average Republican Party supporter (DiMaggio, 2011; Skocpol & Williamson, 2012). The Tea Party is not an extremist political movement in the sense of being antidemocratic, violent, revolutionary, or self-consciously xenophobic.[1] However, an analysis of the rise of the Tea Party within the context of the global economic crisis is relevant to understanding how events that trigger widespread uncertainty can move people toward relatively more extreme ideological positions.

The Tea Party is an internally heterogeneous social movement composed of at least three distinct underlying ideologies: libertarianism, nationalism, and religious conservatism (Skocpol & Williamson, 2012). Thus, although Tea Party members share an intense concern about current and future conditions within the United States, they are not of one mind. Indeed, U.S. conservative populist movements have long been a complex blend of conflicting libertarian, nationalist, and religious conservative ideologies (Zernike, 2010). These ideologies are unified by their common opposition to modern liberalism but they often disagree in their more positive agendas. The conflicts among these distinct ideologies were evident in the dynamics of the Republican Party's recent Presidential nomination contest. The greater intensity of Tea Party-identified voters compared to centrist Republican voters led many political analysts to predict that this movement would influence Republicans to select a more ideologically extreme nominee than the establishment frontrunner, former Massachusetts governor Mitt Romney. However, ideological divisions within the Tea Party movement hampered its ability to unify behind a single alternative candidate, and over the course of the Republican primary elections, polls showed Republican voters rapidly cycling through opposition candidates, with one candidate emerging as a favorite only to be replaced in the

---

[1] Although Tea Party spokespeople strongly denied that racist or xenophobic motives were a significant factor within their movement, opinion surveys have found that identification with the Tea Party is associated with standard measures of racial resentment (Williamson, Skocpol, & Coggins, 2011).

course of a few weeks or even days by a different favored candidate. Romney's rivals for the Republican nomination seemed to appeal to one or the other of the distinct ideological camps within the movement, but none were able to capture enduring support from all three camps and the Tea Party vote was consequently split.

The fact that a political movement arising in response to an economic crisis could embody such distinct and often conflicting libertarian, nationalist, and religious conservative ideologies highlights the question of whether ideologies with such manifestly different contents nevertheless function to fulfill a common psychological need. In other words, do these distinct ideologies hang together not because of logical or practical coherence but because of an underlying psychological coherence in relation to a fundamental psychological need? Moreover, if such different ideologies do fulfill the same psychological need, is it possible to explain why an individual might be increasingly drawn to one of these ideologies over another when either would suffice to fulfill that need? The present article reviews a new functionalist model of ideological content that seeks to answer these fundamental questions.

There have been numerous psychological models seeking to explain how diverse sociopolitical ideologies might function to fulfill a common psychological need, including the need to cope with existential anxieties regarding mortality (Greenberg, Solomon, & Pyszczynski, 1997), the need to maintain meaning (Heine, Proulx, & Vohs, 2006; Proulx & Major, 2013), the need for social identity (Hogg & Adelman, 2013; Hogg & van Knippenberg, 2003), and the need to manage uncertainty (Doosje, Loseman, & van den Bos, 2013; Esses, Medianu, & Lawson, 2013; van den Bos & Lind, 2002). Though all of these perspectives have heightened our understanding of the motivational bases of ideology, they offer little insight into variability in the manifest content of ideology. Indeed, these accounts typically provide no explanation for why variability in ideological content should exist and they provide little theoretical guidance for predicting patterns of variation in ideological content. Compensatory control theory (CCT), a new functionalist model of ideology, seeks to overcome these limitations of previous models.

CCT proposes that people defensively embrace ideologies that emphasize personal, societal, or religious control in order to alleviate anxieties they experience when they perceive randomness and disorder in their lives. Thus, according to CCT, the need to perceive the world as controllable, nonrandom, and orderly is a latent human need that is commonly fulfilled by social and political ideologies that differ in their manifest contents. A major contribution of CCT is spotlighting the common theme of control in this set of otherwise distinct ideologies.

For example, the different varieties of right-wing populist ideologies contained within the Tea Party each appear to emphasize different sources of control, with the libertarian camp emphasizing personal control, the nationalist camp emphasizing control by strong government, and the religious right camp emphasizing supernatural control. However, unlike other functionalist theories of ideology, CCT not only accounts for what diverse ideologies share in common (i.e., the theme of control) but it also explains why their contents differ (i.e., specific sources of control emphasized). We now turn to a deeper explanation of the underlying logic and hypotheses derived from CCT.

Overview of Compensatory Control Theory

CCT draws inspiration from a number of theoretical precursors, including just world theory (Lerner, 1980), system justification theory (Jost & Banaji, 1994), and the dual process model of control (Rothbaum, Weisz, & Snyder, 1982). But its theoretical foundations, most simply, derive from two waves of social, clinical, and personality psychology research. The first wave, covering a period from the 1960s to the 1990s, strongly argued for a human need to believe that individuals control their environment. Many influential studies supported the existence of a fundamental need for people to believe that they personally control what happens to them, even when they do not, and provided evidence that believing otherwise is psychologically aversive and associated with dysfunctional outcomes (e.g., Janoff-Bulman, 1992).

Why, one may wonder, would people be so strongly driven to believe in personal control? Several answers to this question have been offered, but the one most relevant to CCT postulates that belief in personal control represents an ideal means for shielding the individual from the threatening idea that life is random and arbitrary. Belief in personal control is psychologically desirable, according to this account, because personal control necessarily implies an orderly world—one in which whatever happens, good or bad, will have a determinable cause (Lerner, 1980). Personal control beliefs both shield people from anxieties that would be evoked by perceiving the world as random, arbitrary, or haphazard and also gives them confidence in their pursuit of long-term goals (Laurin, Fitzsimons, & Kay, 2011). Beliefs in personal control, therefore, function to satiate an overarching, broad need to perceive a nonrandom, orderly world, in which events do not happen randomly but follow clear rules of cause-and-effect (see Kay, Gaucher, Napier, Callan, & Laurin, 2008).

Somewhat contradicting these findings is a second wave of research that demonstrated that perceptions of personal control are more variable than researchers who postulated a fundamental need to perceive control originally assumed. Perceptions of personal control and their impact on psychological functioning, this research demonstrated, vary across individuals, cultural contexts, socioeconomic status, and in relation to situational constraints (e.g., Burger, 1989; Ji, Peng, & Nisbett, 2000; Snibbe & Markus, 2005). In short, beliefs in personal control and the motivation to maintain them fluctuate, both chronically and temporarily. If the need to perceive an orderly, nonrandom world is presumed to be a fundamental, relatively constant human need and belief in personal control fulfills this need, then how do people fulfill this need when their belief in personal control is low? The first wave of research on personal control provided no clear answer to this question.

CCT was developed, at least in part, to address this problem. At its essence, it asserts that, in the absence of perceived personal control, an alternative means for maintaining perceptions of order is through endorsement of culturally recognized sources of secular or religious control. Endorsing belief in the power of social institutions or supernatural agents to control events can provide individuals the security of knowing that, even though their personal control may be low, some external agency can ensure that events and outcomes are nonrandom (Antonovsky, 1979; Rothbaum, Weisz, & Snyder, 1982). Indeed, belief in external control agents, much like belief in personal control, has been tied to healthy psychological functioning (Schwartz, 2000). Thus, if personal control is not an available or attractive means for assuaging anxieties associated with randomness, an individual can instead invest their confidence in external systems that impose order upon the world. Thus, with respect to fulfilling the overarching motive to believe in an orderly world there exists a substitutability between cognitions about the self and cognitions about the world, such that threatened or lowered beliefs in personal control can be compensated with increased belief in and support of external control. Compensatory control, then, offers a novel approach to uncertainty management but is distinct from models of *personal* uncertainty. The uncertainty it addresses is not about the individual's personal goals, identity, or self-clarity, but focuses solely on uncertainty about the world external to the self—the extent to which that world is a manageable, nonrandom, understandable place.

This straightforward proposition of CCT holds powerful implications for understanding and predicting the content and strength of people's ideological attachments. When combined with recent functional and cognitive perspectives on the operation of ideology (Kay & Eibach, 2012), it can shed light, we submit, on both which ideologies people adopt in situations of uncertainty or control threat and how zealously they cling to these ideologies. But before turning to a discussion of these applications, we briefly survey the empirical support for CCT. In so doing, we hope to not only demonstrate the emerging body of support for the main tenets of this theory, but also illustrate its various nuances as well as how it diverges from other theories of defensive ideological processes.

CCT: Empirical Support

Although it is a relatively new theory, there are now several sources of evidence supporting the basic tenets of CCT and testing its implications for sociopolitical and religious ideologies.

One area of research has tested the most basic tenet of CCT: that threatened or lowered levels of personal control should lead to heightened support for external secular or religious systems of control. For example, experimental manipulations that temporarily lower feelings of personal control heighten people's beliefs in a controlling God (Kay et al., 2008; Kay, Laurin, & Moscovitch, 2010; Laurin, Kay, & Moscovitch, 2008), their preferences for government control, and their support for current government structure and policies (Kay et al., 2008). Manipulations that lower personal control have also been shown to affect belief in a wide range of other sources of external control, including heightened beliefs in the existence and importance of powerful enemies (Sullivan, Landau, & Rothschild, 2010), endorsement of conspiracy theories to explain seemingly arbitrary events (Whitson & Galinsky, 2008), and faith in origins of life theories that suggest orderly rather than random causes (Rutjens, van der Pligt, & van Harreveld, 2010). Importantly, the reverse also holds true: participants led to believe that their government (i.e., an external source of control) was unable to assure order demonstrated increased illusions of personal control in a modified contingency task (Kay et al., 2008).

All of the effects listed above, however, could be interpreted as byproducts of rational information processing rather than defensive, compensatory processes. That is, whereas CCT posits a motivational process whereby emotional discomfort associated with lowered levels of control triggers compensatory control strivings, none of the original findings provided direct evidence for this defensive mechanism. However, more recent research, using a wide variety of methods, has supported the role of emotion, anxiety, and defensiveness in mediating compensatory control phenomena (e.g., Kay et al., 2008; Kay, Moscovitch, & Laurin, 2010; Laurin, Kay, & Moscovitch, 2008).

According to CCT, people flexibly draw upon various types of beliefs to maintain perceptions of an orderly, nonrandom world. As we have reviewed, this includes substituting beliefs about personal control with beliefs about external sources of control. There is no reason to assume, however, that this substitutability should apply only to that particular combination. If beliefs in personal control are substitutable with various different external sources of control precisely because all of these sources (internal and external) reaffirm nonrandomness, then external systems of control should also be substitutable for one another. This prediction of CCT has received considerable support. It has been observed, for example: that naturally occurring events that threaten the perceived stability of governments (e.g., upcoming elections) increase belief in religious sources of control; experimental manipulations that threaten beliefs in God's control increase belief in government control and support for extant government policy; and experimental manipulations that affirm the ability of the government to provide order lessen belief in religious sources of control (Kay, Shepherd, Blatz, Chua, & Galinsky, 2010). Furthermore, electroencephalograph measures find that exposure to religious and nonreligious sources of control are equally effective at reducing anterior cingulate cortex activity—a brain region implicated in feelings of distress and anxiety (Bush, Luu, & Posner, 2000; Critchley et al., 2003; Critchley, 2005; Shackman et al., 2011)—when compared to exposure to reminders of randomness (Inzlicht, McGregor, Hirsh, & Nash, 2009; Inzlicht & Tullett, 2010).

Research has also established the specificity of the predictions offered by CCT compared to other motivated ideological responses to threat. In particular, CCT suggests that, following threats that suggest disorder, people do not defensively affirm just any culturally prevalent worldview or meaning system (Greenberg, Solomon, & Pyszczynski, 1997; Heine, Proulx, & Vohs, 2006), nor do they more zealously adopt whatever beliefs they presently hold (McGregor, Zanna, Holmes, Spencer, 2001; also see McGregor, Prentice, & Nash, 2013), rather they more specifically affirm worldviews that emphasize personal or external sources of control. In other words, when events suggest a random, disorderly existence, people should prefer belief systems that emphasize the theme of control and not necessarily belief systems that express other needs, such as needs for self-certainty, symbolic immortality, or personal significance.

This presumed specificity of compensatory control effects has been demonstrated across a variety of studies. For example, whereas threats to personal control increase belief in a controlling God, this effect disappears when God's control is not emphasized in the dependent measure (Kay et al., 2008). Similarly specific effects have been observed in the context of many different outcomes, ranging from political beliefs to scientific theories to consumer products (Kay et al., 2010; Shepherd, Kay, Landau, & Keefer, 2011). In each case, control threat led to increased endorsement of the order conferring aspects of the relevant construct or ideology (e.g., the parts of the government that establish and maintain law and order), but did not affect attributes tied more directly to other needs, such as symbolic immortality, individuality, group identity, or personal significance.

To summarize, CCT suggests a motivated substitutability between personal control and secular and religious sources of external control. Considerable evidence supports the hypothesized substitutability of these belief systems, the function of these belief systems in defending against perceived randomness, and distinguishes these effects from other motivated ideological processes. It is important to note, however, that although compensatory control processes often manifest in beliefs that may have positive outcomes for the individual, the motivation, at its most basic level, is not for positivity but for perceiving order rather than randomness. In fact, several recent studies have demonstrated that when personal control is threatened people even turn to negative sources of control—e.g., powerful enemies, conspiracy theories, and even pessimistic medical prognostications—if they represent the best available means to restoring perceived order.

In the remainder of this article, we shift our focus to an analysis of different ideologies, with the aim of pinpointing how and when they may function as sources of compensatory control. We first present a functionalist, socio-cognitive model of ideological content that can be used to shed light on when people turn to one or another of the many sources of compensatory control that exist, and then, we illustrate this perspective with examples of ideological orientations that may fulfill compensatory control needs.

A Functionalist, Sociocognitive Model of Compensatory Control Processes

Our application of CCT to the study of ideological extremism is based on a recent model of ideological reasoning (Kay & Eibach, 2012), which proposes that in modern, pluralistic cultures individuals have access to and flexibly draw upon a diverse set of ideological tools to solve relevant functional problems. Thus, everyday ideologies are often "scavenger ideologies" (Mosse, 1995) in the sense that people sample ideas from a variety of sources to support their political goals or fulfill their psychological needs. These sampled ideological fragments are brought together not because they logically cohere, indeed they often do not, but rather because they commonly contribute to meeting the individual's psychological needs or justifying his or her political goals. These ideologies cannot be considered hybrid ideologies because their users often make little or no attempt to integrate or synthesize the sampled ideological fragments into a coherent whole. Rather, like scavengers, individuals sample these ideological fragments in an ad hoc, opportunistic way and then deploy them as needed to advance an agenda, fulfill a psychological need, or score rhetorical points.

Drawing on social cognition theory, this functionalist model of ideological reasoning proposes that the individual's use of ideological tools in everyday problem solving is influenced by two critical determinants: (1) the cognitive accessibility of those tools, and (2) the degree of fit between the tool and the specific functional problem the user faces. When the functional problem is coping with the threat of seemingly random life events, the relevant tools are ideologies of personal, government, and supernatural control. According to CCT, these ideologies of control provide reassurance that events are not as random as they may initially appear and so individuals should be motivated to access these ideological tools when threatened by evidence of randomness in their lives. The particular control ideology that an individual selects when threatened by randomness will in part be influenced by the cognitive accessibility of that ideology, both chronic and situational. Chronic influences on the accessibility of a control ideology include: variability in the quantity of previous exposure to that ideology within one's culture, and variability in one's own habitual use of that ideology. Situational influences on the accessibility of a control ideology include exposure to a recent event in which that ideology was directly or indirectly invoked, and immediate cues within the setting that favor that ideology over alternative control ideologies.

In addition to the relative accessibility of alternative control ideologies, the other critical determinant of ideology selection is the functional fit between the ideological tool and the immediate problem confronting the individual. For example, invoking an ideology of supernatural control should provide more reassurance about the prospects of controlling natural disasters than would an ideology of personal or government control, insofar as there are recognized limits to human, but not divine, control over natural events. Functional fit may also help explain why people are less likely to invoke government control to cope with randomness when the government is perceived to be corrupt, untrustworthy or unstable (Kay et al., 2008; Sullivan, Landau, & Rothschild, 2010). In such circumstances, government control is unlikely to be reassuring and so individuals should get more satisfaction from endorsing a more reliable source of control, such as personal or supernatural control (Kay et al., 2008).

To summarize, this model proposes that an individual will express more extreme ideological investment in a given control source when an event triggers anxiety about disorder and randomness in an important life domain, and that control source is both cognitively accessible and seems to provide a better functional fit to the immediate problem than other accessible sources of control. In other words, according to this model, randomness threats provide the stimulus that motivates individuals to endorse control ideologies (which is the thrust of CCT), and cognitive accessibility and functional fit provide the selection mechanisms that determine the specific content of the control ideology that the individual expresses.

The Control Conferring Characteristics of Ideology

At the outset of this article, we noted that conservative populism in the United States, as currently embodied in the Tea Party movement, is a mixture of libertarian, nationalist, and religious conservative elements, and these different elements emphasize different sources of control. In the next sections, we examine each of these distinct ideological tendencies within U.S. conservative populist culture to better illustrate how accessibility and functional fit influence the use of ideological resources to cope with control threats. We briefly describe the historical background and current cultural context within the United States that may influence how accessible these control ideologies are for an individual coping with specific threats. Afterwards, we discuss the circumstances, from a CCT perspective, that should promote more extreme expressions of these and other ideologies. Before turning to this analysis, though, it is important to point out that we focus on American right-wing populism not because we believe it to be an uniquely extreme movement, but because all three of the main types of control ideologies emphasized in CCT are represented within this movement and it thus serves as a convenient case for illustrating variability in expressions of these control ideologies.

Ideologies Emphasizing Personal Control

Personal control is likely to be a chronically accessible ideological coping resource for many Americans, including and perhaps especially conservatives, because of America's deeply rooted individualist ethos. Explicit expressions of individualist values and idealization of self-reliance have been highly resonant cultural themes throughout American history. For example, Ralph Waldo Emerson (1841/1993) strongly advocated the virtue of self-reliance, writing,

> It is only as a man puts off all foreign support, and stands alone, that I see him to be strong and to prevail... He who knows that power is inborn, that he is weak because he has looked for good out of him and elsewhere, and so perceiving, throws himself unhesitatingly on his thought, instantly rights himself, stands in the erect position, commands his limbs, works miracles... In the Will work and acquire, and thou hast chained the wheel of Chance, and shall sit hereafter out of fear of her rotations. (pp. 37–8).

In contemporary U.S. politics self-reliance is a particularly strong theme in conservative populist movements (Lakoff, 1996). Indeed, Lilla (2010) attributed the emergence of the conservative Tea Party movement to "two classic American traits that have grown much more pronounced in recent decades: blanket distrust of institutions and an astonishing—and unwarranted—confidence in the self" (p. 53). The libertarian segment of the Tea Party especially emphasizes this personal control ideology.

The Obama administration's immediate responses to the collapse of the U.S. housing market may have provoked opposition from adherents to this ideology, in part, because many of those emergency policies could be readily framed as contradicting the notion that individuals control their own destiny. Indeed, this was a prominent concern expressed in one of the critical events that was believed to inspire the Tea Party movement, in which journalist Rick Santelli passionately spoke against government intervention to relieve individuals' mortgage burdens. Santelli said,

> The government is promoting bad behavior... How about this, President and new Administration, why don't you put up a website to have people vote ... as a referendum to see if we really want to subsidize the losers' mortgages, or would we like to at least buy cars and buy houses in foreclosure and give them to people who might have a chance to actually prosper down the road and reward people who actually carry the water instead of drink the water... This is America. How many of you people want to pay for your neighbors' mortgages that has an extra bathroom and can't pay their bills?

The fact that during a national crisis—one which, given the extent to which it was fraught with reminders of economic instability and volatility, should motivate people to embrace control ideologies—Obama was enacting policies that seemed to explicitly undermine libertarians' most chronically accessible control ideology (i.e., personal control/responsibility) may help to explain the otherwise surprising intensity of libertarian opposition to Obama's administration.

Ideologies Emphasizing Government Control

The idea that a strong state can provide vital protection from the chaos, disorder, and unpredictability of natural existence was the key rationale behind Hobbes's *Leviathan*, one of the most influential modern, secular defenses of a strong, interventionist, centralized state. To escape this chaotic existence, people elect to live under the imposed order of a powerful sovereign state. Faith in the power of social institutions to control events may, therefore, function as a crucial buffer against the seeming randomness of life, a point Ellison (1948/2003) emphasized when he wrote that social institutions constitute "one of the bulwarks which men place between themselves and the constant threat of chaos. For whatever the assigned function of social institutions, their psychological function is to protect the citizen against the irrational, incalculable forces that hover about the edges of human life like cosmic destruction lurking within an atomic stockpile" (p. 324).

Thus, economic crises and other national threats may motivate people to amplify their commitment to government control to reduce their anxieties regarding these threats. This may explain why in the aftermath of economic crises, support sometimes rises for left-wing political movements that promote government control in the form of economic redistribution and greater regulation of financial markets, as recently seen in the rise of the Occupy Wall Street movement. For example, during the Great Depression, Americans evidenced increased support for socialist parties, increased circulation of socialist newspapers, stronger labor union support for government intervention in the economy, and more class-differentiated voting patterns (Lipset & Marks, 2000; but see Jost, Glaser, Kruglanski, & Sulloway, 2003, for evidence that this response may have been specific to the United States).

Although government control is a potentially powerful ideological resource for coping with national threats, it may not be a chronically accessible resource for many Americans due to a pervasive anti-government strain within their culture. Investigating the historical roots of this anti-government theme, Wills (1999) proposes a confluence of influences including:

> The lack of a symbolic center (religious or political) at our origins, the air of compromise in our Constitution's formation (which made it vulnerable to the reversal of Federalist and Anti-Federalist values), the Jeffersonian suspicion of the Constitution (which Madison abetted at one stage), a jostling of competitive states' claims (reaching a climax in the secession of the South), a frontier tradition, the "Lockean" individualism of our political theory, a fervent cult of the gun.

Wills suggests that "the instinctive urge that kept all of these forces quick to the touch" was a "cluster of anti-governmental values," including the values of "authenticity, amateurism, spontaneity, candor, tradition, rights, and religion" which, he suggests, "grew out of the [historical elements] just listed, but ... took on a life of their own, especially as they cross-pollinated in mutually confirming ways" (p. 318). Wills' analysis is consistent with recent cultural psychology models, which propose that cultural values that arise as adaptations to ecological and historical circumstances encountered during the formative stages of a society can become self-perpetuating, exerting a persisting influence even when the functional context of a society changes (Cohen, 2001).

This skepticism of "big government" has traditionally been a particularly strong theme within American conservatism. Thus, it is not surprising that during the current economic crisis only 20% of American conservatives reported positive attitudes toward "socialism" compared to 61% of liberals (Newport, 2010). However, while there are strong anti-government themes within American conservatism, to label even conservatives as "anti-government" would be an oversimplification that ignores the fact that, although conservatives are often skeptical of certain forms of government intervention in the economy, they invest strong support in other domains of government control, notably criminal justice, immigration control, and national defense (Hagan, 2010; Harcourt, 2011). Indeed, the application of the "anti-government" label to American conservatives loses much of its credibility when one considers their strong support for severe anticrime policies that have erected a massive and expensive prison system that incarcerates nearly 1% of the population, and for a U.S. national defense system the annual maintenance costs of which are greater than the next 45 highest-spending countries combined (Hellman & Sharp, 2008; Wacquant, 2009). In recent decades within the United States, when conservative administrations have been in power they have substantially expanded investments in criminal punishment and national security while at the same time reducing economic regulations (Hagan, 2010). Seen from this perspective, liberals and conservatives do not differ in their support for "big government," rather they differ in what specific forms of strong government intervention they prefer.

To be sure, then, the relation between ideology and preferences for government control is a complex one. By distinguishing between different forms of government control, however, it may be possible to clarify this relationship from a CCT perspective. American conservatives may be more skeptical of governmental control in the domain of the economy than they are in the domains of public order and national security because they believe that order emerges naturally and spontaneously within the economic domain (Jost, Blount, Pfeffer, & Hunyady, 2003), but not in these other domains. Classic liberal philosophy and social science theories popularized by conservative scholars and commentators emphasize that, whereas in the economic domain misbehavior tends to be most efficiently controlled by market mechanisms, maintaining public order and national security requires intervention by the state to severely punish criminals and defend against foreign enemies (Hartcourt, 2011). Given these cultural assumptions about where order naturally does and does not emerge, the patterns of conservatives' preferences for government control are consistent with the idea that functional fit influences the use of government control ideology to cope with randomness threats. Consistent with CCT, conservatives tend to resist using government control to solve problems in domains, such as the economy, which they believe are regulated by a natural, spontaneous source of order, namely the invisible hand of the free market. Far from being necessary to produce order within the economy, conservatives often accuse government regulation of undermining natural sources of economic order by introducing "uncertainty" into markets. Indeed, this was a charge that Tea Party activists commonly leveled against the Obama administration's attempts to tighten regulations on trading markets in the aftermath of the U.S. housing crisis. However, conservatives are more enthusiastic about using government as a tool for solving problems in domains such as public safety, border control, and national security, where they tend to believe natural sources of order are less reliable or nonexistent (Harcourt, 2011).

Conservatives' belief that government control provides a better functional fit for addressing public safety and national security problems than economic problems may explain why threatening events related to public order or national security reliably increase conservative support for government control, while economic threats do not. For example, research shows that when individuals perceive signs of increasing public disorder and criminality, they adopt more authoritarian attitudes that license government violations of civil liberties (Altemeyer, 1988) and they favor more punitive measures against criminals (Tetlock et al., 2007).

Ideologies Emphasizing Supernatural Control

The idea that supernatural beliefs function to help people cope with the anxieties evoked by randomness and unpredictability in life has a distinguished history in the social sciences (e.g., Malinowski, 1954). The accessibility of supernatural control beliefs as a tool for fulfilling control needs is likely to vary between individuals based on their socialization experiences. For example, Evangelical Christians make extensive efforts to develop the skill to hear the voice of God during prayer and feel His presence in their lives (Luhrmann, 2012). The process of developing a rich spiritual life through such practices is likely to make religious control a more chronically accessible resource for dealing with control threats, whenever they occur.

Religious control should also be a more chronically accessible coping resource for people from faith traditions with well-established rituals for invoking supernatural intervention in the everyday world. Such rituals cultivate a spiritual imagination that sees the world as an enchanted place, with manifestations of the divine in events that might otherwise seem ordinary (Greeley, 1995). For example, Ault (2004) noted how the prayer life of the members of a fundamentalist Baptist church helped them attribute order and cause to otherwise random-seeming events:

> In whatever ways these interconnected discourses of prayer, testimony and spiritual discernment were applied to life, they cultivated in our group a radically supernatural view of the world and a keen consciousness of the presence of God (and Satan) in everyday life. It encouraged us to recognize as [one member] put it, that ... "There's no luck with the Lord." In every presumably "lucky" or "chance" occurrence we could see, instead, the hand of God – or Satan. (p. 179).

To the extent that developing this perception of the world makes religion a more valuable resource for fulfilling control needs, it should tend to motivate believers to draw upon religious resources to cope with relevant problems. Consistent with this hypothesis, beliefs about the functional fit of religious control to specific problems seem to influence religious believers' use of religion to cope with control threats. The relevance of functional fit in the application of religious control ideology is reflected in people's beliefs about when faith-based organizations are preferable to government or private secular organizations as social service providers. For example, Christian conservatives rate faith-based organizations more favorably than government or private secular organizations for services such as prison counseling, youth mentoring, and teen pregnancy counseling—that is, domains in which personal transformation, which is often thought to occur via religion, are emphasized (Wuthnow, 2004). By contrast, Christian conservatives claim no special role for religious organizations for other services such as job training (Wuthnow, 2004) where religion is presumed to be less uniquely suited to influence.

Religious control ideology is a prominent theme in much of the rhetoric and activism associated with conservative populism in the United States, including the Tea Party movement. An influential segment of the Tea Party movement is composed of Christian conservatives who often invoke religious control as a resource for coping with national threats. A vivid example of this was a prayer rally where Texas Governor Rick Perry asked for God's intervention to resolve America's ongoing economic and political problems praying,

"You are our only hope, and we stand before you today in awe of your power and in gratitude for your blessings, and humility for our sins. Father, our heart breaks for America. We see discord at home. We see fear in the marketplace. We see anger in the halls of government, and as a nation we have forgotten who made us, who protects us, who blesses us, and for that we cry out for your forgiveness", (quoted in Hernandez, 2011, August 11, p. A12). According to CCT religious conservatives like Governor Perry are likely to rely strongly on God's control during times of threat such as the present economic crisis. This may explain why this group of conservatives reacted with such hostility toward the Obama administration which they perceived as threatening America's Judeo-Christian traditions through symbolic acts, such as Obama's support for the right to build a Muslim educational center nearby the September 11th attack site, and policies that seemed to contradict traditional religious teachings, such as Obama's recent endorsement of same-sex marriage rights.

To summarize, the historical and cultural evidence we reviewed suggests ways that distinct personal and external control ideologies are likely to vary in their accessibility when contemporary American conservatives are coping with particular control threats. Specifically, this evidence suggests that when American conservatives are coping with control threats: (1) personal control ideologies will be chronically accessible, (2) national control ideologies will be accessible when they perceive law and order or national security threats but not economic threats, and (3) religious ideologies will be chronically accessible tools for those who were socialized into intensive faith communities.

CCT and Extreme Commitment to Control Ideologies

We have emphasized that themes of personal and external control are prominent features of sociopolitical ideologies. CCT proposes that the need to defend oneself against anxieties regarding randomness in life is the engine that drives people to endorse these ideologies of control. If this is the case, then individual and situational variables that heighten the salience of concerns about randomness should predict more extreme endorsement of these ideologies. And, indeed, as described earlier, considerable research has demonstrated that when one control source is undermined people increase their reliance on other sources (for reviews, see Kay, Gaucher, McGregor, & Nash, 2010a; Kay, Whitson, Gaucher, & Galinsky, 2009).

What are the implications of this model for understanding ideological extremism? Although function and accessibility should generally guide people toward the adoption of one dominant control ideology, most people have multiple sources of control available and they draw on each to some extent. For many people, that is, their perceptions of order are buffered by a blend (even if unequal) of secular, supernatural, and personal control ideologies. Indeed, it has even been argued that the healthiest psychological functioning occurs when people do not rely too much on internal or external modes of control, but strike a balance between them (Schwarz, 2000). In certain cases, however, the totality of people's control needs may be funneled into only one of these control-affirming ideologies. In such cases, CCT would suggest, we should see especially vigorous attachment to and defense of the relevant ideology—that is, extremism. This funneling could happen for a number of reasons.

For many people, accessibility of personal control ideologies may be limited or entirely absent. In many cultural contexts, ideologies of personal control simply are not widely available (Weisz, Rothbaum, & Blackburn, 1984). For example many collectivist cultures (Markus & Kitiyama, 1991) and lower socioeconomic communities within highly individualist cultures (Stephens, Markus, & Townsend, 2007) tend to emphasize interdependent models of selfhood and are thus less inclined to see themselves as the sole controllers of their destiny (e.g., Young & Morris, 2004).

Access to external sources of control—both secular and religious—may also vary depending on a person's social background. For some individuals and communities, government control may be especially untrustworthy or ineffectual. For example, people are less inclined to amplify their support for government in response to control threats if government corruption is known to be high (Kay et al., 2008) or the government is temporarily unstable (Kay et al., 2010). It has also been suggested that regions of the United States that were settled well before organized law arrived and were far away from central government, such as the Western frontier, developed cultures with little faith in the power of government and strong anti-government leanings (Lipset, 1990; Vandello & Cohen, 1999).

Access to religious and supernatural control ideologies can also vary, generally as a function of socialization. Due to historical contingencies, some sociocultural contexts simply make notions of supernatural control more accessible than others. Also, religions vary in how much control over human events they attribute to God and these variations in religious content influence the efficacy of religion as a control resource. It should be noted, however, that even those who do not affiliate with official religions may hold less formalized superstitious and paranormal beliefs that serve a similar compensatory control function (Burger & Lynn, 2005). Indeed, such paranormal beliefs and practices may be more common among individuals and within regions with lower levels of traditional religious belief (Bainbridge & Stark, 1980) and they may increase as traditional religiosity declines (Houtman & Mascini, 2002).

For various reasons, then, people's access to control ideologies—whether personal or external—can be constrained. This becomes particularly problematic, we submit, when it leaves an individual with only one predominant means of imbuing the world with order. That is, when alternative options of control are cut off extreme endorsement of the only available ideology is likely to be seen, especially in contexts of temporary or prolonged control threat, as we next illustrate with examples of extreme versions of personal, religious, and government control ideologies.

Libertarianism is an example of an ideology that very strongly emphasizes personal control and the individual's right and capacity to live a self-determined, unencumbered life. Interestingly, libertarianism is often accompanied by explicit denial of religion and a firm philosophical belief that government intervention prevents, rather than facilitates, optimal human functioning (Critchlow, 2007). For example, the novelist Ayn Rand and her many followers strongly rejected religious and government control while glorifying the solitary individual's ability to control his or her own fate as illustrated by the heroic protagonist John Galt from Rand's novel *Atlas Shrugged* (Burns, 2009). Given these libertarians' rejection of the two main *external* control ideologies, it makes sense, from the perspective of CCT, that they would express more extreme confidence in *personal* control compared to others, such as moderate conservatives, who balance belief in personal control with belief in religious and/or government control.

Extreme religious ideologies are likely to be adopted by individuals who live in sociocultural contexts that limit both the ability to believe in personal control and confidence in the power of government. Certain countries in the Middle East, for example, combine unstable governments with economies that provide restricted access to resources and, therefore, minimal opportunity for individual social mobility. From a CCT perspective, these reality constraints on belief in personal and governmental control may cause people to funnel the entirety of their control needs toward religious control. Of course, this effect need not be limited to more economically and politically unstable nations. Even within wealthy countries with stable governments individuals often vary in their access to personal and government resources. Members of lower socioeconomic status communities, for example, may feel both disenfranchised by the government and have little experience of personal control in their lives. Thus, as CCT would expect, religious belief tends to be higher among individuals who are low in socioeconomic status or otherwise marginalized (Pargament, 1997).

Finally, more extreme ideologies of government control, such as state socialism, should tend to be endorsed more strongly by individuals whose belief in personal control and religious faith are chronically low. Consistent with this prediction, research finds that liberals report higher levels of support for state socialism (Newport, 2010) but lower faith in personal control (e.g., Bryant, Dweck, Ross, Kay, & Mislavsky, 2009) and lower levels of religious faith (Malka, Lelkes, Srivastava, Cohen, & Miller, 2012) compared to conservatives. However, as noted above conservatives may endorse a strong State in domains, such as controlling crime, border security, and defense against foreign enemies, where they believe that the State is the most effective mechanism of control. For example, right-wing authoritarians endorse severe government security policies because they believe these are the only available means of controlling the spread of chaos and disorder (Alyemeyer, 1988).

Thus, CCT offers unique insights for predicting extreme ideological conviction by highlighting the importance of control motivations and the manner in which various ideologies can collectively and interchangeably satisfy this motivation. Any reminder of randomness, according to CCT, should increase reliance upon control ideologies. However, although extreme threats may at times engender extreme responses, compensatory control processes need not always (or even usually) result in extremism. But when threats occur in combination with sociocultural constraints that lead individuals to channel all of their compensatory control strivings into a single outlet, rather than a blend of many, extremism is a more likely result.

We must be cautious in drawing strong conclusions from these case studies illustrating associations of extreme ideology with limited options for meeting control needs. In case studies, it is impossible to disentangle causality and there may be exceptions to the observed pattern. However, it demonstrates the generative capacity of CCT that it sensitizes us to look for otherwise ignored patterns. Moreover, as we reviewed earlier, considerable evidence from controlled laboratory studies provides evidence for the causal mechanisms that we hypothesize produce ideological extremism. Ultimately, further studies are needed to more definitively test the hypothesized joint role of compensatory control motivations and funneling processes in producing extreme ideological conviction. For example, this account of ideological extremism predicts that experiments that simultaneously threaten multiple sources of control should yield especially extreme defense of whatever control source remains available. For example, threats to both personal and government control should yield more extreme religiosity than threats to either source alone yields. Also, more systematic macrolevel studies are needed to test whether ideological extremism is especially likely to emerge when control is threatened and individuals' options for meeting their control needs via multiple sources are severely constrained. These and many other implications of CCT for understanding ideological extremism remain to be tested.

Summary and Conclusion

By highlighting the common theme of control in otherwise diverse social, political, and religious ideologies, CCT makes an important contribution toward understanding the psychological functions of ideological extremism. The theory proposes, and research has shown, that when people experience random, threatening events they defensively embrace ideologies that restore their faith in internal or external sources of control in their lives, and these sources of control are substitutable. Drawing on CCT, we developed a new functional sociocognitive model that explains how the dynamics of people's ideological responses to control threats are structured by individual and situational constraints on the accessibility and functional fit of ideological resources. We reviewed several examples to illustrate the hypothesized dynamics of this functional sociocognitive model and we used the model to generate novel predictions about the circumstances that are likely to promote ideological extremism. Finally, by proposing that variability in ideological content interacts with psychological needs to predict ideological extremism this model takes ideological content more seriously than many previous functionalist models.

References

Altemeyer, B. (1988). *Enemies of freedom: Understanding right-wing authoritarianism.* San Francisco, CA: Jossey-Bass.
Antonovsky, A. (1979). *Health, stress and coping.* San Francisco: Jossey-Bass.
Ault, J. (2004). *Spirit and flesh: Life in a fundamentalist Baptist church.* New York: Vintage.
Bainbridge, W. S., & Stark, R. (1980). Superstitions: Old and new. *Skeptical Inquirer, 4,* 18–32.
van den Bos, K., & Lind, E. A. (2002). Uncertainty management by means of fairness judgments. In M. P. Zanna (Ed.), *Advances in experimental social psychology* (Vol. 34, pp. 1–60). San Diego, CA: Academic Press. doi: 10.1016/S0065-2601(02)80003-X
Bryan, C. J., Dweck, C. S., Ross, L., Kay, A. C., & Mislavsky, N. (2009). Political mindset: Effects of schema priming on liberal-conservative political positions. *Journal of Experimental Social Psychology, 45,* 890–895. doi: 10.1016/j.jesp.2009.04.007
Burger, J. M. (1989). Negative reactions to increases in perceived personal control. *Journal of Personality and Social Psychology, 56,* 246–256. doi: 10.1037/0022-3514.56.2.246
Burger, J. M., & Lynn, A. L. (2005). Superstitious behavior among American and Japanese professional baseball players. *Basic and Applied Social Psychology, 27,* 71–76. doi: 10.1207/s15324834basp2701_7
Burns, J. (2009). *Goddess of the market: Ayn Rand and the American Right.* New York: Oxford University Press.
Bush, G., Luu, P., & Posner, M. I. (2000). Cognitive and emotional influences in anterior cingulate cortex. *Trends in Cognitive Sciences, 4,* 215–222. doi: 10.1016/S1364-6613(00)01483-2
Cohen, D. (2001). Cultural variation: Considerations and implications. *Psychological Bulletin, 127,* 451–471. doi: 10.1037/0033-2909.127.4.451
Critchley, H. D., Mathias, C. J., Josephs, O., O'Doherty, J., Zanini, S., Dewar, B.-K., Cipolotti, L., Shallice, T., & Dolan, R. J. (2003). Human cingulate cortex and autonomic control: Converging neuroimaging and clinical evidence. *Brain, 126,* 2139–2152. doi: 10.1093/brain/awg216
Critchley, H. D. (2005). Neural mechanisms of autonomic, affective, and cognitive integration. *Journal of Comparative Neurology, 493,* 154–166. doi:10.1002/cne.20749
Critchlow, D. T. (2007). *The conservative ascendancy: How the GOP right made political history.* Cambridge, MA: Harvard University Press.
DiMaggio, A. (2011). *The rise of the Tea Party: Political discontent and corporate media in the Age of Obama.* New York: Monthly Review Press.
Doosje, B., Loseman, A., & van den Bos, K. (2013). Determinants of radicalization of Islamic youth in the Netherlands: Personal uncertainty, perceived injustice, and perceived group threat. *Journal of Social Issues, 69,* 586–604.
Ellison, R. (1948/2003). Harlem is nowhere. In J. F. Callahan (Ed.), *The collected essays of Ralph Ellison* (pp. 320–327). New York: Modern Library.
Emerson, R. W. (1841/1993). *Self-reliance and other essays.* New York: Dover.
Esses, V. M., Medianu, S., & Lawson, A. S. (2013). Uncertainty, threat, and the role of the media in promoting dehumanization of immigrants and refugees. *Journal of Social Issues, 69,* 518–536.
Fernandez, M. (2011, August 11). Perry leads prayer rally for "Nation in crisis." *The New York Times,* p. A12.
Greeley, A. M. (1995). *Religion as poetry.* New Brunswick, NJ: Transaction.
Greenberg, J., Solomon, S., & Pyszczynski, T. (1997). Terror management theory of self-esteem and cultural worldviews: Empirical assessments and conceptual refinements. In M. P. Zanna (Ed.), *Advances in experimental social psychology* (Vol. 29, pp. 61–139). New York: Academic Press. doi: 10.1016/S0065-2601(08)60016-7
Hagan, J. (2010). *Who are the criminals? The politics of crime policy from the Age of Roosevelt to the Age of Reagan.* Princeton, NJ: Princeton University Press.

Harcourt, B. F. (2011). *The illusion of free markets: Punishment and the myth of natural order.* Cambridge, MA: Harvard University Press.

Heine, S. J., Proulx, T., & Vohs, K. D. (2006). The meaning maintenance model: On the coherence of social motivations. *Personality and Social Psychology Review, 10*, 88–110. doi: 10.1207/s15327957pspr1002_1

Hellman, C., & Sharp, T. (2008). The FY 2009 Pentagon Spending Request—Global military spending. Retreived January 12, 2012 from http://armscontrolcenter.org/policy/securityspending/articles/fy09_dod_request_global/

Hogg, M., & Adelman, J. (2013). Uncertainty–Identity Theory: Extreme Groups, Radical Behavior, and Authoritarian Leadership. *Journal of Social Issues, 69,* 436–454.

Hogg, M. A., & van Knippenberg, D. (2003). Social identity and leadership processes in groups. In M. P. Zanna (Ed.), *Advances in experimental social psychology* (Vol. 35, pp. 1–52). San Diego, CA: Academic Press. doi: 10.1016/S0065-2601(03)01001-3

Houtman, D., & Mascini, P. (2002). Why do churches become empty, while New Age grows? Secularization and religious change in The Netherlands. *Journal for the Scientific Study of Religion, 41*, 455–473. doi: 10.1111/1468-5906.00130

Inzlicht, M., McGregor, I., Hirsh, J. B., & Nash, K. (2009). Neural markers of religious conviction. *Psychological Science, 20*, 385–392. doi: 10.1111/j.14679280.2009.02305.x

Inzlicht, M., & Tullett, A. M. (2010). Reflecting on God: Religious primes can reduce neurophysiological response to errors. *Psychological Science, 21*, 1184–1190. doi: 10.1177/0956797610375451

Janoff-Bulman, R. (1992). *Shattered assumptions: Towards a new psychology of trauma.* New York: Free Press.

Ji, L., Peng, K., & Nisbett, R. E. (2000). Culture, control, and relationships in the environment. *Journal of Personality and Social Psychology, 78*, 943–955. doi: 10.1037/0022-3514.78.5.943

Jost, J. T., & Banaji, M. R. (1994). The role of stereotyping in system justification and the production of false consciousness. *British Journal of Social Psychology, 33*, 1–27. doi: 10.1111/j.2044-8309.1994.tb01008.x

Jost, J. T., Blount, S., Pfeffer, J., & Hunyady, G. y. (2003). Fair market ideology: Its cognitive-motivational underpinnings. In R. M. Kramer, B. M. Staw (Eds). *Research in organizational behavior: An annual series of analytical essays and critical reviews,* (Vol. 25, pp. 53–91). Oxford, England: Elsevier Science.

Jost, J. T., Glaser, J., Kruglanski, A. W., & Sulloway, F. (2003). Political conservatism as motivated social cognition. *Psychological Bulletin, 129*, 339–375. doi: 10.1037/0033-2909.129.3.339

Kay, A. C., & Eibach, R. P. (2012). The ideological toolbox: Ideologies as tools of motivated social cognition. In S. T. Fiske & C. N. Macrae (Eds.), *Handbook of social cognition,* (pp. 495–515). London, UK: Sage.

Kay, A. C., Gaucher, D., McGregor, I., & Nash, K. (2010a). Religious belief as compensatory control. *Personality and Social Psychology Review, 14*, 37–48. doi: 10.1177/1088868309353750

Kay, A. C., Gaucher, D., Napier, J. L., Callan, M. J., & Laurin, K. (2008). God and the government: Testing a compensatory control mechanism for the support of external systems. *Journal of Personality and Social Psychology, 95*, 18–35. doi: 10.1037/0022-3514.95.1.18

Kay, A. C., Moscovitch, D. M., & Laurin, K. (2010). Randomness, attributions of arousal, and belief in God. *Psychological Science, 21*, 216–218. doi: 10.1177/0956797609357750

Kay, A. C., Shepherd, S., Blatz, C. W., Chua, S. N., & Galinsky, A. D. (2010). For God (or) country: The hydraulic relation between government instability and belief in religious sources of control. *Journal of Personality and Social Psychology, 99*, 725–739. doi: 10.1037/a0021140

Kay, A. C., Whitson, J. A., Gaucher, D., & Galinsky, A. D. (2009). Compensatory control: Achieving order through the mind, our institutions, and the heavens. *Current Directions in Psychological Science, 18*, 264–268. doi: 10.1111/j.1467-8721.2009.01649.x

Lakoff, G. P. 1996. *Moral politics: What conservatives know that liberals don't.* Chicago: University of Chicago Press.

Laurin, K., Fitzsimons, G. F., & Kay, A. C. (2011). Social disadvantage and the self-regulatory function of justice beliefs. *Journal of Personality and Social Psychology, 100*, 149–171. doi: 10.1037/a0021343

Laurin, K., Kay, A. C., & Moscovitch, D. M. (2008). On the belief in God: Towards an understanding of the emotional substrates of compensatory control. *Journal of Experimental Social Psychology*, *44*, 1559–1562. doi: 10.1016/j.jesp.2008.07.007

Lerner, M. J. (1980). *The belief in a just world: A fundamental delusion*. New York: Plenum.

Lilla, M. (2010). The Tea Party Jacobins. *The New York Review of Books*, *57*, 50–54.

Lipset, S. M. (1990). *Continental divide: The values and institutions of the United States and Canada*. New York: Routledge.

Lipset, S. M., & Marks, G. (2000). *It never happened here; Why socialism failed in the United States*. New York: St. Martin's Press.

Luhrmann, T. M. (2012). *When God talks back: Understanding the Evangelical relationship with God*. New York: Knopf.

Malinowski, B. (1954). *Magic, science, and religion*. New York: Doubleday.

Malka, A., Lelkes, Y., Srivastava, S., Cohen, A. B., & Miller, D. T. (2012). The association of religiosity and political conservatism: The role of political engagement. *Political Psychology*, *33*, 275–299. doi: 10.1111/j.1467-9221.2012.00875.x

Markus, H. R., & Kitayama, S. (1991). Culture and the self: Implications for cognition, emotion, and motivation. *Psychological Review*, *98*, 224–253. doi:10.1037/0033 295X.98.2.224

McGregor, I., Prentice, M., & Nash, K. (2013). Anxious uncertainty and reactive approach motivation (RAM) for religious, idealistic, and lifestyle extremes. *Journal of Social Issues*, *69*, 537–563.

McGregor, I., Zanna, M. P., Holmes, J. G., & Spencer, S. J. (2001). Compensatory conviction in the face of personal uncertainty: Going to extremes and being oneself. *Journal of Personality and Social Psychology*, *80*, 472–488. doi: 10.1037/0022-3514.80.3.472

Mosse, G. (1995). Racism and nationalism. *Nations and Nationalisms*, *1*, 163–173. doi: 10.1111/j.1354-5078.1995.00163.x

Newport, F. (2010). Socialism viewed positively by 36% or Americans. Gallup politics. Retrieved January 18, 2012 from http://www.gallup.com/poll/125645/socialism-viewed-positively-americans.aspx.

Pargament, K. I. (1997). *The psychology of religion and coping: Theory, research, practice*. New York: Guilford Press.

Proulx, T., & Major, B. (2013). A raw deal: Heightened liberalism following exposure to anomalous playing cards. *Journal of Social Issues*, *69*, 455–472.

Rothbaum, R., Weisz, J. R., & Snyder, S. S. (1982). Changing the world and changing the self: A two-process model of perceived control. *Journal of Personality and Social Psychology*, *42*, 5–37. doi: 10.1037/0022-3514.42.1.5

Rutjens, B. T., van der Pligt, J., & van Harreveld, F. (2010). Deus or Darwin: Randomness and belief in theories about the origin of life. *Journal of Experimental Social Psychology*, *46*, 1078–1080. doi: 10.1016/j.jesp.2010.07.009

Shackman, A. J., Salomons, T. V., Slagter, H. A., Fox, A. S., Winter, J. J., & Davidson, R. J. (2011). The integration of negative affect, pain and cognitive control in the cingulate cortex. *Nature Reviews Neuroscience*, *12*, 154–167. doi: 10.1038/nrn2994

Schwartz, B. (2000). Self-determination: The tyranny of freedom. *American Psychologist*, *55*, 79–88. doi: 10.1037/0003-066X.55.1.79

Shepherd, S., Kay, A. C., Landau, M. J., & Keefer, L. A. (2011). Evidence for the specificity of control motivations in worldview defense: Distinguishing compensatory control from uncertainty management and terror management processes. *Journal of Experimental Social Psychology*, *47*, 949–958. doi: 10.1016/j.jesp.2011.03.026

Skocpol, T., & Williamson, V. (2012). *The Tea Party and the remaking of Republican conservatism*. New York: Oxford University Press.

Snibbe, A. C., & Markus, H. R. (2005). You can't always get what you want: Educational attainment, agency, and choice. *Journal of Personality and Social Psychology*, *88*, 703–720. doi: 10.1037/0022-3514.88.4.703

Stephens, N. M., Markus, H. R., & Townsend, S. S. M. (2007). Choice as an act of meaning: The case of social class. *Journal of Personality and Social Psychology*, *93*, 814–830. doi: 10.1037/0022-3514.93.5.814

Sullivan, D., Landau, M. J., & Rothschild, Z. (2010). An existential function of enemyship: Evidence that people attribute influence to personal and political enemies to compensate for threats to control. *Journal of Personality and Social Psychology, 98*, 434–449. doi: 10.1037/a0017457

Tetlock, P., Visser, P., Singh, R., Polifroni, M., Scott, A., Elson, S., & Rescober, P. (2007). People as intuitive prosecutors: The impact of social-control goals on attributions of responsibility. *Journal of Experimental Social Psychology, 43*, 195–209. doi: 10.1016/j.jesp.2006.02.009

Vandello, J. A., & Cohen, D. (1999). Patterns of individualism and collectivism across the United States. *Journal of Personality and Social Psychology 72*, 279–292. doi: 10.1037/0022-3514.77.2.279

Wacquant, L. J. D. (2009). *Punishing the poor: The neoliberal government of social insecurity*. Durham, NC: Duke University Press.

Weisz, J. R., Rothbaum, F. M., & Blackburn, T. C. (1984). Standing out and standing in: The psychology of control in America and Japan. *American Psychologist, 39*, 955–969. doi: 10.1037/0003-066X.39.9.955

Whitson, J. A., & Galinsky, A. D. (2008). Lacking control increases illusory pattern perception. *Science, 322*, 115–117, 268. doi: 10.1126/science.1159845

Williamson, V., Skocpol, T., & Coggins, J. (2011). The Tea Party and the remaking of Republican conservatism. *Perspectives on Politics, 9*, 25–43. doi: 10.1017/S153759271000407X

Wills, G. (1999). *A necessary evil: A history of American distrust of government*. New York: Touchstone.

Wuthnow, R. (2004). *Saving America: Faith-based services and the future of civil society*. Princeton, NJ: Princeton University Press.

Young, M. J., & Morris, M. W. (2004). Existential meanings and cultural models: The interplay of personal and supernatural agency in American and Hindu ways of responding to uncertainty. In J. Greenberg, S. L. Koole, & T. Pyszczynski (Eds.), *Handbook of experimental existential psychology* (pp. 215–230). New York: Guilford Press.

Zernike, K. (2010). *Boiling mad: Inside Tea Party America*. New York: Times Books.

AARON C. KAY (PhD 2005, Stanford University) is an Associate Professor of Management and Associate Professor of Psychology and Neuroscience at Duke University. His research centers on the application and development of social cognitive and social psychological theories, principles and processes to the understanding of individual and societal motivations, beliefs and behaviors. For this research, Aaron Kay has been awarded the Janet T. Spence Award for Transformative Early Career Contributions from the American Psychological Society (2012), and the SAGE Young Scholar Award from the Foundation of Personality and Social Psychology (2010).

RICHARD P. EIBACH (PhD, Cornell University) is an Associate Professor of Psychology at the University of Waterloo. His research focuses on social judgment, with an emphasis on the study of construal processes, naive realism, and egocentrism. He applies a constructivist perspective, investigating how psychological biases interact with dominant cultural frames to influence judgments of change. Eibach's research examines individual biases that cause people to perceive illusory patterns of societal decline, intergroup biases that polarize perceptions of progress toward racial and gender equality, social movement dynamics, the development of moral panics, and the relative success of competing ideologies.

Determinants of Radicalization of Islamic Youth in the Netherlands: Personal Uncertainty, Perceived Injustice, and Perceived Group Threat

Bertjan Doosje*

University of Amsterdam

Annemarie Loseman and Kees van den Bos

Utrecht University

In this study among Dutch Muslim youth (N = 131), we focus on the process of radicalization. We hypothesize that this process is driven by three main factors: (a) personal uncertainty, (b) perceived injustice, and (c) perceived group threat. Using structural equation modeling, we demonstrate that personal uncertainty, perceived injustice, and group-threat factors are important determinants of a radical belief system (e.g., perceived superiority of Muslims, perceived illegitimacy of Dutch authorities, perceived distance to others, and a feeling of being disconnected from society). This radical belief system in turn predicts attitudes toward violence by other Muslims, which is a determinant of own violent intentions. Results are discussed in terms of the role of individual and group-based determinants of radicalization.

When people decide to join radical groups, this can have dramatic consequences. For example, radical groups can decide to let their actions speak. Radical groups as diverse as Tamil Tigers, IRA, Al-Qaeda, FARC, and ETA all have in

---

*Correspondence regarding this article should be addressed to Bertjan Doosje, Department of Social Psychology and Department of Political Science, University of Amsterdam, Weesperplein 4, Amsterdam 1018 XA, The Netherlands. Tel: +31 20-5256685 [e-mail: doosje@uva.nl].

We thank the Ministry of Justice of the Netherlands (NCTb/WODC) for awarding a grant to finance this research. We thank the head (A. W. A. Erkens) and members of the supervising committee (F. Beijaard, D. Carabain, J. Dagevos, F. van Gemert, J. J. van Miert, C. Nassau, and C. J. de Poot) for their useful comments during this research project. This research was also funded in part by a VICI innovational research grant from the Netherlands Organization for Scientific Research (NWO, 453.03.603) awarded to Kees van den Bos.

Annemarie Loseman and Kees van den Bos, University of Utrecht, Van Unnik Building, Heidelberglaan 2, Utrecht, 3584 CS, The Netherlands; a.loseman@live.nl; k.vandenbos@uu.nl.

common their willingness to use violence to achieve their goals. As a consequence, we have witnessed the actions of such groups in the form of numerous violent attacks on innocent people designed to instigate fear and terror.

Not surprisingly, understanding why people become radicalized and decide to join terrorist groups, have become important questions in the social and behavioral sciences (e.g., Bongar, Brown, Beutler, Breckenridge, & Zimbardo, 2006; De Wolf & Doosje, 2010; Hogg, Sherman, Dierselhuis, Maitner, & Moffitt, 2007; Kruglanski & Fishman, 2006; McCauley, 2002; Moghaddam, 2005; Silke, 2008). At first, scientists have considered the explanation of terrorism in terms of psychopathology: a terrorist must be a deviant and "sick" person. However, interviews with and tests of former terrorists showed consistent and remarkable results: there were no systematic differences between former terrorists and "normal people" in terms of psychopathology (e.g., Ruby, 2002; Sageman, 2004; Silke, 2008). Building on this observation we investigate the role of "normal" psychological variables that may lead nonradical youth to become susceptible to adopting a radical belief system.

In the present empirical study, we focus on one specific group of people who might be open to endorsing a radical belief system, namely Islamic youth living in the Netherlands. Specifically, we examine three important determinants of radicalization: personal uncertainty, perceived injustice, and perceived intergroup threat. We argue below that a combination of these three factors can contribute to support for a radical belief system, and that this belief system forms the basis of attitudes toward violent behavior by other Muslim extremists, and ultimately, intentions to actually engage in violent behavior toward other people.

Radical Belief System

Silber and Bhatt (2007, p. 16) define radicalization as "the progression of searching, finding, adopting, nurturing, and developing this extreme belief system to the point where it acts as a catalyst for a terrorist act." In applying this to the present context, namely Islamic youth living in the Netherlands, there are at least four elements that may be important in terms of content of a radical belief system.

Perceived illegitimacy of authorities. First, when people support a radical belief system, they begin to perceive the wider authorities as illegitimate (Buijs, Demant, & Hamdy, 2006; De Wolf & Doosje, 2010; Loza, 2007). This may be due to perceived mistreatment or perceived discrimination, which leads to mistrust of the authorities. In addition, from a radical Islamic person's point of view, there is a strong prescription to obey the laws and rules of Allah only, which implies that one does not have to respect the laws of unbelievers, such as the authorities in the Netherlands. For example, one extreme Islamic Dutch person states in an interview (Buijs et al., 2006, p. 83): "I do not know the Dutch laws. I consider them as nothing. I do not acknowledge the Dutch laws." Similarly, Mohammed

B. (who murdered the Dutch moviemaker and critic of Islam Theo van Gogh in November 2004) argues that "You cannot expect anything from the government. I have had enough of the institutions" (Buijs et al., 2006, p. 35).

Perceived in-group superiority. Second, an important component of a radical belief system is the perceived superiority of the in-group: all other groups are perceived as clearly inferior to the ingroup (e.g., Loza, 2007; Mazarr, 2004). In most religions, people typically make a distinction between believers and unbelievers. The group of "believers" consider themselves to be superior to the group of "unbelievers" (in most believers' view, the group unbelievers includes the people who believe in another religion). For example, when an extreme Islamic person living in the Netherlands (Jason W.) talked about Dutch people, he indicates that "These people are nothing. Worthless. You cannot trust them" (Buijs et al., 2006, p. 28).

Perceived distance to other people. Third, we argue that when people adopt a radical belief system, they start to develop a feeling of great distance toward other people who live differently (De Wolf & Doosje, 2010). There are several possible reasons for this. One is that Islamic people living in the Netherlands may experience a glass ceiling effect, because they face serious obstacles in climbing the societal ladder to the most senior leadership positions. In addition, they are likely to perceive their culture as quite different from the main stream culture. In their view, their in-group's norms and values conflict with the dominant cultural belief system. For example, an extreme Islamic person living the Netherlands states: "Working together is important, but it does not really work. Dutch people talk and gossip too much, our characters do not go well together." And another person argues that "their [Dutch] behavior is different from what I am used to" (both quoted in Buijs et al., 2006, p. 64).

Perceived societal disconnectedness. Fourth, we argue that in a radical belief system, people often start to feel disconnected from society. Related to the third component, this factor encapsulates a perception that one does not belong (Mazarr, 2004). Partly due to their different norms and values, Islamic Dutch people can feel disconnected from mainstream society. This idea of alienation is of course very influential in sociology—it has been described by Durkheim (1951) as a cause of suicide, but it has also been linked to increased susceptibility to extreme ideologies (e.g., Hoffer, 1951). Hoffer (p. 21) argues that, after a period of alienation, people can become "true believers" in the sense that "their innermost craving is for a new life—a rebirth—or, failing this, a chance to acquire new elements of pride, confidence, hope, a sense of purpose and worth by an identification with a holy cause." In line with this argument, one extreme Islamic person living in the Netherlands indicates that "sometimes I long for a place where

I am allowed to practice my religion without a fuss. It is becoming more and more difficult for us in the Netherlands" (quoted in Buijs et al., 2006, p. 68), while another extreme Dutch Islamic person states "If you are against them, you are a radical. You are a stranger. You have to be a stranger. They see you as strange, even at home you are strange. Everywhere they look at you with a strange eye, at home and in the metro. That is the way of the person who tells the truth" (quoted in Buijs et al., 2006, pp. 127–128).

To summarize, we consider four components of radicalization: (1) perceiving the authorities as illegitimate, (2) perceiving the in-group as superior, (3) experiencing a distance towards other people, and (4) feeling alienated and disconnected from society. We argue that these components of radicalization are associated with violent tendencies. In our study, we distinguish between general attitude toward Islamic violence (as perpetrated by *other* Islamic people), and *own* inclinations to become violent and engage in violent behavior. We expect the four components to be associated with general attitudes towards Islamic violence, and that this, in turn, will predict people's own tendency to become violent.

Our conceptual model shares features of the narcissism-aggression link formulated by Baumeister, Smart, and Boden (1996). Their notion that people are inclined to use violence when their ego is threatened is very much in line with our own argument that people from radical groups are inclined to use violence when the ego of their group is threatened. Similarly, Golec de Zavala, Cichoka, Eidelson, and Jayawickreme (2009, p. 1074) argue that groups might be likely to use violence when their members have a "high but ambivalent group esteem."

Determinants of a Radical Belief System

We now turn to our three main determinants of a radical belief system: personal uncertainty, perceived injustice, and perceived intergroup threat.

Personal uncertainty. In our model, personal uncertainty is the first determinant of a radical belief system. There are several different versions of personal uncertainty and related concepts in the literature (see, e.g., Hogg, 2007, 2012; Hogg, Kruglanksi & van den Bos, 2013; Marigold, McGregor, & Zanna, 2009; McGregor, Zanna, Holmes, & Spencer, 2001; Sedikides, De Cremer, Hart, & Brebels, 2009). We define personal uncertainty as a subjective sense of doubt or instability in self-views, world-views, or the interrelation between the two (Arkin, Oleson, & Carroll, 2009; Van den Bos & Lind, 2009). Furthermore, personal uncertainty, as we conceive of it, involves the implicit and explicit feelings and other subjective reactions people experience as a result of being uncertain about themselves (Van den Bos, Poortvliet, Maas, Miedema, & Van den Ham, 2005). In short, personal uncertainty is the feeling that you experience when you feel uncertain about yourself (Van den Bos, 2009) and we argue that typically experiencing personal uncertainty constitutes an aversive or at least an uncomfortable feeling (Hogg & Adelman, 2013; Van den Bos & Lind, 2002).

Personal uncertainty may concern people's questions about their identity ("Who am I?"), what they are doing in this world (existential uncertainty; Van den Bos, 2009), what the future might bring for them, etc. When people are in such a state or period in their lives, they are more susceptible for extreme ideas and extreme groups (e.g., Hogg, Meehan, & Farquharson, 2010; Hogg, Sherman, Dierselhuis, Maitner, & Moffitt, 2007). Why? The reason is that these extreme ideas and groups can provide clear and straightforward answers and solutions to their questions and worries. They provide uncertain people with a clear Black-and-White-ideology, including norms and values (what is good and what is bad) and strict codes of behavior. In this manner, these norms, values and behavioral rules can reduce their uncertainty.

In other words, when uncertainty arises, people cling to their cultural worldview. That is, uncertainty increases worldview defense (Stillman & Baumeister, 2009). The assumption is that personal uncertainty indicates that life is meaningless and absurd, and defending one's worldview allows the sense that life is meaningful to prevail. In other words, people manage feelings of uncertainty, via worldview defense, in order to make sense of life. In line with this idea is this quote from an extreme Dutch Islamic person: "Islam is everything. Without Islam I would go insane (...) I would not know what to do" (Buijs et al., 2006, p. 107), while another person states that "Deep inside me, I missed something, there was a kind of emptiness in me (...) But in mosques I felt differently. I need religion, my religion gives me meaning and peace" (Buijs et al., 2006, p. 100).

A similar argument has been formulated by Kruglanski, Pierro, Mannetti, and De Grada (2006) stating that to the extent people experience a high need for closure (which is related to high levels of uncertainty), they are more likely to opt for cohesive groups (i.e., groups with a clear identity). Finally, Van den Bos et al. (2005) have argued that feelings of uncertainty make people more likely to protect their worldview, for example, their religious worldview. Thus, we hypothesize that to the extent that people feel personally uncertain, they are more likely to endorse a radical belief system. In particular, we argue that this uncertainty will predict perceived in-group superiority, because this membership of a group that is perceived as superior is a viable manner to reduce this uncertainty.

Perceived injustice. Most theories of radicalization take into account some element of perceived injustice, the second determinant that we consider. For example, in Moghaddam's (2005) staircase metaphor of radicalization, he argues that perceived injustice is an important element on the "ground floor," and thus a basic determinant. We argue that perceived injustice will be associated with a radical belief system, in particular that they perceive the Dutch authorities are illegitimate, and that they feel disconnected in society. The following statement from an extreme Islamic person living in the Netherlands provides support for this notion: "We [Islamic people living in the Netherlands] try so hard but they [non-Islamic Dutch people] just do not understand us. Discrimination at school and at work are happening on a daily basis (. . .) A lot of Muslims do not have a job, they are being put aside" (Buijs et al., 2006, p. 68).

Perceived group threat. Perceived group threat is the third and final determinant of a radical belief system. In most ideologies, people learn that an eminent threat to their group is present. This perceived group threat may take different forms. We follow Stephan et al. (2002)'s distinction between symbolic threat, realistic threat, and intergroup anxiety. Symbolic threat refers to the threat to the Islamic culture. Realistic threat refers to threat to the economic status of one's group. Intergroup anxiety is defined that the fear one can experience when one has to interact with a person from another group. Previous research has demonstrated the link from (perceived and manipulated) group threat to negative out-group attitudes (see for a review Riek, Mania, & Gaertner, 2006). In addition, Kruglanski, Chen, Dechesne, Fishman, and Orehek (2009) argue that people are more likely to endorse violence and engage in violent actions themselves in order to restore threatened significance.

In line with these ideas, in this study, we argue that to the extent that Islamic people feel that their group is being threatened, they are more likely to endorse a radical belief system. Specifically, this perceived threat is expected to translate into a perception of the Dutch authorities as illegitimate, while the in-group is being perceived as superior. At the same time, it might make people more likely to perceive a distance to other people, and to feel disconnected from society. For example, an extreme Islamic person living in the Netherlands argues that: "I am worried about the oppression of Muslims. I empathise with my brothers in faith. Islam is just like a body, the pain is being felt by all parts of the body. That is why I feel the pain of Muslims" (Buijs et al., 2006, p. 65).

Background variables. Apart from these three main determinants of radicalization, it is important to consider the potential predictors of these determinants. In the current study, we have included three potential predictors of the determinants, namely in-group identification (e.g., Doosje, Spears, & Ellemers, 2002; Ellemers, Spears, & Doosje, 1997), and individualistic and collective forms of relative deprivation (e.g., Crosby, 1976; Grant & Brown, 1995), a feeling that people may experience when they perceive that they themselves (as an individual and/or as a group member) receive less than they consider to be just and deserved. We have included these background variables because previous research has observed correlations between ingroup identification and two components of group threat, namely symbolic threat and realistic threat (and less so for intergroup anxiety; Stephan et al., 2002). In addition, perception of individual and collective relative deprivation can been linked to feelings of injustice (Grant & Brown, 1995) and perceived illegitimacy of authorities (Tyler, 2006).

To summarize, we aim to predict a radical belief system among Islamic youth living in the Netherlands using three determinants. Specifically, we hypothesize that Islamic youth will endorse a radical belief system to the extent that they experience high levels of perceived injustice, personal uncertainty, and group threat.

Method

Sample

Participants in this study were 131 young Islamic people from the Netherlands. Their mean age was 17.27 years ($SD = 2.21$), ranging from 12 to 21. There were 80 males (61%) and 51 females (39%). Most of them (95.5%) were high school students. All of them categorized themselves as "Muslim."

Procedure

The questionnaire was administered online. Most participants were approached to take part in the study via high schools at different locations in the Netherlands. They were not paid. In addition, in order to increase the sample size, we paid 5 Euro (approximately 6.53 US Dollars) to some other participants. They were all requested to fill in the online questionnaire, and after completion were thanked and debriefed.

Predictors and Dependent Variables

Unless specified otherwise, for all items, participants were requested to indicate their agreement with a statement, ranging from 1 "totally disagree," to 5 "totally agree."

Individual relative deprivation. We measured this construct using six items. For example: "I don't think I get as many chances as others in the Netherlands." The six items formed a reliable scale (alpha = .82).

Collective relative deprivation. This construct was assessed with six items. An example item is: "I think Muslims are less well off than other groups in the Netherlands." With these six items, we created a reliable scale (alpha = .86).

In-group identification. We measured in-group identification with two items from Doosje, Ellemers, and Spears (1995). One item measured the perceived importance: "Being a Muslim is important for me." The two items were highly correlated ($r = .76$, alpha $= .86$).

Perceived procedural injustice. We used the items from Moorland (1991) to measure perceived procedural injustice. Our version consists of eight items, for example "I think I am treated fairly most of the time" (reverse coded). The alpha of the scale was high (.87).

Emotional uncertainty. Greco and Roger's (2001) measure of emotional personal uncertainty was used in this study. An example item is "I get worried when a situation is uncertain." The 15 items formed a highly reliable scale (alpha $= .89$).

Perceived group threat. We administered perceived group threat in terms of the model proposed by Stephan et al. (2002). This model distinguishes three types of threat: symbolic threat, realistic threat, and interpersonal anxiety. *Symbolic threat* was assessed with 12 items, such as: "Islamic and non-Islamic people in the Netherlands have different family values" (alpha $= .88$). We measured *realistic threat* with 3 items, one of them being: "Non-Islamic Dutch people have too many positions of power and responsibility in this country" (alpha $= .70$). The *interpersonal anxiety* scale consisted of 14 items. Participants were asked to indicate whether or not they experienced certain emotions when interacting with a non-Islamic person. Example emotions are anxious, nervous, relaxed (reverse coded), and calm (reverse coded). After recoding the positive emotions, the 14 items formed a reliable scale of interpersonal anxiety (alpha $= .70$).

Perceived in-group superiority. We used 4 items to assess perceived in-group superiority. For example, the following item was presented: "I believe that Muslims are better people than people who endorse another religion." Alpha was satisfactorily (.71).

Perceived illegitimacy of Dutch authorities. "I respect the Dutch government" was one example of the 3 items we used to measure perceived illegitimacy of Dutch authorities (derived from "respect for authorities" scale by Tyler, 1990). The items formed a reliable scale (.81).

Perceived distance to other people. Three items were administered to capture this construct. One example is: "I feel a great distance to people who live and think differently than I do." The scale was not that reliable (.56), probably due to the fact we only used three items for this construct. As it was not possible to increase the alpha by deleting items, we decided to use this scale, but interpret the results with some caution.

Societal disconnection. We tailored this construct specifically to disconnection from Dutch society and the Netherlands. One of the four items we used was: "I feel at home in the Netherlands" (reverse coded). Alpha was high (.84).

Attitude towards muslim violence by others. We assessed attitude towards Muslim violence by others with four items, one of them being: "What is your attitude towards the murder of Theo van Gogh, in November 2004?" answer options ranged from 1 "very negative" to 5 "very positive," as was the case with a more general item: "What is your attitude towards Muslim radicalization?" The reliability was high (.85).

Own violent intentions. Own violent intentions were measured with three items. For example, we presented the items "I am prepared to use violence against other people in order to achieve something I consider very important," and "I am prepared to disturb the orderliness in order to achieve something I consider very important." The three items formed a reliable scale (.76).

Results

Table 1 presents the means, standard deviations and inter-correlations of all constructs in this study. Using Structural Equation Modeling (SEM), we tested a model in which we predict own violent behavioral intentions from positive attitudes towards Muslim violence by others. In turn, we hypothesized this attitude towards Muslims' violence to be predicted by a radical belief system (perceived illegitimacy of the Dutch authorities, perceived Muslim superiority, distance to other people, and societal disconnectedness). We expected this radical belief system to be predicted by personal uncertainty, perceived injustice and group threat. We explored the predictors of these latter three variables (potential predictors were in-group identification, individual and collective deprivation). We allowed for associations within sets of predictors (for example between threat components; and between components of the radical belief system).

The hypothesized model had a good fit: Chi-square $(65) = 76.58, p = .154$, CFI $= .98$, NFI $= .87$, GFI $= .93$, SRMR $= .082$, and RMSEA $= .037$. La Grange Multiplier Test suggested including two direct paths: from collective deprivation to perceived illegitimacy of Dutch authorities, and from perceived distance to own violent intentions. When we included these paths, the fit became better. Our final model is presented in Figure 1. It has a very good fit: Chi-square $(62) = 58.13$, $p = .650$, CFI $= 1.00$, NFI $= .90$, GFI $= .94$, SRMR $= .070$, and RMSEA $= .000$. All paths included in the model are significant. We discuss this model in steps from left to right.

Table 1. The Means, Standard Deviations, and Inter-Correlations of All the Constructs

	M	SD	1	2	3	4	5	6	7	8	9	10	11	12	13	14
1. Identification	4.56	0.85	—	−.19*	.08	−.25*	.42*	.07	.08	−.06	−.28*	.09	−.17	−.25*	−.04	−.07
2. Ind. Rel. Depri.	2.39	0.81		—	.49*	.36*	.23*	.50*	.21*	.50*	.25*	.12	.17	.21*	.12	.09
3. Col. Rel. Depri.	3.31	0.92			—	.11	.54*	.62*	.26*	.38*	.21	.31*	.18*	.09	.20*	.10
4. Int. Anxiety	−0.20	0.17				—	.01	.15	.19*	.21*	.35*	.08	.22*	.26*	.18*	.14
5. Symbolic Threat	3.46	0.76					—	.64*	.21*	.24*	.07	.39*	.01	.04	.17	−.01
6. Realistic Threat	3.10	0.88						—	.27*	.34*	.16	.35*	.19*	.14	.26*	.16
7. Per. Em. Uncertain.	2.84	0.67							—	.10	.08	.29*	.18	.00	.30*	.14
8. Perc. Proc. Injustice	2.38	0.68								—	.15	.01	.03	.23*	.04	.06
9. Perc. Illegitimacy	2.37	0.02									—	.22*	.17*	.35*	.35*	.24*
10. Perc. Ingr. Super.	3.26	0.93										—	.34*	.08	.53*	.30*
11. Distance	2.32	0.66											—	.08	.44*	.39*
12. Disconnected	2.79	0.96												—	.24*	.00
13. Moslim Violence	2.89	1.06													—	.47*
14. Violent Intentions	2.08	0.91														—

Note. 2 = *Individual Relative Deprivation*, 3 = *Collective Relative Deprivation*, 4 = *Intergroup Anxiety*, 5 = *Symbolic Threat*, 6 = *Realistic Threat*, 7 = *Personal Emotional Uncertainty*, 8 = *Perceived Procedural Injustice*, 9 = *Perceived Illegitimacy*, 10 = *Perceived Ingroup Superiority*. *p < .05.

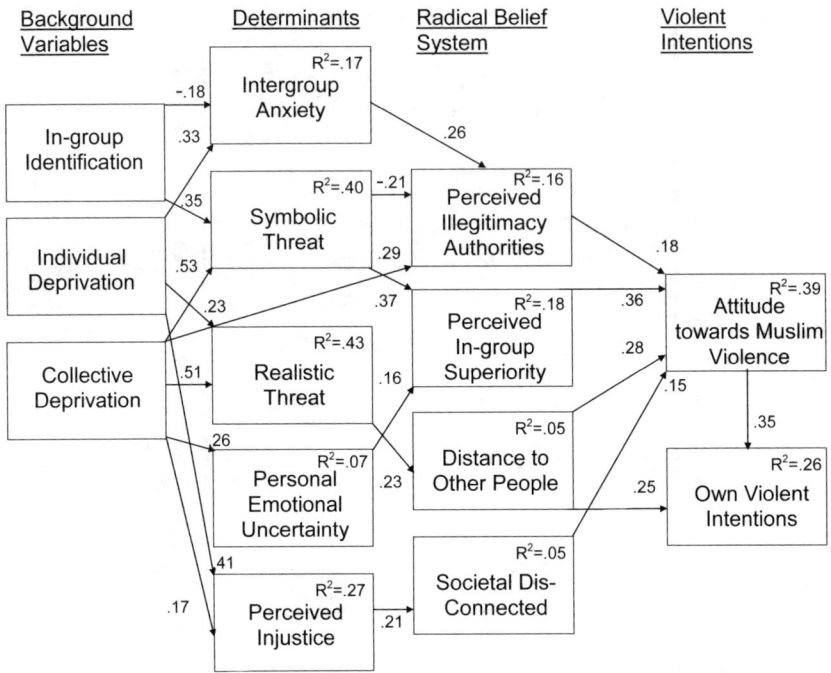

Fig. 1. Final structural equation model. All paths are significant. $R^2 = \%$ variance explained.

Determinants of perceived injustice, personal uncertainty, and group threat. As hypothesized, perceived injustice is predicted most strongly by individual deprivation. When people feel personally deprived, they experience this as unjust. Collective deprivation was another significant predictor of perceived injustice. Collective deprivation was the only predictor of personal uncertainty: to the extent that people experience deprivation as group members, they feel personally uncertain. As expected, realistic group threat was most strongly predicted by collective deprivation, and individual deprivation constituted another significant predictor. Again in line with hypotheses, when people perceived a high level of collective deprivation and in-group identification, they experienced high levels of symbolic threat. Finally, high intergroup anxiety was associated with high levels of individual deprivation, and unexpectedly, *low* in-group identification was associated with higher levels of intergroup anxiety.

Determinants of radical belief system. As expected, perceived illegitimacy of Dutch authorities was predicted by symbolic threat as well as intergroup anxiety. Thus, to the extent that people feel symbolically threatened and experience anxiety when interacting with out-group members, they perceive the Dutch authorities as less legitimate. There was also a direct path from collective deprivation to perceived illegitimacy. When people feel deprived, they perceive the Dutch authorities as less legitimate. As hypothesized, personal emotional uncertainty was a predictor of perceived Muslim in-group superiority. In line with the expectations, perceived in-group superiority was predicted by symbolic threat as well. Thus, both personal emotional uncertainty and perceived symbolic threat were associated with higher levels of perceived in-group superiority. Realistic threat was a predictor of perceived distance towards other people. Finally, perceived procedural injustice was the only predictor of societal disconnectedness: When people experienced higher levels of procedural injustice they felt less connected to Dutch society.

Determinants of attitudes towards muslim violence by others and own violent intentions. All four components of the radical belief system were significant predictors of attitudes towards Muslim violence by others. Thus, to the extent that people perceived the Dutch authorities as illegitimate, perceived the in-group as superior, perceived distance to others, and felt socially disconnected, they were more likely to have a favorable attitude towards violence by other Muslims. In-group superiority was the strongest predictor (Beta = .36), while perceived illegitimacy was the weakest, but still significant, predictor (Beta = .18).

Intentions to use violence themselves were predicted most strongly by attitude towards Muslim violence by others and, to a lesser extent, by perceived distance to others. Finally, it is important to note that the variables in this model explain 39% of the variance of attitudes towards Muslim violence by others, and 26% of own violent intentions.

Discussion

In this study, we focused on the radicalization of young Islamic people living in the Netherlands. We specified a model in which we distinguished between background variables, determinants of a radical belief system, a radical belief system, and violent behavioral intentions. In terms of a radical belief system, we identified four key components: (1) the perceived illegitimacy of Dutch authorities, (2) the perception of the in-group as superior, (3) the perceived distance towards other people, and (4) a feeling of alienation and disconnectedness from society. These components were only weakly inter-correlated (correlations ranged from .08 to .35). All four components were significant predictors of general attitude towards Muslim violence by others. This attitude was a good predictor of own intentions to use violence, as was the perceived distance to other people.

The three determinants of a radical belief system that were examined in this study, namely personal emotional uncertainty, perceived procedural injustice, and group threat were, in combination, a good set of predictors of a radical belief system. Specifically, perceived injustice was associated with perceived societal disconnectedness, personal emotional uncertainty and symbolic group threat were related to in-group superiority, realistic group threat was a predictor of perceived distance to other people, and intergroup anxiety was associated with lower levels of perceived legitimacy of Dutch authorities.

While these relations were in the expected direction, one path was not: to the extent that people experience more symbolic threat, they perceive the Dutch authorities as *less* illegitimate (Beta = −.21). This path may have popped up due to the strong correlation between symbolic and realistic threat ($r = .64$). This creates an overlap between these two constructs. While this overlap had no influence of other paths (compare the raw correlations in Table 1 and Betas in Figure 1), this particular path did change, possibly due to this overlap. In support of this argument, the simple correlation between symbolic threat and perceived illegitimacy was *not* significant, and if anything, slightly positive and in the expected direction ($r = .07$).

In terms of background variables, we studied the role of in-group identification, together with individual and collective forms of relative deprivation. These background variables were significant predictors of our radical belief system, as suggested by Moghaddam (2005). In line with previous research, in particular the *collective* form of relative deprivation was highly influential in this study (e.g., Quillian, 1995). It predicted not only group forms of threat (i.e., symbolic and realistic group threat), it also predicted personal emotional uncertainty and perceived procedural unfairness. In addition, collective deprivation had a direct link with perceived illegitimacy of Dutch authorities.

Only one path from the background variables was unexpected: higher levels of in-group identification are associated with *less* intergroup anxiety (Beta = −.18). In this case, the simple correlation is in the same magnitude ($r = −.25$). Even though we did not anticipate this effect, we offer the following post hoc explanation. Previous research has shown a link between in-group identification and self-esteem (e.g., Abrams & Hogg, 1988; Branscombe & Wann, 1991; Rubin & Hewstone, 1998). This increased self-esteem might reduce intergroup anxiety when interacting with out-group members. In future research it might be possible to disentangle the potential positive *and* negative consequences of in-group identification in intergroup contexts.

It is interesting to focus on certain paths in our model. For example, there is a path from collective relative deprivation, to personal emotional uncertainty, to perceived in-group superiority, to attitudes towards Muslim violence by others, to own violent intentions. In this case then, a group- oriented background variable, namely collective deprivation, is associated with a person-oriented variable, namely personal emotional uncertainty. This personal emotional uncertainty in turn is a predictor of group-oriented variable again, namely in-group superiority (see also Federico, Hunt, & Fisher, 2013). This indicates how intertwined personal and group-oriented variables can be in real life contexts: individual-based issues (such as personal uncertainty) can make people search for group-based answers (such as supporting a radical belief system; Hogg et al., 2007; Van den Bos et al., 2005). These radical groups can present people with a clear–cut world view or ideology. Ultimately, such an extreme ideology may provide people with meaning and a focus in their lives, and as such, reduce their personal uncertainty (see Klein & Kruglanski, 2013).

Another conclusion from this present study concerns the important role of the perceived distance to other people, even though the particular scale we have used was only marginally reliable. It predicts both support for Muslim violence by others, and own intention to use violence. Perceived distance is defined here as a psychological detachment to out-group members. Importantly, when people experience a distance to others, it becomes easier for them to inflict harm upon them (e.g., Staub, 1989). This may be particularly so when people no longer perceive out-group members as humans, but rather as animals. Indeed, this dehumanization process has been linked with increased support for in-group violence against an out-group (Leyens, Paladino, Rodriguez-Torres, Vaes, Demoulin, Rodriguez-Perez, & Gaunt, 2000). In addition, when people dehumanize an outgroup, they experience less guilt after violence towards that group perpetrated by in-group members (Zebel, Zimmermann, Viki, & Doosje, 2008). Thus, by perceiving a great distance to out-group members, people are more likely to adopt a violent solution when facing difficult situations.

Perceived in-group superiority was the best perdictor of attitude towards violence displayed by other group members, and, even though it did not show up in the final structural equation model it was significantly related to own violent intentions. This is in line with ego threat – aggression link formulated by Baumeister et al. (1996), extended to the group level by Golec de Zavala et al. (2009) and in line with findings among right wing extremists (Doosje, Van den Bos, Loseman, Feddes, & Mann (2012).

It is important to note that for this study we recruited *nonradical* young Islamic people as participants. While certain observed patterns can be explained in terms of theory or previous research, we cannot of course be certain that these patterns can be generalized to *radical* people. Rather, we have identified certain determinants of susceptibility for adopting a radical belief system. Our participants merely self-categorized as Muslims—they were in no manner radical or extreme. Thus, our study shows how people can become vulnerable for extreme ideas—it does not show how people have committed terrorist attacks. This noted, from qualitative interviews with ten young radical Muslims we have some indication that our proposed model may also hold for more radical samples (Van den Bos, Loseman, & Doosje, 2009). Future research is needed to test all the relations between the concepts studied here as a function of the phase of radicalization.

Similarly, it is interesting to discuss how our findings might be generalized to other contexts and groups. We argue that perceived in-group superiority may play a role in many other groups. For example, the important role of perceived in-group superiority has been observed in many extreme right-wing groups (e.g., Doosje et al., 2012). Golec de Zavala et al. (2009) have examined the role of in-group superiority in national group in the US, and in terms of white/black identity in Great Britain.

A clear limitation of our work is its correlational design. Even though we have tested a structural equation model, it is not possible to draw any firm causal conclusions. While it is certainly possible to experimentally manipulate some variables, we suspect it might be difficult if not impossible to do justice to the full complexity of the societal features incorporated in the presented model in this study.

Another limitation of this study is that, while we can address a large number of variables, we are not in a position to thoroughly examine the influence of each variable separately and in combination with other variables. Thus, in the current study, it is possible to examine simple correlations between variables (for example that uncertainty is associated with different forms of group threat – see Esses, Medianu, & Lawson, 2013). However, we do not adress the potential interaction between the variables.

In addition, a further limitation of the present study is that we have used self-resport measures. As such, we are not able to examine the validity of the answers as would have been possible if we had collected other data as well (e.g., impressions of them by their teachers, their parents and/or their friends). Similarly, as another limitation, we have measured violent behavioral *intentions*, but not registered actual violent *behavior*. One can never be certain how behavioral intentions are translated into actual behavior.

Still, in terms of practical implications, we argue that our findings can inform first line workers (i.e., police, teachers, youth workers) about potential psychological characteristics of people who might be susceptible to embracing a radical belief system. Such youngsters may show signs of personal uncertainty, combined with a sense of personal or group-based injustice, and experience a threat to the image of their in-group. It is important to stress that this should never lead to excessive profiling practices, as it is completely legal to voice one´s attitudes, even when they have an extreme nature, as long as one is not disobeying the law.

To conclude, we have demonstrated how people can start to feel attracted towards adopting a radical belief system. This radical belief system comprises four elements: (1) perceiving out-group authorities as illegitimate; (2) perceiving the in-group as superior, (3) perceiving distance towards other people, and (4) feeling alienated and disconnected from society. We have shown how personal uncertainty, perceived injustice, and perceived in-group threat are associated with embracing such a radical belief system. When people support such a radical belief system, they are more likely to be in favor of violence by other in-group members, which ultimately predicts people's own violent intentions. Although violent intentions are of course not the same as violent behavior, research on attitude-behavior relations does suggest that under appropriate conditions intentions can be relatively good predictors of actual behavior (e.g., Banaji & Heiphetz, 2010).

References

Abrams, D., & Hogg, M. A. (1988). Comments on the motivational status of self-esteem in social identity and intergroup discrimination. *European Journal of Social Psychology, 18*, 317–334, doi: 10.1002/ejsp.2420180403
Arkin, R. M., Oleson, K. C., & Carroll, P. J. (Eds.). (2009). *Handbook of the uncertain self*. New York: Psychology Press.
Banaji, M. R., & Heiphetz, L. (2010). Attitudes. In S. T. Fiske, D. T. Gilbert, & G. Lindzey (Eds.), *Handbook of social psychology* (5th ed., Vol. 1, pp. 353–393). New York: Wiley.
Baumeister, R. F., Smart, L., & Boden, J. M. (1996). Relation of threatened egotism to violence and aggression: The dark side of high self-esteem. *Psychological Review, 103*, 5–33, doi: 10.1037/0033-295X.103.1.5
Bongar, B., Brown, L. M., Beutler, L. E., Breckenridge, J. N., & Zimbardo, P. G. (2006). *Psychology of terrorism*. Oxford: Oxford University Press.
Branscombe, N. R., & Wann, D. L. (1991). The positive social and self concept consequences of sports team identification. *Journal of Sport & Social Issues, 15*, 115–127, doi: 10.1177/019372359101500202
Buijs, F. J., Demant, F., & Hamdy, A. (2006). *Warriors from own soil: Radical and democratic Muslims in The Netherlands*. Amsterdam: Amsterdam University Press.
Crosby, F. J. (1976). A model of egoistical relative deprivation. *Psychological Review, 83*(2), 85–112, doi: 10.1037//0033-295X.83.2.85
De Wolf, A., & Doosje, B. (2010). *Aanpak van radicalisme: A psychological analysis* [Dealing with radicalization: A psychological analysis]. Amsterdam: SWP.
Doosje, B., Spears, R., & Ellemers, N. (2002). The dynamic and determining role of ingroup identification: Responses to anticipated and actual changes in the intergroup status hierarchy. *British Journal of Social Psychology, 41*, 57–76, doi: 10.1348/014466602165054
Doosje, B., van den Bos, K., Loseman, A., Feddes, A. R., & Mann, L. (2012). "My In-group is Superior!" Susceptibility for radical right-wing attitudes and behaviors in Dutch Youth. *Negotiation and Conflict Management Research, 5*, 253–268, doi: 10.1111/j.1750-4716.2012.00099.x
Durkheim, E. (1951 [1897>]). *Suicide*. London: Routledge.
Ellemers, N., Spears, R., & Doosje, B. (1997). Sticking together or falling apart: Ingroup identification as a psychological determinant of group commitment versus individual mobility. *Journal of Personality and Social Psychology, 72*, 617–626, doi: 10.1037/0022-3514.72.3.617
Esses, V. M., Medianu, S., & Lawson, A. S. (2013). Uncertainty, threat, and the role of the media in promoting the dehumanization of immigrants and refugees. *Journal of Social Issues, 69*, 518–536.
Federico, C. M., Hunt, C. V., & Fisher, E. L. (2013). Uncertainty and status-based asymmetries in the distinction between the "good" us and the "bad" them: Evidence that group status strengthens the relationship between the need for cognitive closure and extremity in intergroup differentiation. *Journal of Social Issues, 69*, 473–494.
Golec de Zavala, A., Cichocka, A., Eidelson, R., & Jayawickreme, N. (2009). Collective narcissism and its social consequences. *Journal of Personality and Social Psychology, 97*, 1074–1096, doi: 10.1037/a0016904
Grant, P. R., & Brown, R. (1995). From ethnocentrism to collective protest: Responses to relative deprivation and threat to social identity. *Social Psychology Quarterly, 58*, 195–211. Available online http://www.jstor.org/stable/2787042.
Hoffer, E. (1951). *The true believer*. New York: HarperCollins.

Hogg, M. A. (2007). Uncertainty-identity theory. In M. P. Zanna (Ed.), *Advances in experimental social psychology* (Vol. 39, pp. 70–126). San Diego, CA: Academic Press. doi: 10.1016/S0065-2601(06)39002-8

Hogg, M. A. (2012). Uncertainty-identity theory. In P. A. M. Van Lange, A. W. Kruglanski, & E. T. Higgins (Eds.), *Handbook of Theories of Social Psychology* (pp. 62–80). Thousand Oaks, CA: Sage.

Hogg, M. A., & Adelman, J. (2013). Uncertainty-identity theory: Extreme groups, radical behavior, and authoritarian leadership. *Journal of Social Issues, 69*, 436–454.

Hogg, M. A., Kruglanksi, A., & van den Bos, K. (2013). Uncertainty and the roots of extremism. *Journal of Social Issues, 69*, 407–418.

Hogg, M. A., Meehan, C., & Farquharson, J. (2010). The solace of radicalism: Self-uncertainty and group identification in the face of threat. *Journal of Experimental Social Psychology, 46*, 1061–1066, doi: 10.1016/j.jesp.2010.05.005

Hogg, M. A., Sherman, D. K., Dierselhuis, J., Maitner, A. T., & Moffitt, G. (2007). Uncertainty, entitativity, and group identification. *Journal of Experimental Social Psychology, 43*, 135–142, doi:10.1016/j.jesp.2005.12.008

Klein, K. M., & Kruglanski, A. W. (2013). Commitment and extremism: A goal systemic analysis. *Journal of Social Issues, 69*, 419–435.

Kruglanski, A. W., Chen, X., Dechesne, M., Fishman, S., & Orehek, E. (2009). Fully committed: Suicide bombers' motivation and the quest for personal significance. *Political Psychology, 30*, 331–357, doi: 10.1111/j.1467-9221.2009.00698.x

Kruglanski, A. W., Pierro, A., Mannetti, L., & De Grada, E. (2006). Groups as epistemic providers: Need for closure and the unfolding of group-centrism. *Psychological Review, 113*, 84–100, doi: 10.1037/0033-295X.113.1.84

Kruglanski, A. W., & Fishman, S. (2006). The psychology of terrorism: "Syndrome" versus "tool" perspectives. *Terrorism and Political Violence, 18*, 193–215, doi: 10.1080/09546550600570119

Leyens, J.-P., Paladino, P. M., Rodriguez-Torres, R., Vaes, J., Demoulin, S., Rodriguez-Perez, A., & Gaunt, R. (2000). The emotional side of prejudice: The attribution of secondary emotions to ingroups and outgroups. *Personality and Social Psychology Review, 4*, 186–197, doi: 10.1207/S15327957PSPR0402_06

Loza, W. (2007). The psychology of extremism and terrorism: A Middle-Eastern perspective. *Aggression & Violent Behavior, 12*, 141–155, doi: 10.1016/j.avb.2006.09.001

Marigold, D. C., McGregor, I., & Zanna, M. P. (2009). Defensive conviction as emotion regulation: Goal mechanisms and interpersonal implications. In R. M. Arkin, K. C. Oleson, & P. J. Carroll (Eds.), *Handbook of the uncertain self* (pp. 232–2480). New York: Psychology Press.

Mazarr, M. J. (2004). The psychological sources of Islamic terrorism: Alienation and Identity in the Arab World. *Policy Review, 125*, 39–60. Available online http://www.hoover.org/publications/policy-review/article/6864

McCauley, C. (2002). Psychological issues in understanding terrorism and the response to terrorism. In C. E. Stout (Ed.), *The psychology of terrorism: Theoretical understandings and perspectives (psychological dimension to war and peace)*, Vol. III. (pp. 3–29). Connecticut: Praeger.

McGregor, I., Zanna, M. P., Holmes, J. G., & Spencer, S. J. (2001). Compensatory conviction in the face of personal uncertainty: Going to extremes and being oneself. *Journal of Personality and Social Psychology, 80*, 472–488, doi: 10.1037/0022-3514.80.3.472

Moghaddam, F. M. (2005). The staircase to terrorism: A psychological exploration. *American Psychologist, 60*, 161–169, doi: 10.1037/0003-066X.60.2.161

Quillian, L. (1995). Prejudice as a response to perceived group threat: Population composition and anti immigrant and racial prejudice in Europe. *American Sociological Review, 60*, 586–611. Available online http://www.jstor.org/stable/2096296.

Riek, B. M., Mania, E. W., & Gaertner, S. L. (2006). Intergroup threat and outgroup attitudes: A meta-analytic review. *Personality and Social Psychology Review, 10*, 336–353, doi: 10.1207/s15327957pspr1004_4

Rubin, M., & Hewstone, M. (1998). Social identity theory's self-esteem hypothesis: A review and some suggestions for clarification. *Personality and Social Psychology Review, 2*, 40–62, doi: 10.1207/s15327957pspr0201_3

Ruby, C. L. (2002). Are terrorists mentally deranged? *Analysis of Social Issues and Public Policy, 2,* 15–26, doi: 10.1111/j.1530-2415.2002.00022.x

Sageman, M. (2004). *Understanding terror networks.* Philadelphia: University of Pennsylvania Press.

Sedikides, C., De Cremer, D., Hart, C. M., & Brebels, L. (2009). Procedural fairness responses in the context of self-uncertainty. In R. M. Arkin, K. C. Oleson, & P. J. Carroll (Eds.), *Handbook of the uncertain self* (pp. 142–159). New York: Psychology Press.

Silber, M. D., & Bhatt, A. (2007). *Radicalization in the West: The homegrown threat.* New York: New York Police Department.

Silke, A. (2008). Holy warriors: Exploring the psychological processes of Jihadi radicalization. *European Journal of Criminology, 5,* 99–123, doi: 10.1177/1477370807084226

Staub, E. (1989). *The roots of evil: The origins of genocide and other group violence.* Cambridge, England: Cambridge University Press.

Stephan, W. G., Boniecki, K. A., Ybarra, O., Bettencourt, A., Ervin, K. S., Jackson, L. A., McNatt, P. S., & Renfro, C. L. (2002). The role of threats in the racial attitudes of Blacks and Whites. *Personality and Social Psychology Bulletin, 28,* 1242–1254, doi: 10.1177/01461672022812009

Stillman, T. F., & Baumeister, R. F. (2009). Uncertainty, belongingness, and four needs for meaning. *Psychological Inquiry, 20,* 249–251, doi:10.1080/10478400903333544

Tyler, T. R. (1990). *Why do people obey the law? Procedural justice, legitimacy, and compliance.* New Haven, CT: Yale University Press.

Tyler, T. R. (2006). Psychological perspectives on legitimacy and legitimation. *Annual Review of Psychology, 57,* 375–400, doi: 10.1146/annurev.psych.57.102904.190038

Van den Bos, K. (2009). Making sense of life: The existential self trying to deal with personal uncertainty. *Psychological Inquiry, 20,* 197–217, doi:10.1080/10478400903333411

Van den Bos, K., & Lind, E. A. (2002). Uncertainty management by means of fairness judgments. In M. P. Zanna (Ed.), *Advances in experimental social psychology* (Vol. 34, pp. 1–60). San Diego, CA: Academic Press. Available online http://dx.doi.org/10.1016/S0065-2601(02)80003-X.

Van den Bos, K., & Lind, E. A. (2009). The social psychology of fairness and the regulation of personal uncertainty. In R. M. Arkin, K. C. Oleson, & P. J. Carroll (Eds.), *Handbook of the uncertain self* (pp. 122–141). New York: Psychology Press.

Van den Bos, K., Loseman, A., & Doosje, B. (2009). *Waarom jongeren radicaliseren en sympathie krijgen voor terrorisme: Onrechtvaardigheid, onzekerheid en bedreigde groepen* [Why young people engage in radical behavior and sympathize with terrorism: Injustice, uncertainty, and threatened groups]. The Hague: Research and Documentation Centre of the Dutch Ministry of Justice.

Van den Bos, K., Poortvliet, P. M., Maas, M., Miedema, J., & Van den Ham, E.-J. (2005). An enquiry concerning the principles of cultural norms and values: The impact of uncertainty and mortality salience on reactions to violations and bolstering of cultural worldviews. *Journal of Experimental Social Psychology, 41,* 91–113, doi: 10.1016/j.jesp.2004.06.001

Zebel, S., Zimmermann, A., Viki, G. T., & Doosje, B. (2008). Dehumanization and guilt as distinct but related predictors of support for reparation policies. *Political Psychology, 29,* 193–219, doi: 10.1111/j.1467-9221.2008.00623.x

BERTJAN DOOSJE is a Professor of Radicalization Studies (FORUM Frank Buijs Chair) at the Political Science Department and Social Psychology Department at the University of Amsterdam, The Netherlands. His research interests include radicalization, group-based emotions, and terror management theory. He is an Associate Editor of *Group Processes and Intergroup Relations* and an Editorial Board Member of *Peace and Conflict: Journal of Peace Psychology*.

ANNEMARIE LOSEMAN received her PhD from the Utrecht University in The Netherlands. Her research mainly focused on processes of fairness reactions and radicalization. Currently, she works as a researcher on the national healthcare insurance in the Netherlands.

KEES VAN DEN BOS is Professor of Social Psychology at Utrecht University. His main research interests focus on fair and unfair treatment, morality, cultural worldviews, behavioral disinhibition, radical behavior and terrorism. He examines these issues in both basic research studies and projects for government agencies. He received his PhD from Leiden University. Currently, he is an Associate Editor of the *Journal of Experimental Social Psychology*.

A Millennial Challenge: Extremism in Uncertain Times

Susan T. Fiske*
Princeton University

This comment highlights the relevance and importance of the uncertainty-extremism topic, both scientifically and societally, identifies common themes, locates this work in a wider scientific and social context, describes what we now know and what we still do not, acknowledges some limitations, foreshadows future directions, and discusses some potential policy relevance. Common themes emerge around the importance of social justice as sound anti-extremism policy.

Uncertainty and Extremism, this *Journal of Social Issues* volume, is a disturbing, must-read compilation of millennial, unprecedented insights. Addressing a life-and-death mystery of our era, the tragedy of terrorism nevertheless yields to scientific analysis. We can understand why desperate people blow up thousands of their fellow human beings.

This concluding article has several aims: highlighting the relevance and importance of the topic both scientifically and societally, identifying common themes, locating this work in a wider scientific and social context, identifying what we now know and what we still do not, acknowledging some limitations, foreshadowing future directions, and discussing some potential policy issues.

Relevance to Science and Society

Scientific understandings can and must inform societal policies, if humans are to survive each other's violence. Make no mistake: Understanding is not condoning. As someone who sought to understand why ordinary people torture enemy prisoners (Fiske, Harris, & Cuddy, 2004), I learned the hard way that the public assumes that the understanding excuses the doing. In a painful BBC interview, victims of torture accused us of collusion: by explaining the circumstances

---

*Correspondence concerning this article should be addressed to Susan T. Fiske, Psychology Department, Princeton University, Princeton, NJ 08540 [e-mail: sfiske@princeton.edu].

that could drive almost anyone to commit immoral heinous acts, we were letting them off the hook. I tried unsuccessfully to argue that understanding the circumstances motivating extreme behavior extends the blame—beyond the actors who allow themselves to be manipulated by dire situations—to those who control the situations, in the case of torturers, their supervisors and policymakers. In the case of terrorists, this would be their leaders and the host country policies that worsen their situation. More on that later.

Social science is particularly vulnerable to this understanding = excusing view because we explain how situations cause behavior, even extreme behavior. Observers prefer to blame other humans for horrible outcomes, the more horrible, the more human responsibility must be blamed (belief in a just world: Lerner & Miller, 1978; defensive attributions: Shaver, 1970; retributive justice: Darley & Pittman, 2003; moral psychology: Haidt & Kesebir, 2010; Knobe et al., 2012). If someone, even a bad actor, is responsible, then presumably someone is in control and future malfeasance can be prevented. Circumstances seem too random to be controlled, so social context is a dissatisfying explanation, especially for the most hideous events.

This speaks precisely the point of the current work, as well as other social issues analyses that offer context to explain our shared problems. We can change contexts more effectively than merely by restraining bad actors, simply incarcerating or executing a few evil-doers. As long as the wrong contexts prevail, other bad actors will rise up to take their places. For society, citizens and policymakers need to get the message that explanations by circumstances do not excuse, but call for changing those toxic circumstances.

For scientists, this means that as we seek to understand what drives extreme behavior, we must explain the societal implications of our contextual explanations, as the final section of this comment—and many of the authors—try to do. First, however, consider what the authors tell us about how contextual uncertainty drives extremism.

Identifying Common Themes

Social justice appears key, defining social justice as equality, voice, respect for individuals, and respect for all groups. Violations of social justice sow the seeds of uncertainty and extremism. According to Gelfand, LaFree, Fahey, and Feinberg (2013), terrorism is more likely in cultures that are fatalistic (low personal control), tight (less tolerance, more humiliation, less access, no gradual change), and rigid in gender roles valuing masculinity (high aggression). Social justice has a short reach in a tight society that does not tolerate deviance or change, and fatalism reflects outgroups having no hope. To reduce extremism, give certainty about social justice in terms of democratic representation, and individual personal agency. (Gender equality is more complex, a point we will revisit.)

Among the most important candidates for social justice are immigrants, especially those who are in the host country a minority ethnicity, religion, or nationality. Esses, Medianu, and Lawson (2013) show how easily civilized societies such as Canada can dehumanize immigrants as animals (infectious, amoral, and violent), lacking human sensibility. Our American data support the Esses et al. interpretation: Immigrants land in the stereotypically least warm, least competent cluster of societal groups, along with dehumanized homeless people (Lee & Fiske, 2006). Dehumanizing immigrants (or anyone else) is opposite of the most useful policy because it reinforces their humiliation. Esses et al.'s link to social dominance orientation shows how dehumanizing immigrants solidifies the status quo.

Social injustice is not lost on its targets. As Doosje, Loseman, and van den Bos (2013) note, when society's outgroups perceive social injustice, combined with threat to their own group, and resulting uncertainty, this creates a toxic set of beliefs: authorities are illegitimate, one's oppressed ingroup is morally superior to them, mainstream society and its members seem distant, and voluntary isolation results. Doosje et al. show that this toxic context radicalizes immigrant youth.

Immigrant young men are especially under threat by social injustice, as they suffer disproportionately high unemployment and ill-defined futures, being of an age when time horizons are short and a gender for whom agency and aggression are expected. This makes certainty all the more appealing. Especially attractive are particular ideologies that promise personal control or societal control over seemingly random misfortunes, as Kay and Eibach (2013) show. Functionally relevant ideologies will particularly appeal if they counteract feelings of arbitrary victimization.

Not just relevant, control-enhancing ideologies, but extreme ones intrinsically promise the most relief from uncertainty and perceived social injustice. McGregor, Prentice, and Nash (2013) propose that attraction to extremes stems from a motivational state termed reactive approach. That is, personal motivational conflict results from frustration of one's active goals (e.g., accomplishment) through salient threat (e.g., disruption). Frustration's resulting uncertainty and anxiety are aversive, creating vigilance and inhibition. But relief lies in the behavioral approach system, which down-regulates the vigilance and anxiety. Approaching extremes is rewarding because they provide clear action plans to counter the fallout from goal obstruction. Righteous anger plays a role here. But respect for one's values averts this process: social justice again.

Attraction to extremes may well be an implicit, unconscious process, as Proulx and Major (2013) suggest. Faced with even trivial anomalies that violate accustomed meanings, people express more extreme commitment to ideologies they already endorse. Perhaps being embedded in what seems a socially just, certain context would mitigate the need for an extreme ideology commitment.

Particular goals also promise certainty and efficacy. As Klein and Kruglanski (2013) demonstrate, actions that uniquely serve only one goal, despite costs to other goals, seem especially instrumental to that goal. Extremism exemplifies goal commitment despite the costs of deviance within larger society. Loyalty and commitment to larger society might mitigate these reactions; we will come back to this point. For now, the foundational point remains that seeking epistemic certainty motivates extremism.

Particular groups likewise create certainty, Hogg and Adelman (2013) show. Groups that are entitative (groupy), structured, action-oriented, autocratic—and thus extreme—offer more appealing identities under uncertainty. This crucial idea explains how an uncertain identity seeks a clear, well-defined action plan. Again, an alternative identification with the mainstream society would counteract the appeal of fringe extremist groups.

If we must go beyond the potential extremists as individual bad actors to their toxic circumstances, this demands knowing: Who is responsible for creating conditions conducive to uncertainty and extremism? Violators of minorities' social justice are also themselves likely to be extremists, most likely high-status groups oriented toward clarity and conviction, that is, those with a need for closure. Federico, Hunt, and Fisher (2013) show that high status exaggerates need for closure effects on outgroup derogation. This explains both states' and ruling classes' extremism, as in dictatorships, but also the most likely perpetrators of social injustice.

In short, social injustice appears as a common element producing uncertainty and fueling attraction to extreme ideologies, goals, and groups that seem to promise certainty, dignity, voice, and traction on frustrated hopes. The uncertainty-extremism connection ranks as a millennial insight, not because humans have never faced terrorism before, but because the current technology makes terrorism an all-the-more deadly global threat, and because the problem now belongs to all of us. Answers as comprehensive as this one are a service to humanity.

Locating within the Wider Scientific and Social Context

Some broader social scientific and historical perspective helps place these social psychological findings. Turning to history, societal uncertainty has encouraged populist movements on both extremes in the past (Fiske, 2002). Given inequality and instability, discontent and uncertainty sow the seeds for groups claiming to represent "the people" against the elites. Representing the people as uncertain and out of control lays the ground for providing certainty and control through an ideological movement that promises revenge against those with more control.

Inequality not only deprives subordinate groups of control, but it also undermines societal unity. Inequality, as one form of social injustice, ruins societies: increasing violence, damaging health, and undermining communities (Wilkinson

& Pickett, 2009). Lack of control includes an inability to predict what will happen (uncertainty), as well as an inability to affect one's fate (influence). Of course, utterly predictable inequality could eliminate uncertainty if the powerholders oppress the subordinates in utterly predictable ways, but the lesson from this special issue is that unpredictability will make matters worse.

Identifying What We Now Know and What We Still Don't

To be sure, the answers offered here provide only one piece of the complex puzzle. As the editors Hogg, Kruglanski, and van den Bos (2013) note, not all uncertainty leads to extremism, and not all extremism is "determined" by uncertainty. For example, uncertainty can redouble people's efforts but it can eventually induce passivity, depending on the amount and duration of randomness. And extremism can stem from uncertainty but also from reasoned political discourse: Principled extremism may be complex and sophisticated, from having to defend itself intellectually (Sidanius, 1984). Interest and information search can correlate with extreme positions, in some contexts. We do not know what happens when.

We know that affirming one's values can undercut attraction to extremes in the face of uncertainty (McGregor et al., 2013). But how does a society tolerate, even encourage, the expression of minority values antithetical to its mainstream values? In the United States, freedom of speech protects most value expression, even hate speech. Europe has mostly decided against allowing hateful speech, but in practice this mostly applies to minorities hating the majority, upward hate, not the other direction, downward hate. From a scientific perspective, we do not know the impact of minority hate speech, though we can guess. The point is that the expression of views distasteful to the majority may benefit the minority, but it also has costs to their public image (divisiveness, prejudice) and possibly to their action intentions (fomenting disruption); we need to know more about all this. How do we assure value affirmation when values are counter to host values?

A particular place of value conflict lies in some minority groups' attitudes toward women. For example, immigrant cultures that endorse rigid patriarchy do not fit well with developed nations' gender equality. Gelfand et al. (2013) note that rigid gender roles and masculine culture encourage terrorism. The obvious answer might seem to be empowering women, but how does a society change gender inequality without threatening the very men most at risk for extreme reactions? Male threat based on changing gender roles constitutes part of the uncertainty that plagues many vulnerable but proud immigrant groups. We need to know more about how to do this. How do we empower women without threatening patriarchal men?

We know that social and societal distance contribute to extremism (Doosje et al., 2013). Costs of deviance to the larger society are minimized (Klein &

Kruglanski, 2013). How do we create links and loyalty to larger host societies? We know that immigrant youth who fare the best have dual identities, integrating both origins and host as ingroups (Berry, Phinney, Sam, & Vedder, 2006). But how do we offer them opportunities to show that both identities are legitimate and not zero-sum?

If we create opportunities to move up in the larger world, how do we prevent forming elites with high need for closure and outgroup derogation (Federico et al., 2013)? Giving power to the formerly powerless may create dictatorial monsters unaccustomed to tolerance, compromise, and moderation necessary to govern modern developed societies. Pluralism does not come spontaneously, yet our globalized societies require all of us to tolerate the uncertainties it creates.

Limitations and Future Directions

Collectively and individually, this volume is a tour-de-force. Across the contributions, this volume provides the ideal combination of laboratory experiments' causality and real-world correlations' generalizability. Within a given contribution, the ideal combination remains of course hard to create. Future efforts will doubtless strive to use such converging operations to triangulate on combined internal and external validity.

An impressive array of applicable theory appears here. As noted, uncertainty-extremity insights might profit from some additional perspectives. For example, as noted, the context hypothesis for sophisticated extremists posits that the position of having to defend an unpopular position correlates with political interest and information (Sidanius, 1984), belying the idea that extremism necessarily reflects uncertainty. Likewise, the attitude polarization approach posits that more thought leads to more extremity, as long as information can fit into a well-developed framework (Tesser, 1978). As a counterpoint, perhaps the complexity–extremity theory also has a role here (Linville, 1982), contributing the idea that simplicity (few dimensions) about an outgroup, here the dominant culture, allows extremity. Understanding how all these prior theories play off might help explaining uncertainty and extremism.

Attitude strength and certainty approaches might also generate some traction here (Tormala & Rucker, 2007). Many of the papers imply that extremism links to attitude strength, conviction, and commitment to action. Attitude certainty may instead amplify the attitude in whatever direction it tended, strengthening univalent attitudes but weakening ambivalent attitudes' resistance to persuasion (Clarkson, Tormala, & Rucker, 2008). Even uncertain attitudes might also foster extremism because they can motivate selective exposure to confirmatory information in times of doubt (Sawicki, Wegener, Clark, Fabrigar, Smith, & Bengal, 2011). Future work might profitably connect to the attitude strength literature.

Ambivalent attitudes have another role to play in uncertainty and extremism. The dynamics of disenfranchised groups' envy upward creates a volatile mix of perceptions. The dominant groups' higher status makes them seem to possess some enviable competences (but not morality and trustworthiness), creating a mix of grudging respect and resentment (Fiske, 2011; Fiske et al., 2002). Although passive associations may prevail in stable times, in uncertain times, the envious attack the envied. Uncertainty combined with this volatile form of ambivalence is dangerous for society, but we do not know enough about ambivalence, uncertainty, and extremism toward envied outgroups.

None of the papers come from anyone personally committed to extremism, to the best of my knowledge. While it might seem heretic, the science might benefit from understanding any principled perspectives that attempt to defend extremism on its own terms. The editors justly note that extremism is contested but inflicting violence is decried. Nevertheless, an extremist partisan might detect a status-quo bias in terms such as "cling to ....rigid, intolerant ... " versus their own self-view of coming to firm convictions, respecting authority, and being loyal to their oppressed group. Cited briefly, fusion theory might provide some leverage here (Swann, Jetten, Gómez, Whitehouse, & Bastian, 2012). When personal identity fuses with group identity, maintaining individual autonomy and agency in the service of group goals, people are capable of extraordinary self-sacrifice in the service of the collective. Whether describing a fused extremist as a terrorist or a freedom fighter or a national hero, the processes of identity fusion can be useful here.

Finally, we have not begun to understand the micro-level processes involved. Perhaps this level of analysis is premature or irrelevant, but if the uncertainty-extremity process seems right—and it does—then it must be basic enough that it even has neural correlates (Fiske & Taylor, 2013). For example, activation of the brain's reward areas to an envied outgroup's misfortunes (even without ingroup gain) correlates with self-reports of having personally harmed the envied outgroup (Cikara, Botvinick, & Fiske, 2011). Perhaps we are wired for uncertainty to abet extreme actions toward superordinate groups.

Found in Translation: Policy Issues and Strategies

Here's a radical policy implication: Domestic social justice and stable equality create certainty and moderation. Social welfare and value expression promote certainty and allow dialogue among reasonable groups. Creating social justice is not easy because uncertainty also stems from crises, conflicts, and disasters. But the inevitability of these disruptions, if not their timing, suggests preparing society for them via rich, complex, and interconnected social networks of mutual respect, even or especially in the face of profound disagreement. Socially just domestic policy may be the best anti-terrorism and foreign policy.

References

Berry, J. W., Phinney, J. S., Sam, D. L., & Vedder, P. (2006). Immigrant youth: Acculturation, identity, and adaptation. *Applied Psychology: An International Review, 55*(3), 303–332. doi: 10.1111/j.1464-0597.2006.00256.x

Cikara, M., Botvinick, M. M., & Fiske, S. T. (2011). Us versus them: Social identity shapes neural responses to intergroup competition and harm. *Psychological Science, 22*, 306–313. doi: 10.1177/0956797610397667

Clarkson, J. J., Tormala, Z. L., & Rucker, D. D. (2008). A new look at the consequences of attitude certainty: The amplification hypothesis. *Journal of Personality and Social Psychology, 95*(4), 810–825. doi: 10.1037/a0013192

Darley, J. M., & Pittman, T. S. (2003). The psychology of compensatory and retributive justice. *Personality and Social Psychology Review, 7*(4), 324–336. doi: 10.1207/S15327957PSPR0704_05

Doosje, B., Loseman, A., & van den Bos, K. (2013). Determinants of radicalization of Islamic youth in the Netherlands: Personal uncertainty, perceived injustice, and perceived group threat. *Journal of Social Issues, 69*, 586–604.

Esses, V. M., Medianu, S., & Lawson, A. S. (2013). Uncertainty, threat, and the role of the media in promoting the dehumanization of immigrants and refugees. *Journal of Social Issues, 69*, 518–536.

Federico, C. M., Hunt, C. V., & Fisher, E. L. (2013). Uncertainty and status-based asymmetries in the distinction between the "good" us and the "bad" them: Evidence that group status strengthens the relationship between the need for cognitive closure and extremity in intergroup differentiation. *Journal of Social Issues, 69*, 473–494.

Fiske, S. T. (2002). *Envy up, scorn down: How status divides us.* New York: Russell Sage Foundation.

Fiske, S. T., Cuddy, A. J., Glick, P., & Xu, J. (2002). A model of (often mixed) stereotype content: Competence and warmth respectively follow from perceived status and competition. *Journal of Personality and Social Psychology, 82*, 878–902. doi: 10.1037/0022-3514.82.6.878

Fiske, S. T., Harris, L. T., & Cuddy, A. J. C. (2004). Policy Forum: Why ordinary people torture enemy prisoners. *Science, 306*, 1482–1483. doi: 10.1126/science.1103788

Fiske, S. T., & Taylor, S. E. (2013). *Social cognition: From brains to culture* (2nd ed.). London: Sage.

Gelfand, M. J., Lafree, G., Fahey, S., & Feinberg, E. (2013). Culture and extremism. *Journal of Social Issues, 69*, 495–517.

Haidt, J., & Kesebir, S. (2010). Morality. In S. T. Fiske, D. T. Gilbert, & G. Lindzey (Eds.) *Handbook of Social Psychology* (5th ed., pp. 797–832). Hoboken, NJ: Wiley.

Hogg, M. A., & Adelman, J. (2013). Uncertainty-identity theory: Extreme groups, radical behavior, and authoritarian leadership. *Journal of Social Issues, 69*, 436–454.

Hogg, M. A., Kruglanski, A. W., & van den Bos, K. (2013). Uncertainty and the roots of extremism. *Journal of Social Issues, 69*, 407–418.

Kay, A., & Eibach, R. P. (2013). Compensatory control and its implications for ideological extremism. *Journal of Social Issues, 69*, 564–585.

Klein, K. M., & Kruglanski, A. W. (2013). Commitment and extremism: A goal systemic analysis. *Journal of Social Issues, 69*, 419–435.

Knobe, J., Buckwalter, W., Nichols, S., Robbins, P., Sarkissian, H., & Sommers, T. (2012). Experimental philosophy. *Annual Review of Psychology, 63*, 81–99. doi: 10.1146/annurev-psych-120710-100350

Lee, T. L., & Fiske, S. T. (2006). Not an outgroup, but not yet an ingroup: Immigrants in the stereotype content model. *International Journal of Intercultural Relations, 30*, 751–768. doi: 10.1016/j.ijintrel.2006.06.005

Lerner, M. J. Miller, D. T. (1978). Just world research and the attribution process: Looking back and ahead. *Psychological Bulletin, 85*, 1030–1051. doi: 10.1037/0033-2909.85.5.1030

Linville, P. W. (1982). The complexity–extremity effect and age-based stereotyping. *Journal of Personality and Social Psychology, 42*(2), 193–211. doi: 10.1037/0022-3514.42.2.193

McGregor, I., Prentice, M., & Nash, K. (2013). Anxious uncertainty and reactive approach motivation (RAM) for religious, idealistic, and lifestyle extremes. *Journal of Social Issues, 69*, 537–563.

Proulx, T., & Major, B. (2013). A raw deal: Heightened liberalism following exposure to anomalous playing cards. *Journal of Social Issues, 69*, 455–472.
Sawicki, V., Wegener, D. T., Clark, J. K., Fabrigar, L. R., Smith, S. M., & Bengal, S. T. (2011). Seeking confirmation in times of doubt: Selective exposure and the motivational strength of weak attitudes. *Social Psychological and Personality Science, 2*(5), 540–546. doi: 10.1177/1948550611400212
Shaver, K. G. (1970). Defensive attribution: Effects of severity and relevance on the responsibility assigned for an accident. *Journal of Personality and Social Psychology, 14*(2), 101–113. doi: 10.1037/h0028777
Sidanius, J. (1984). Political interest, political information search, and ideological homogeneity as a function of sociopolitical ideology: A tale of three theories. *Human Relations, 37*(10), 811–828. doi: 10.1177/001872678403701003
Swann, W. B., Jr., Jetten, J., Gómez, Á., Whitehouse, H., & Bastian, B. (2012). When group membership gets personal: A theory of identity fusion. *Psychological Review, 119*(3), 441–456. doi: 10.1037/a0028589
Tesser, A. (1978). Self-generated attitude change. *Advances in Experimental Social Psychology, 11*, 289–338. doi: 10.1016/S0065-2601(08)60010-6
Tormala, Z. L., & Rucker, D. D. (2007). Attitude certainty: A review of past findings and emerging perspectives. *Social and Personality Psychology Compass, 1*(1), 469–492. doi: 10.1111/j.1751-9004.2007.00025.x
Wilkinson, R. G., & Pickett, K. E. (2009). Income inequality and social dysfunction. *Annual Review of Sociology, 35*, 493–511. doi: 10.1146/annurev-soc-070308-115926

SUSAN T. FISKE – Eugene Higgins Professor, Psychology and Public Affairs, Princeton University (Ph.D., Harvard University; honorary doctorates, Université Catholique de Louvain-la-Neuve, Belgium; Universiteit Leiden, Netherlands)—investigates social cognition at cultural, intergroup, interpersonal, and neural levels. Policy applications include the U.S. Supreme Court citing her gender-bias testimony, presenting to President Clinton's Race Initiative Advisory Board, editing Beyond Common Sense: Psychological Science in the Courtroom, and authoring the Guggenheim- and Russell-Sage-funded Envy Up, Scorn Down: How Status Divides Us. Upper-level texts are Social Beings: Core Motives in Social Psychology and Social Cognition: From Brains to Culture. She has just been elected to the National Academy of Sciences.

NYU PRESS
Keep reading.

Deviant and Criminal Behavior in the Workplace
Edited by STEVEN M. ELIAS

"A *valuable* volume for anyone with interest in the issues inherent to complex people working together within complex systems."
—Deborah E. Rupp, Purdue University

$30.00 • PAPER
In the *Psychology and Crime* series

Mastering the Semi-Structured Interview and Beyond
From Research Design to Analysis and Publication
ANNE GALLETTA
Foreword by WILLIAM E. CROSS

"A *beautifully crafted* book....Will surely be a classic, widely used in methods courses."
—Susan Opotow, John Jay College of Criminal Justice and The Graduate Center, CUNY

$24.00 • PAPER
In the *Qualitative Studies in Psychology* series

NYU PRESS IS A MEMBER OF THE University Press Content Consortium

www.nyupress.org

Save Time and Let the Research Come to You

Sign up for new content alerts for all of your favorite journals:

- ✓ Be the first to read Early View articles
- ✓ Get notified of Accepted Articles when they appear online
- ✓ Receive table of contents details each time a new issue is published
- ✓ Never miss another issue!

Follow these 3 easy steps to register for alerts online:

1 Log into **Wiley Online Library**. If you are not already a registered user, you can create your profile for free.

2 Select "**Get New Content Alerts**" from Journal Tools on the top left menu on any journal page or visit the Publications page to view all titles.

3 Submit your preferences and you are done. You will now receive an email when a new issue of the journal publishes.

wileyonlinelibrary.com